REMEMBERING SHAKESPEARE

ESSENTIAL ESSAYS SERIES 68

Canada Council   Conseil des arts
for the Arts   du Canada

ONTARIO ARTS COUNCIL
CONSEIL DES ARTS DE L'ONTARIO

an Ontario government agency
un organisme du gouvernement de l'Ontario

Guernica Editions Inc. acknowledges the support of the Canada Council
for the Arts and the Ontario Arts Council. The Ontario Arts Council is an
agency of the Government of Ontario.

We acknowledge the financial support of the Government of Canada.

JOHN O'MEARA

REMEMBERING SHAKESPEARE

The Scope of His Achievement
from *Hamlet* through *The Tempest*

GUERNICA
EDITIONS

ESSENTIAL ESSAYS

GUERNICA
TORONTO – BUFFALO – LANCASTER (U.K.)
2016

Michael Mirolla, general editor
Interior design: Aline Francoeur
Guernica Editions Inc.
1569 Heritage Way, Oakville, (ON), Canada L6M 2Z7
2250 Military Road, Tonawanda, N.Y. 14150-6000 U.S.A.
www.guernicaeditions.com

Distributors:

University of Toronto Press Distribution,
5201 Dufferin Street, Toronto (ON), Canada M3H 5T8
Gazelle Book Services, White Cross Mills, High Town,
Lancaster LA1 4XS U.K.

First edition.
Printed in Canada.

Legal Deposit – Second Quarter
Library of Congress Catalog Card Number: 2016941119
Library and Archives Canada Cataloguing in Publication:

O'Meara, John, 1953-, author
Remembering Shakespeare: the scope of his achievement
from Hamlet through The Tempest / John O'Meara.—1st edition.

(Essential essays series ; 68)
Issued also in electronic formats.
ISBN 978-1-77183-227-4 (paperback)—ISBN 978-1-77183-228-1
(epub).—ISBN 978-1-77183-229-8 (mobi)

1. Shakespeare, William, 1564-1616—Criticism and interpretation.
2. Anthroposophy in literature. I. Title. II. Series: Essential essays series
(Toronto, Ont.) ; 68

PR2976.O44 2016   822.3'3   C2016-902899-2
                                          C2016-902900-X

CONTENTS

I so gratefully acknowledge the support over these many years of

Joanne Zuckerman
John Broadbent
Nicholas Brooke
Anthony Gash
D. J. Palmer
Owen Barfield
R.W. Desai
Alex Newall
Judith Herz
Charles Forker
Edward Pechter
John Astington
Joanna Dutka
Randall McLeod
Richard Greene
Alexandra Gunther
Arthur Kinney
Ted Hughes
Sergei O. Prokofieff
Richard Ramsbotham
and
Aline Francoeur

AUTHOR'S NOTE

The three Parts of this volume and the Overview were written at different periods, with a significant spread of time lying in between each piece. Even so, the three Parts were conceived as a Trilogy, and as with other trilogies in which the parts originate separately, each with its own individual starting-point, the reader can expect a looser form of structural unity than in the case of the singly developed text and its uniform continuity. As for the Overview, written when Part Three was nearing completion, it was conceived with the idea of covering the full range of material in the three Parts more generally, without the further applications from Steiner. The Overview constitutes, in this respect, the exoteric counterpart to the more esoteric explorations of the Parts. Bringing all of this material together in one volume has been, among other things, my personal act of remembering Shakespeare by revisiting some of the work I had done on my author after more or less 'scanting' him in more recent years. It seemed especially fitting to be returning to him in this extraordinary year of the 400th anniversary of Shakespeare's death. Significantly this volume has a moral: we will remember Shakespeare best by re-thinking how we have forgotten to do him justice.

In memory of
my father and my mother

Lord, we know what we are
but know not what we may be.

Preface

The comprehensive scope of Shakespeare's achievement has, over the centuries, been acknowledged by almost everyone, and yet in respect of one dimension of this achievement what especially concerned Shakespeare at the last, to the point of tragedy for himself, we have consistently passed by. One could well imagine the Ghost of Shakespeare appearing to us today, and especially in this year, to clamour to be 'remembered' especially in this respect. Given the depth of our unknowing resistance in this matter, there would needs be 'a Ghost come from the grave to tell us this'; to put it fancifully, no other omission on our part would call for so extraordinary a deviation from the process of our day-to-day immersion in all of our usual notions and concerns. Indeed, the issues involved go beyond Shakespeare's own will *or* that of the Ghost in *Hamlet* through whom these issues first come to light: both the Ghost and Shakespeare would have had to submit to a universe that requires much more of us than we seem ever ready to admit. This was to be Hamlet's great tragic lesson, as it was also, as I show below, Shakespeare's lesson on taking up with *Hamlet*. Hamlet would put it in this way: 'There are more things in heaven and earth ... than are dreamed of in your philosophy'. It was to be a very hard lesson for Hamlet, one that even he would not be ripe enough to handle fully. Nor would Shakespeare, for many years after. For years he would continue, in the tragedies that follow, to 'unpack his heart with words', in protest and outrage that so much would have to be renounced to satisfy the will of a universe that, for our instruction, had taken him over. And that would turn out to be Shakespeare's tragedy: that over the whole of the time since, we have not let ourselves *be* instructed, for all the nearly imponderable pains he finally took in this matter.

Only the most deep-seated prejudices could divert us from finally recognizing Shakespeare's assumed mission in this respect. In spite of our profession of complete open-mindedness today, we continue, as always, to favour a certain range of plays, if not quite to the exclusion of others, at least to their detriment, insofar as we fail to have any clear sense of the final significance these plays have in comparison with the more privileged groups. Among these groups, which we can reasonably say we understand very well, are the histories, the comedies, even the very early types of these, and—at least we think so—the tragedies. As for what we used to call the romances, by which I intend *Pericles*, *The Winter's Tale*, and *The Tempest*, as well as *Cymbeline*: while we respect these plays for their unearthly charm and bewildering freedom from the generic conventions, we have to confess, in fact, no real understanding of them in the last analysis. There have been many historical-cultural reasons for this over the centuries, but one essential reason will explain it: our fundamental inability to live *through* tragedy the way Shakespeare did, who used the tragic characters of Hamlet, Othello, Lear, and Macbeth to deliberately give himself that experience. It is not a question here of passing beyond tragedy, not a question of anything like what would produce the catharsis that leads one back to one's 'place' in society, nor of moving on 'in spite of' tragedy, but of fully passing through tragedy without any holding back or holding on to this or that consolation. The result of this exemplary ability was that Shakespeare was, without his even anticipating that anything of the sort was possible, further able to come into those extraordinary and almost unknown *higher* evolutionary states of being that are so elaborately represented in the later romances—which is the very reason why they were written.

In practical terms, as participants in Shakespeare's plays, what this has meant is that we have not really known how to value, though we think we have, the plays that stand at the very centre of the mission Shakespeare suddenly inherited, which is to say the plays that proceed from *Hamlet* onwards. I can cite the case of a woman who, having heard me lecture years ago on the material presented in this book, came up to me to say how my presentation had explained much for her. It had been *her* experience precisely that she had never been able to witness the frightful events in *Macbeth* without having to look away and to think away from what is presented there. It had seemed to her inexplicable, even cruel, that Shakespeare would ever want to involve us in such a presentation. The same could be said of events in *King Lear*, or *Othello*, or even *Hamlet*: one has but to think of Cordelia dead in Lear's arms, of Desdemona dead in Othello's arms, or Ophelia dead in Hamlet's arms. Why give us things 'too terrible to be endured', as the famous critic Samuel Johnson once put it of *Othello* and *Lear*? Why insist on our participating in these events without mitigation, or comforting perspectives of any sort?—Because that would be the only way to get us, ourselves, to live through, inasmuch as we can, the very worst of human tragedy, as Shakespeare found himself doing.— And to what end? Shakespeare did not know at all at the time, except that he understood it was what he had to bear on behalf of our full humanity.

To do with it what? To lead us where?—To lead us to a threshold where nothing more would happen, or else suddenly everything. The readiness *was* all: consciousness remained, and it would suddenly transmute further, though without Shakespeare's in any way knowing that it would.—But it finally did, yielding with that those astonishing states of being that are symbolically reflected to us in the extraordinary developments offered to us in Shakespeare's last plays. It is on the basis of these states of being that a brave new world *would* emerge and take shape, even if that world still lies in the far future of our human destiny. We cannot speak of the full scope of Shakespeare's achievement, consequently, without our coming to terms also with all that Shakespeare was signifying as to where humanity would have to take itself further, beyond what he had previously given us by way of histories, comedies, and tragedies: taking *us* further through a form of initiation theater that literally enacts the processes of redemption and of resurrection of which we today only tend to speak.

At the heart of this initiation theater is the understanding that not only is human tragedy not to be forgotten, the whole history of human tragedy as such is to be paradigmatically revived: whether as this was known in Denmark, in Venice, Old Britannia, Scotland, or wherever: human destiny would only be vindicated or justified if it could really overcome itself, which is to say if the human spirit could live it all through again in imagination, to the very depths of the knowledge of human perversity and evil, at least in some essential form. So many of our ongoing usual cultural standpoints, preferences, and presuppositions would in this way have to be let go of, and the further question arises: when, then, can we expect to be able to let go of them? It is a question that, in fact, cannot be answered until we do let go; certainly one can say of Shakespeare that everything changes for *him* after *Hamlet*. However, he did not, on that account, abjure all the rest of his life's work even if he *had* passed beyond it. It was, in the meantime, inevitable that we would carry on the way we always have, even if the full scope of Shakespeare's achievement tells us, in fact, that this cannot, will not be able to, last. We may continue to insist on loving each play simply for itself without any at least avowed need to see them as configuring any special development of vision across each other, which has been the direction we are taking today, especially in this our so-called postmodern and posthistorical age. Along the same lines we can decide that we especially treasure the comedies, especially notably what were once called the 'happy' comedies. And so on for all the plays in all the aforementioned groups: the reasons for preference and privileging in these cases, tending to a deliberate attachment—all this will go on for some time yet. But it does not alter the fact that in Shakespeare's case we are dealing at the last with a great renunciation of all this, all the greater because he was the one who gave us all that he then proceeded to renounce.

It becomes necessary, in this context, to attempt at least to push back at many of the cultural prejudices about Shakespeare's achievement that threaten to totally obscure the finally very serious bent of mind and the unqualified gravity that are associated with his ultimate mission. In these times we are re-writing Shakespeare as never before, indeed one could say writing him out of his very self, this in order to satisfy our own need for self-definition or how we want it to be, but Shakespeare remains, for all that, a man of his own time, someone who made full use of the thoughts of his time to explore himself and our inalienable humanity further. It becomes necessary, therefore, to stay true to what he worked with as a historical experience. For example, he belonged to an age that was steeped in an otherworldly perspective that brought on real experience, so that what is given in *Hamlet* as action would not have seemed at all far-fetched, or merely speculative. Involved in this, as *Hamlet* also shows, was a crushing sense of the burden of what continues to lie in wait in human nature by way of tragic perversity and evil, including, and most prominently at first sight, sexual perversity, with the prospect of judgment for this. Here the contemporary perspectives of Martin Luther, the great Protestant reformer, must be all the more seriously considered, as Shakespeare did, wrestling with Luther in this respect in a way that utterly altered the course of his imaginative life. Shakespeare was learning late the extraordinary lesson of Christopher Marlowe's own tangle with Luther (though not overwhelmed by Marlowe's example, as recent cultural presentations have made bold to think, but rather abiding his own time, patiently waiting for all to take shape in him more and more fully so he could emerge in his own right, thereby taking Marlowe's struggle all the further still.) So—I argue fully—it is Shakespeare's own Muse who, to his great dismay, takes him down this dark path, after he had so carefully wound himself up to a pitch of perfect form up to the time of *Hamlet*.[1]

In the meantime, Shakespeare's otherworldly impulses, like Hamlet's, would die hard. He had thought to be able to vindicate humanity, with reference to all that condemned it in its inner nature, simply through

---

1. For a recent distillation of my views on this score, see my contribution to *Shakespeare the Man*, ed. R. W. Desai (Baltimore, ML: Fairleigh Dickinson University Press, 2014): 'Outbraving Luther: Shakespeare's Evolution through the Tragedies into the Last Plays'.

the re-assertion of a deeper integrity of the type Hamlet still hopes to affirm himself in, the evidence of a universal culpability notwithstanding. However, a visionary justification of human integrity such as Hamlet would mastermind, through his supremely elaborate conception of revenge, it is seen, is no longer possible, and Hamlet himself must die in the further tragic knowledge of this. This was the 'new tragedy' of the time, as I have termed it, and Shakespeare understood from this that the battle with inner human nature would unavoidably have to continue. He was no less intent on testing the value, in those circumstances, of other time-honoured solutions to tragic human nature, including what I have called the 'romantic-transcendental' solution, as given in the ending of *Othello*. We think of Shakespeare, likewise, as the author who staked his claim to literary supremacy as the one who could bring everything and anything to its fullest and final expression, but even in his case what I have further dubbed the 'formal-aesthetic' solution to tragedy, which would settle the problem of tragedy by means of a perfect formal control over it, is seen to fail him, disturbingly. Still other time-honoured notions deriving from Romantic tradition are also finally negated, touching on the presumed inalienable value of heroism and of Nature itself. There was nothing to do, in the end, but to see the total reality of human tragedy through, which Shakespeare does, as I have noted, without any given lead in the matter and to this day far beyond what it would seem we are yet able to fathom, sufficiently to make this into our own experience. But there remains, still, a possibility of *understanding* what is involved and what is at stake, and this is where the extraordinary cultural revelations of Rudolf Steiner have had to come into the picture, to set us properly on our course with Shakespeare, so that Shakespeare himself, I have no doubt, would especially have wished in our time to be remembered by means of what Steiner came to reveal, with its applications also to the full scope of Shakespeare's achievement.

JOM

Introductory Overview:
On Shakespeare's Muse

1
The Muse Appears

Recent interest in who Shakespeare's Muse may have been—his personal Goddess, so to speak—prompts one to come forth to dispel the drastically simplistic notions that have been brought forward. In Tom Stoppard's film script for *Shakespeare in Love*, we are asked to imagine Shakespeare as an author who, at a certain point in his career, has become creatively impotent because sexually and romantically dispossessed, and who is especially non-plussed by the overshadowing influence of Marlowe who is presented as actually dictating some of the material of *Romeo and Juliet*. Along comes a lady who, running against the mainstream of contemporary appreciation, is profoundly taken not with Marlowe's dramatic poetry but (of all things) with Shakespeare's. On his discovering this passion, she and Shakespeare fall head over heels in love, but because of their previous respective commitments in marriage, they cannot prosper, so that she must be ultimately cast as the Juliet to Shakespeare's now tragically unfortunate Romeo (each plays his/her respective part in the opening performance). Shakespeare is once again free to be creative also because Marlowe is now dead, and the former is presented as being responsible for the latter's murder (he has willed it and feels profoundly guilty for it). His lady must now leave him, to go overseas, but in departing from him she is transformed into a symbol of an indestructible creative energy that will never leave him. She will survive the great waters of tragic developments in which they are now immersed to return one day to his symbolic shores as the Viola of *Twelfth Night* (the name she actually bears in real life).

What are we to make of a view of Shakespeare's creative development that stops short halfway through his career, at *Twelfth Night*? It is true that the film's final symbolic sequence, depicting the flailing motions of bodies submerged in water, is intended to evoke not just the scene of *Twelfth Night* but also that of *The Tempest*. The suggestion perhaps (it is far from clear) is that Shakespeare is already in possession of a creative potential that will see him through the great tragic sequence that will engage him so profoundly in the long interval between one play and the other. Of this sequence one must say that there is nothing more tremendous or more tremendously distressing in any literature, and yet all this has been very conveniently left out of the presentation in this film, as if we were to understand that the tragic engagement was there to be gotten through but (once again) were not really ready to know it.

Stoppard's popularizing projection of what we may suppose was involved in Shakespeare's growth and transformation at a highly discrete moment of his career is clearly meant as 'entertainment', and it is conveyed to us with a certain (large) measure of tongue-in-cheek license as well as some very deliberate over-dramatization. In that case, we must think the presentation all the more insidious as an influence, since it also purports to offer a serious view of Shakespeare's development (over-grand, one will think, in the case of the film's very last cut that shows Viola taking her very long walk up the beach on which she has landed). No doubt it is the view of Shakespeare's experience that will survive in the large portion of humankind that got to marvel at this film. Stoppard's presentation is full of the most perverse notions about Shakespeare's experience, and I will be addressing only three of these here before I go on to say where I believe our concern with Shakespeare should actually lie or what form of Muse we can suppose it was that commanded his development the way it did.

(1)

That Shakespeare was ever at a loss for creation, in any degree and at any time in his career, must be seen as a suggestion of total absurdity, and not even Marlowe's influence could keep him from continuing monumentally prolific, as from the first. By the time of the period in question, Shakespeare had produced as many as eight full plays over approximately a five year span, two long narrative poems as well as much of his Sonnet-sequence, and he was returning from a hiatus from the stage of almost two years on account of the plague, to immediately produce almost at one time three new plays in three separate genres: in comedy (*A Midsummer Night's Dream*), in tragedy (*Romeo and Juliet*), and in history (*Richard II*). At what point over this short period of time, and with what possible meaning, can we speak of a creative lapse? We may reasonably speak of a significant qualitative transformation in Shakespeare in the period he was away from the stage, and he returns to it with a renewed impulse of considerable power, as everyone will who has had the occasion to break away from some continuous activity for a while. He would have a similar break at the time of the accession of James I, and that moment would mark another highly significant point of transition: from the powerful, but still relatively static mode that we associate with *Hamlet* to the still more profoundly engaging, considerably more dynamic production represented by *Othello*, *King Lear*, and *Macbeth*.

(2)

In the meantime, the sudden absence of Marlowe from the theatrical scene certainly had something to do with the newly-found sense of freedom and release that appear to characterize Shakespeare's creative effort in the period of *Romeo and Juliet*, though it will strike us as paradoxical to say so. No doubt the sudden death of Marlowe, who was so tremendously gifted and so young at the time, would have had an impact of terrible grandeur, aggrandizing the already profound impression his genius had made on his contemporaries. Shakespeare's struggle with Marlowe would have been made all the *more* difficult by this death, which immediately immemorialized his achievement. However, that struggle went so very deep very simply it had to be deferred, since it had little to do with any usual sense of professional rivalry, by which Shakespeare does not seem to have been very affected.[1] In spite of Marlowe's decided advantage in respect of dramatic achievement at the time of his death, Shakespeare reserved quite enough sense of his own genius, which was already monumental and indeed momentous (his address to his personal daemon in the Sonnets bears this out dramatically). He seems to have been quite content to let his own destiny play itself out, and humbled as he may have been for the moment from the comparison with Marlowe, this was a part that otherwise suited him in light of the altogether singular way he was developing.

His own genius was leading him down a path that he sensed would only bear greater and greater fruit as he was going along. On the other hand, Marlowe's work laid down a challenge that Shakespeare would fully take up only in his great tragic period, which lay ten years away. That Shakespeare would require a full decade to come to terms is a measure of the tremendous depth of Marlowe's achievement, which extended from the combination of both *Tamburlaine* and *Dr. Faustus*, though especially from the latter. Shakespeare would not quite fully absorb the achievement in romantic grandeur of the former play until he finally came through with *Othello*. As for the latter play, and especially its ending, in its incomparable projection of the depths of human depravity, it set a standard that not even Shakespeare's great tragic plays from *Othello* onwards, or Donne's *Holy Sonnets* or Milton's *Paradise Lost*, could displace. I shall have more to say about Marlowe's tremendous achievement below, but influence at that depth was not likely at any time to have kept Shakespeare from continuing strongly in his own development.

(3)

There can be no question that Shakespeare returned to the stage at the time of *Romeo and Juliet* personally transformed, and I too happen to believe that he had in the meantime fallen in love, but the evidence of the Sonnets suggests that he fell in love with a man and not with a woman, and in any case he had been transformed more from love of the eternal that this man represented, from love bred of the eternal, than for what this man represented in himself. Perhaps we may attribute to this love the strong development in the representation of (comic) romantic love that follows from *A Midsummer Night's Dream* through *Twelfth Night*, though highly different forms of love were involved. Shakespeare presents the love of the Sonnets as 'builded far from accident' (see Sonnet 124); he seems to have come back to this saving love in the privacy of his time away from what must have been the trying vicissitudes of continual production in the theatre, among numerous other social responsibilities. He would have returned to this love quite as often from his work in the comedies as from his strenuous work in the histories, which also continued strongly at this time.

We have in any case always made too much of his so-called 'happy' comedies and the supposed romantic inspiration that it is only too easy to associate with his dazzling work in the genre that has always made him so popular, overlooking that Shakespeare was also at this time profoundly engaged in a far broader course of development that was driving him into progressively less and less happy regions. He had always been critical, his romantic comedies themselves incorporating at every turn the sharpest critique of the 'happy' world he was indulging, and that critique he was to unfold to the point where he would finally abandon writing comedies (there would be no more comedies written after *Twelfth Night*).[2] Very simply Shakespeare had grown too serious for that kind of play. He had continued strongly over this same period with his monumental project of depicting the long, dark history of England after Richard II, and that project had involved him in a progressively deeper and deeper study of the great fall in human nature that he saw represented in the will to power. His more recent productions—especially *Henry IV, part one* and *Henry V*— had brought this study to marvellous consummation: his psychological technique especially he had brought to a point of great refinement, so that we have no trouble imagining from here the further leap to *Hamlet*. Here indeed is the great line of continuous development on which we should be insisting, in contradistinction to the usual romantic emphasis. What primarily absorbs Shakespeare in his long, ongoing career is a deeper and deeper study of the will to power, and Claudius would be his next major subject in *Hamlet*. The effects of this character's deeds he could now submit to the intense scrutiny of his own highly developed and refined consciousness as reflected in the figure of Hamlet. In respect of this enterprise, Shakespeare's comedies might be seen as a set of brightly lit candles hanging preciously over his work-desk, which might serve as a form of consolation in the face of the great darkness around him that he had now made his principal concern, but they had become in the meantime secondary, even adventitious accomplishments.

Something of the import of Shakespeare's development at this point may be gleaned from what is dramatized over the course of the Sonnets experienced as a totality. Right up to *Hamlet* Shakespeare maintains an especially resistant and rich connection with the universally beautifying capacities of his most intimate self, the ideal personalized daemon, if you will, who appears in the form of the immortalized young man of the Sonnets' first section. It is well-known that the many Sonnets to this young man break off suddenly to make room for a short sequence of intensely problematic Sonnets to a dark lady that have baffled understanding. The labyrinthine efforts made over the years to seek to identify this dark lady have spelled nothing but futility, for the reason that she is an all-embracing, universal symbol and, unlike in the case of the young man, did not have biographical existence outside the scope of Shakespeare's mythical imagination. Standing at the other extreme from the young man who concentrates Shakespeare's idealized spiritual self, Shakespeare's dark lady crystallizes all the length and breadth and abysmal depths of human perversity. Shakespeare imagines himself enthralled to her as to a kind of universal lover from whom he knows nothing good can come, though he remains wilfully hers. What can this import but that he was fated for a certain experience from which he could not extricate himself, even if he had wished to? This dark lady *is* the Muse to his now tragically beleaguered self—not being at all the kind of Muse popular imagination might have wished for its most celebrated author. It is as if Shakespeare had at a certain point, coincident with his turning to *Hamlet*, gathered up all the forces of his best spiritual self, only to be then bewitched and condemned to experience, in some sense for himself (in his mind), the very worst of which human nature could be thought capable. The Sonnets themselves speak of an absolute negation of any hope of redeeming himself in the terms Shakespeare had elaborated up to that point. The very power of self that the young man had inspired, as an eternal entity lying 'beyond accident', has had to succumb to the greater force of experience that now overwhelms our great author, as in Sonnet 134:

> *Him have I lost, thou hast both him and me;*
> *He pays the whole, and yet I am not free.*[3]

2
Linking Up To Luther

Shakespeare's uncanny and rather disturbing mythical account of himself as associated with this dark Muse would soon find expression in an entirely unexpected *cultural* association. One could well imagine Shakespeare pursuing his studies in the will to power in the histories quite on his own, without substantial recourse to any other major thinker of the time, unless that might be Machiavelli. However, in extending his growing understanding of the will to power into areas that now included (more fully than ever before) the whole psychology and metaphysics of lust (beginning with *Hamlet*), Shakespeare reflects back to us a highly significant deference to Luther—the figure who, after Marlowe, exercised the most significant influence on him at any time in his career. The extent of Shakespeare's reference to the dramatic details of Luther's life in *Hamlet* has been well documented[4]; the elaborate correspondence points to the crucial place Luther continued to hold in the cultural make-up of post-Reformation England. This is in spite of what has been pointed out as the decline of Lutheranism, as a devotional church, in Shakespeare's time. Luther remained, in spite of this, the great hero of the European Reformation to which England, as a Protestant nation, belonged. He continued to maintain, in spite of the strong independence of the English Church from its very outset, a pre-eminent position as the central figure who binds together at every juncture the great effort of the Reformation as recounted by John Foxe in his *Acts and Monuments*, the book that after the Bible was the most widely read in Shakespeare's England. How far Shakespeare's exposure to Luther extends is impossible to say, though numerous English translations of Luther's work already existed in Shakespeare's day. One does not have to imagine Shakespeare working directly from any of these, though he may have done so; he could easily have learned all that he wanted to know of and about Luther simply from what (many) others could tell.[5] Shakespeare's dramatizations from *Hamlet* onwards in any case bear witness to a profound intellectual engagement with the great Protestant leader's appalling view of human nature, amidst which one thought in particular seems to represent Shakespeare's obsessive preoccupation at this time, namely the view that 'nothing can cure libido'.[6]

I imagine Shakespeare taking up this thought in particular (from Luther's commentary on *Genesis*) with appalled abandon. He does so, however, from a point of view that requires some elucidation, since at no point does he embrace this thought as a Lutheran—except perhaps, in a highly qualified sense, initially with *Hamlet*. It was especially devastating for Shakespeare to think this thought precisely because he was not Lutheran and so did not have to hand the further elaborate consolations that Lutherans can claim in the face of it. He seems to have come to this thought with the idea that it must be true, or any rate ready to think it true[7], precisely with that full dramatic power of thinking thoughts through that of course belonged only to him. If this thought, which he seemed to have grasped as the worst of thoughts, did indeed account for human nature, then he would have to take hold of that thought in all its potential reality to see what could be made of it. If one were in the meantime disposed at all to thinking well of human nature, let alone idealizing it, one would have first to find a way of disposing of this thought. And so, at a certain point it seemed all that Shakespeare was ready to think or could think of human nature, like the figure of Hamlet himself, with whom Shakespeare first undertakes his quest.

Over the course of his tragic period, Shakespeare would not in fact be able to resolve this thought, which seemed altogether irreducible. At a certain point he seems to have suffered from it without consolation, via all of the tragic figures that now come from his hand, who seem progressively to add to it the sense of a broader and broader range of human perversity.[8] So that we may imagine Shakespeare carrying on as a great Lutheran would, though without the consolations of grace that also awaited the Lutheran faithful. These in any event Shakespeare was not ready to admit into his inquiry as to what might be thought to be the innate potential of humanity. Luther's terrible injunction, which compelled the moral imagination to peer into the very depths of human depravity, and which we may see as driving Shakespeare, must have appeared all the more grandly and distressingly terrible to the author who was to penetrate more deeply into human nature than any other writer before or since:

Come, accept. Be a sinner! 'Esto peccator!' And don't do the
thing by halves; sin squarely and with gusto, 'pecca fortiter!'
Not just playful sins. No, but real, substantial, tremendous
sins![9]

Not that Shakespeare was alone in this investigation. The dramatists who were his immediate contemporaries in the time of James would also add to the inquiry, offering their own spectacular representations of horrible forms of human perversity, so that the question arose as to whether there could be any other way of checking these tendencies than by some severe manner of moral imposition, of the kind finally proposed in plays such as Marston's *The Malcontent* or Tourneur's *The Revenger's Tragedy*, or Shakespeare's own *Measure for Measure*. These plays put forward models of moral solution that reflect something of the severe moral repression practised by James, who would have thought such interventions laudable (missing out on the irony of the dramatists' representations). Luther would have judged such an approach to the problem typical of 'the ways of the Romanizing oppressors' from whose hands he had come to set humanity free. In Luther's view, it could only be by a free act of the imagination that humanity could turn from an intense absorption in its own innate depravity to the grace-bestowing God on whose 'justification' the Lutheran community attended in its hopeful faith. In the meantime, Shakespeare had left aside any and every such faith, so full is his association with our humanity he could not imagine any prospect of hope other than one that might arise from within humanity's own nature.

3
Marlowe's Route

Years earlier, Christopher Marlowe had come to his own proud reckoning with the Protestant experience. His Faustus (ironically dressed in black and from Wittenberg, as Luther was) initially makes short shrift of it. The view that humanity was radically or fundamentally depraved, so that it could not in the last analysis escape judgment, is dismissed out of hand as irrelevant. Humanity would in any case only wish to venture out for itself when confronted with such a prospect. Thus Faustus is presented as the hero who in choosing a path of magic has come to lead a subjected Europe out of the superimposed Hell of the Protestant judgment:

And I, that have with subtle syllogisms
Gravelled the pastors of the German Church
And made the flowering pride of Wittenberg
Swarm to my problems as the infernal spirits
On sweet Musaeus when he came to hell,
Will be as cunning as Agrippa was,
Whose shadow made all Europe honour him.
(I.i.111-117)[10]

This magic is seen as building on the great sense of worldly promise forecast for humanity from a magnificent understanding of its own powerful graces. Marlowe, in this way, projects another potential *romantic* Wittenberg out of the narrowly oppressed and oppressive historical one. Insistent is his vision of the infinite range of action that was thought to be available:

All things that move between the quiet poles
Shall be at my command. Emperors and kings
Are but obeyed in their several provinces.
Nor can they raise the wind or rend the clouds.
But his dominion that exceeds in this
Stretcheth as far as doth the mind of man:
A sound magician is a demi-god.
Here, tire my brains to get a deity.
(I.i.55-62)[11]

The terms of Faustus' quest necessitate that he resolutely stand by his view that the projection of a judgmental hell is a fictive illusion. This would have to be the case when Mephistopheles and Lucifer finally do appear, in all their terrible, compulsive grandeur (appearances that are absolutely extraordinary in themselves). What are we to make, then, of the fact that within a mere scene of the first encounter with Mephistopheles in which Faustus expresses himself admirably in this resolution, and before we are even out of Act One, he should immediately collapse and is thinking himself already damned from his confrontation with these dark forces?

Now, Faustus, must thou needs be damned?
And canst thou not be saved?
What boots it then to think on God or heaven?
(I.v.1-3)[12]

While Faustus returns to his initial faith in this same scene, what the rest of the play dramatizes (beyond the elaborate forms of escape of his actions with Mephistopheles) is a progressively greater and greater intensification of forces of despair in him—until we reach the play's monumentally terrible ending.

In this ending the whole Protestant angst of being hopelessly fallen is concentrated without relief as Faustus seems destined for damnation in a strictly literal sense. Sensationally enough, he has by then swung over entirely to the opposite experience from the one in which he initially bases himself, an about-face that seems to represent an extraordinary capitulation of sorts. There are the most desperate efforts to work a way out of the entrapment. Faustus calls on time to stand still and for mountains to come and fall on him:

> Stand still, you ever-moving spheres of heaven,
> That time may cease and midnight never come.
> Fair nature's eye, rise, rise again, and make
> Perpetual day. Or let this hour be but
> A year, a month, a week, a natural day,
> That Faustus may repent and save his soul ...
> Mountains and hills, come, come, and fall on me,
> And hide me from the heavy wrath of God.
> ....
> Earth, gape! ...
> You stars that reigned at my nativity,
> ....
> Now draw up Faustus ...
> (V.ii.146-169)

So attuned is Marlowe to the terms of the Lutheran experience, he dramatizes in this same moment the terrible incomprehensibleness of that paradoxical turning back to God that Luther was saying was still possible to our humanity in spite of the fundamental condition of depravity in which it would remain right up to the moment of death, inasmuch as one remained bound to the flesh:

> Oh, I'll leap up to my God: who pulls me down?
> See, see, where Christ's blood streams in the firmament.
> One drop would save my soul, half a drop. Ah, my Christ!
> Ah, rend not my heart for naming of my Christ!
> Yet will I call on him. Oh, spare me, Lucifer!
> Where is it now? 'Tis gone:
> And see where God stretcheth out his arm,
> And bends his ireful brows.
> (V.ii.155-162)

Donne, deliberately building on Marlowe's Faustus, would dramatize this acutely strained hope throughout his *Holy Sonnets*, but without the full terror of 'knowing', as Faustus does, that damnation is a certainty. And that 'knowledge' of course is what explains the unsurpassable power of Marlowe's ending and what made it so continually haunting to those who came after Marlowe:

> The clock strikes twelve.
> *Oh, it strikes, it strikes! Now body turn to air,*
> *Or Lucifer will bear thee quick to hell.*
> Thunder and lightning.
> *Oh soul, be changed into little water drops*
> *And fall into the ocean, ne'er be found.*
> Thunder. Enter the Devils.
> *My God, my God, look not so fierce on me.*
> *Adders and serpents, let me breathe awhile.*
> *Ugly hell, gape not, come not, Lucifer!*
> *I'll burn my books. Ah! Mephistopheles!*
> (V.ii.193-200)

Marlowe's overwhelming projection of defeat in *Dr. Faustus* takes on a profounder cast the moment one gets behind the apparent impression created to the actual intention of its author, which was heterodoxical in a deeper way than has been supposed. Certainly the play and its ending were bound to be referred to the overriding concern with depravity and damnation that so fanatically marks the epoch in which Marlowe lived and over which Luther had cast a shadow that would not lift. The fear of damnation had never been so real, and Marlowe was playing directly into this fear by dramatically inverting the longstanding Morality-play tradition on which he was drawing, a tradition in which Everyman, hopelessly perverse as he had been, had always been saved. A new element has obtruded itself, however, in the further concern with magic—a bold stroke that was bound to raise the heat of theological concern of those times. Conventionally-speaking, it would have been too easy to draw the conclusion that such was the fate that awaited one who presumed through magic to circumvent the intentions of a God who could not be gainsaid. It is indeed doubtful that Marlowe would have accomplished the goals that he reserved if he had not first carefully appealed to this response, both in the play's opening Chorus and in his Epilogue. What he presents within these confines, however, puts an altogether different spin on the action, rendering Chorus and Epilogue ambiguous in turn.

All hinges on the dramatic reversal that Faustus undergoes within a mere scene of his first encounter with Mephistopheles.

There is nothing to suggest that, before this moment, Faustus does not fully maintain himself in the resolution he expresses initially to see his way past the illusory thought of hell. From Faustus' assumption, that there could be no reality to a notion of hell for the human spirit, it follows that he must look upon all that Mephistopheles imports as itself an effect of illusion. Hence the contemptuous superiority Faustus expresses about the despair Mephistopheles reveals over losing the joys of heaven, which appears to Faustus either as feigned or the effect of a spirit itself suffering from illusion:

> *What, is great Mephistopheles so passionate*
> *For being deprived of the joys of heaven?*
> *Learn thou of Faustus manly fortitude,*
> *And scorn those joys thou never shalt possess.*
> (I.iii.83-86)

In this scene Faustus continues strongly in his views:

> *This word 'damnation' terrifies not me,*
> *For I confound hell in Elysium.*
> (I.iii.58-59)

Then follows the breakdown I have mentioned, without extenuation, the very next time we see him:

> *Now, Faustus must thou needs be damned?*
> *And canst thou not be saved?*
> *What boots it then to think on God or heaven?*

This extraordinary about-face is the more unbelievable in that Faustus returns to his initial resolution in this same scene, as if he had never known of the breakdown he has only just experienced:

> *Come, I think hell's a fable.*
> ....
> *Why, dost thou think that Faustus shall be damned?*
> ....
> *Think'st thou that Faustus is so fond to imagine*
> *That after this life there is any pain?*
> (I.v.130-137)

It should be clear that in the intervals between his conscious dealings with Mephistopheles Faustus is in the process of being possessed, is indeed already profoundly possessed from the first by those dark forces that Mephistopheles and Lucifer represent. This is happening in a part of Faustus that he does not appear to know about, developments that contrast sharply with the control he assumes he actually possesses over both Mephistopheles and 'that Lucifer' who is presumed to be Mephistopheles' master:

> *Did he not charge thee to appear to me?*
> ....
> *Did not my conjuring speeches raise thee?*
> (I.iii.43-45)

Faustus enters into his dealings assuming (as Blake would, two hundred years later[13]) that he will have the better of these dark forces that only *appear* to him in the guise of Mephistopheles and Lucifer; hence, the distance he assumes from the names they possess:

> *Tell me, what is **that** Lucifer, thy lord?*
> (I.iii.62)

Marlowe's working assumption is that it is in the power of these forces to overwhelm with the illusion of hell, and he has Faustus confidently suppose that he will outwit them from the sheer strength of his better knowledge. (That Marlowe should have assumed it possible to summon these forces to manifestation is altogether extraordinary in itself, especially in light of the fact that he did not think humanity ready for this occult fate, though it is a testimony to what he was seriously considering.) Faustus is dramatically unaware, however, that these very forces are, from his first dealings with them, already taking possession of him, for the most part in those dramatic interstices during which he is away from our view. Something of that power to overwhelm and possess is suggested in the first appearance of 'that Lucifer' who overpowers precisely as an unrecognizable form:

> *Oh what art thou that look'st so terribly?*
> (II.i.90)

His very form suggests the power of possession he is actually exercising, over an unsuspecting Faustus who is suddenly rendered defenseless:

> *Oh Faustus, they are come to fetch away thy soul.*
> (II.i.92)

The problem for Marlowe, then, lies not in any actual depravity that may be thought of human nature but in the fact that humanity is compelled to *think* depravity from a power of suggestion that he associates with dark forces who are in control and who limit human power in this way.[14] Marlowe's presentation goes so far as to insinuate that all the voices and visions that are represented in the play are the projected suggestions of those dark forces with which Faustus is in communication. This is the case from the very first appearance of Good Angel and Bad that sound as unheard voices to Faustus, as Mephistopheles confesses at the end:

> ... *when thou took'st the book*
> *To view the scriptures, then I turned the leaves*
> *And led thine eye.*
> (V.ii.102-104)

Even the Old Man who appears at the end and who would seem to offer the greatest impression of objectivity constitutes another of the manifold manifestations of these forces: if not, how is it that he appears fully aware of Faustus' dealings with these forces, when no one else has been made aware of them—a point that is emphasized in the scene between Faustus and the Scholars that follows?[15] In fact, none of the voices and visions that are obtruded into the play's scene have any other effect on Faustus than to combine in the most varied ways to compound and aggravate the progressive despair that has been so powerfully suggested to him, destabilizing him beyond any possible power of control over himself. In this way, Faustus is placed, at the end, at the centre of the most massive phantasmagoria of suggested despair this literature had ever seen and was to see for some time to come, which explains the tremendous status Marlowe's ending was to have for some of the greatest writers for years to come. Otherwise, Marlowe's presentation suggests, God is not there: there is no effective presence or reality to any such 'God' or to the 'heaven' that are spoken of so casually in this play, and humanity has in the meantime been left to itself, to deal with forces that can only get the better of a defenseless and unsuspecting human psyche.

4
Lutheran Hamlet

It would take many years before Shakespeare could finally assimilate Marlowe's achievement in *Dr. Faustus* in respect of what it imports of a hopelessly overwhelmed humanity. Shakespeare would not come to terms fully until he came through with *Macbeth*, and in the meantime there was his own extremely complex route to this point from *Hamlet*—a route on which we find him struggling not only with Marlowe but also, profoundly, with Luther. *Hamlet*, as I have said, marks that extraordinary juncture in Shakespeare's career at which, having gathered up the best of his own forces, he suddenly plunges into a Luther-like confrontation with the very worst of human nature. Something of those best forces are projected in the figure of Hamlet, who is described in terms that compare directly with those ascribed to the young man of the Sonnets:

> *Th' expectancy and rose of the fair state*
> *The glass of fashion and the mould of form*
> *Th' observ'd of all observers...*
> (III.i.153-155)

However, these forces are now overwhelmingly referred to the depravity that is supposed to dwell at the heart of human nature as its fundamental condition. This is a new direction in vision that we may see as the effect of the commanding action of the dark Muse to whom Shakespeare has been made accountable.

Hamlet's meeting with the Ghost of his dead father is in this respect a first initiation. He learns of the profound corruptive force of lust at work not only in his mother and in his uncle Claudius, but in his very father, who on account of it has already submitted to the universal judgment that awaits everyone, and so Hamlet himself (and Ophelia).[16] Needless to say Hamlet is greatly disturbed by this revelation, which he bears alone, overwhelmed and possessed by it as Faustus had been overwhelmed and possessed, though in Hamlet's case, unlike what Marlowe makes of Faustus' situation, what is revealed turns out to be really true. At the same time, as the product of a greater maturity, Hamlet has far greater resources for dealing with his experience. As I have suggested, *Hamlet* is the play in which Shakespeare comes closest to actually adopting a Lutheran standpoint inasmuch as the horror expressed about the extent of human degeneracy is complemented on the other side by a highly sophisticated effort to find some form of 'justification' in the face of it. That effort of 'justification' is expressed through the play's profound concern with Hamlet's striving after an otherworldly validation for revenge.[17] That prospect failing Hamlet, he is drawn down by the forces of despair that have otherwise possessed him, with fatal consequences for almost everyone concerned, at the other extreme from the otherworldly justification he has been seeking. We watch him vacillating violently between one extreme consideration and the other. The effect clearly recalls Faustus' analogous condition, though we are as yet far from seeing our way through to the limits of the exploration of human nature on which Shakespeare was now bent.

5
Thinking Depravity

A significant gap interposes itself between *Hamlet* and *Othello*, during which period we may imagine Shakespeare going through a transformation of an intensity unlike any experienced by any artist before or since. Three years after *Hamlet*, and after almost a year away from the stage, he would return to produce in regular succession *Othello*, *King Lear*, and *Macbeth*—incontestably the most intense works of literature we are ever likely to know. We grasp something of his monumental transformation in technique at this time from the fact that in *Othello* he now accomplishes in one scene (Act Three, scene three) what it had taken Marlowe five years to achieve—taking Othello the whole route from the tremendous heights of the Marlovian magnificence in which he initially invests his hero (and in this greatly outdoing Marlowe for the first time) right through to the abysmal depths of the possession, by Iago, in which we find Othello by the time the scene has closed, with extensive allusion made to the controlling power exercised by Mephistopheles over Faustus.

There is a crucial difference, however, bearing on the fact that, in between Marlowe and Shakespeare, Luther had interposed himself with his own great overweighing claim, so that it is not finally for Othello, as it is for Faustus with Mephistopheles, simply a matter of a self-created thinking gratuitously imposed by the dark forces with which Iago is aligned. Othello falls into the possession of Iago, thinking depravity of Desdemona, because Iago's suggestion is profoundly based in reality— not in that Desdemona is guilty of unfaithfulness of course, but in that depravity may be supposed *even of her*, in that it is possible to think it. The suddenly overwhelmingly sensual nature of her engagement with Othello, after a whole history of severe withdrawal from suitors, lends itself profoundly to the suggestion that it is her sexual will, which violently comes over her, that impels her in the first place.[18]

Shakespeare's working assumption in *Hamlet* was that all are steeped in lust at bottom, from the very fact that we are conceived in it ('it were better my mother had not borne me'—III.i.123-124)[19]. It is a matter in this play of an actual condition we all bear in us, even if Hamlet has much trouble thinking it. Something of this point of view is now carried over to *Othello*, with a similar application, if with a profounder irony. In a single passage in this new play, Shakespeare rehearses the material both of Hamlet's confrontation with Ophelia (cf. Act Three, scene one) and his confrontation with Gertrude (cf. Act Three, scene four) :

> DESDEMONA. *I hope my noble lord esteems me honest.*
> OTHELLO. *O, ay, as summer flies are in the shambles,*
> *That quicken even with blowing ...*
> ....
>   *... would thou hadst ne'er been born!*
> DESDEMONA. *Alas, what ignorant sin have I committed?*
> OTHELLO. *Was this fair paper, this most goodly book,*
> *Made to write 'whore' upon? What committed!*
> *Committed? O thou public commoner!*
> *I should make very forges of my cheeks*
> *That would to cinders burn up modesty*
> *Did I but speak thy deeds. What committed!*
> *Heaven stops the nose at it, and the moon winks,*
> *The bawdy wind that kisses all it meets*
> *Is hushed within the hollow mine of earth*
> *And will not hear't. What committed!*
> (IV.ii.66-81)[20]

Later in this same scene, Desdemona, by then overwhelmed by the influence of the profound suggestion at work in this play, will apply *to herself* the thought of her own depravity, in a way that we must see functions also apart from the force of Othello's imposition:

> DESDEMONA. *Am I that name, Iago?*
> ....
> *Such as she said my lord did say I was.*
> EMILIA. *He called her whore ...*
> IAGO. *Why did he so?*
> DESDEMONA. *I do not know; I am sure I am none such.*
> (IV.ii.119-125)

This last statement especially should be seen as spoken in a tone that reveals Desdemona desperately wondering that it may somehow *or at some level* be true. We are returned at this point, in a way that forces the suggestion on us again, to the ambiguous circumstances of her initial choice of Othello, on which Iago had harped so strategically:

> EMILIA. *Hath she forsook so many noble matches,*

Her father, and her country, and her friends,
To be called whore?...
DESDEMONA. *It is my wretched fortune.*
(IV.ii.127-130)[21]

Thinking depravity of Desdemona, Othello is of course himself steeped in his own unconscious share in it, and in this way the thought of it in her profoundly taints him, as Hamlet himself was tainted. The spirit of revenge in Othello bears all the marks of being corrupted by the very vice it sets out to judge. This is unlike in the case of Hamlet who strives strenuously to keep free of that corruption, though he does so only with an ambiguous success. Othello, what is more, in his further deliberate killing of Desdemona goes far beyond the kind of judgment Hamlet expresses of Ophelia and of his mother, horrible as that is in itself. For the first time in Shakespeare in the fullest sense we may say that a hero whom we had thought inherently and profoundly noble is exposed to us in the irreversible depravity of his action.

However, Othello is still far from confronting the actual depravity of which he has become guilty. A very large gap remains between the new degree of depravity Shakespeare suddenly represents and any self-perception in the hero that we might suppose would accompany it, that might persuade us that the depravity has in some way been dealt with. Until this moment, Shakespeare's hero has for the most part been 'merely' thinking depravity, immersed in that thinking in a way that is profoundly disturbing. Now he is plunged into an actual depravity with which he appears, superficially at least, to be unable to come to terms at all.

Equally significant about *Othello* is the way in which Shakespeare for the first time foregrounds a character—in Desdemona—who comes right up to meet the thought about depravity head on. Ophelia is given something of this function in *Hamlet*, but she herself falls prey psychologically to the impact this thought makes through the figure of Hamlet. Strangely, it is Hamlet who in an initial phase bears Desdemona's function. *He* is Shakespeare's idealized self ('That unmatched form and feature of blown youth') submitting to the prospect of depravity that yawns before him. After that, Othello takes us fully into that abyss, relinquishing in doing so the kind of magnificent dignity he stands for. In the figure of Desdemona Shakespeare's idealized self returns yet again, pretending to balance out this prospect from the other side, for while her life may be defeated in the face of this prospect, not so, she says, her love:

... Unkindness may do much,

And his unkindness may defeat my life
But never taint my love.
(IV.ii.161-163)

Her love, however, will itself be of no immediate consequence at least, in the face of the appalling, extreme violence with which she is finally done away with (on which more below, in Part Two).[22]

6
Defeated Life

King Lear takes us one step further than *Othello* in respect of an actual depravity that is now fully expressed, by now by quite a sizable assortment of characters. That representation is, also, accompanied now by a more or less conscious perception in the hero of what is involved both in the scope and import of that depravity. *King Lear* is, in this respect, the play of greatest Lutheran reach and impact, taking us about as far into violent depravity as we can imagine. Speaking of Lear's daughters, Albany says:

Tigers, not daughters, what have you performed?
(IV.ii.41)

And Lear too fully grasps the extent of their actions:

The fitchew, nor the soiled horse, goes to't with a more
riotous appetite ... But to the girdle do the gods inherit,
beneath is all the fiend's: there's hell, there's darkness, there is
the sulphurous pit, burning, scalding, stench, consumption!
Fie, fie, fie! Pah, pah! Give me an ounce of civet, good
apothecary, to sweeten my imagination ...
(IV.vi.120-127)

Of course Lear himself partakes in a very substantial degree in this depravity. There is his initial rejection of Cordelia in which he is overwhelmingly hideous and through which all are plunged into the unstemmable chaos of depraved motives that ensue:

... The barbarous Scythian,
Or he that makes his generation messes
To gorge his appetite, shall to my bosom
Be as well neighboured, pitied, and relieved,
As thou my sometime daughter.
(I.i.117-121)

And at the end of it all, Cordelia lies dead in Lear's arms, Lear inheriting the completeness of his rejection of her. All that Cordelia might have offered of hope in the face of the general depravity is crushed, and she herself has become in her death the profoundest symbol of life defeated by the grossest elements of human nature that prevail. It is the furthest point to which Shakespeare's dark Muse has led him. The further element of love, fitfully thrown up from the depths of Shakespeare's idealized self, is also wiped away by the sheer force of accumulated violence represented over the course of the play and the impact this violence has when Cordelia is herself done away with.

Beyond *King Lear* Shakespeare imagines a still greater precipitation in depraved chaos such as we are given in Macbeth who will 'tumble in confusion', as Marlowe puts it in *Dr. Faustus* (see V.ii.142). Macbeth is driven by a force of actual depravity that entirely overtakes and possesses him as the thought of depravity had once overtaken and possessed Faustus. Shakespeare had indeed taken on Luther's challenge to imagine real depravity to the fullest, while he had also fully incorporated Marlowe's lesson as to the part that would be played in human tragedy by the human psyche in thinking depravity in the first place. Indeed much of the power of 'merely thinking' depravity goes into precipitating Macbeth deeper and deeper into his own tragedy. Such power of thinking is at work in Macbeth from the first, though it stems in his case, in an extraordinary way, from the violence of his actions on the battlefield.[23] However, Shakespeare had by then already passed the point of greatest devastation, the farthest extremities of a stifled humanity, in the ending of *King Lear*. It is a wonder that Shakespeare had anywhere to go from there. Compelled ruthlessly by his dark Muse, and desperately following Luther's lead, he had brought himself to the point of imagining an action in which, as one critic has shown, horrible death finally prevails over 'all forms of hope'[24]:

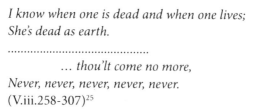

> *I know when one is dead and when one lives;*
> *She's dead as earth.*
> ....
>   *... thou'lt come no more,*
> *Never, never, never, never, never.*
> (V.iii.258-307)[25]

By no obvious route does Shakespeare then imagine his way beyond this point of utter hopelessness. He had done all that Luther could expect in the way of an imagination of human depravity and its devastating consequences. He had come to that point entirely on the strength of his own thinking, without further recourse to a faith that might either console him or allow him, by any mechanism of compensation, to come *away* from the spectacle of human depravity he had opened up. He had been brought to it by his Muse and by his unconscious will to prove the Lutheran indictment of human nature incomplete if not wrong. Could Shakespeare now show that he could plumb further than Luther ever supposed a human imagination might go? Could there be anything else or anything more than what Luther had spoken, about the irreclaimable hopelessness of human nature? Could Shakespeare, that is, pass beyond the worst hopelessness imaginable and, in doing so, thereby prove humanity capable of something by which it could redeem itself in the face of the spectacle of depravity by which it seemed otherwise inculpated? The process by which this prospect finally opens up must be counted among the greatest events in our literature and, as we shall see, expresses an almost unimaginable faith in the power of human self-justification before the most withering indictment of human nature history had yet known.[26]

7

The Transmutation of the Muse

With his seemingly interminable string of tragedies, which had run their course as far as *Timon of Athens*, it appeared for a while as if Shakespeare's career had come to an end. Tragedy in him had spent itself, without further recourse—or so it seemed. The obituary Alcibiades pronounces about Timon might almost apply to Shakespeare himself, who had gone as far in despair about human nature as one could go, far beyond what *we* might think ourselves capable of:

> *Though thou abhorr'dst in us our human griefs,*
> *Scorn'dst our brains' flow and those our droplets which*
> *From niggard nature fall, yet rich conceit*
> *Taught thee to make vast Neptune weep for aye*
> *On thy low grave*
> (V.iv.75-79)

It seems fitting that Shakespeare would see himself by the time of *Timon of Athens* as finally settled close up to the verge of that great 'sea' of troubles of acutest human perversity into which he had peered more fearlessly than any author had before.

Then suddenly, with *Pericles*, a light appears out of the darkness as, out of that 'sea' of ultimate tragedy by which Shakespeare had been claimed, there emerges, by an extraordinary turn, a new *transfigured* life, to replace that which was lost for good. Desdemona had gone down, as had Cordelia, and Shakespeare's tragic heroes with them. No further life could be supposed in those terms. Shakespeare would not in the least deny the ultimate power of tragedy: for him human tragedy finally focuses in the extremest form of violent death of the loved one. With that form of death the love that, out of Shakespeare's idealized self, goes out to meet tragedy is also wiped out. But beyond the extinction of Shakespeare's self in these terms lies the enduring power of Shakespeare's Muse who has led him this far *and who now transmutes in and through the death of the loved one.*

Structurally, the new developments are conveyed through the fact that the loved one—Thaisa in *Pericles*; Hermione in *The Winter's Tale*—now 'returns' from death, having in some sense then 'borne' that death, while leaving behind her in her sacrificial 'bearing' a new redeeming power in the form of her 'daughter'—Marina in *Pericles*; Perdita in *The Winter's Tale*. Pericles focuses around himself the impact human tragedy has made on Shakespeare in respect of our innocence of it—given the way it strikes without regard to our responsibility for it. It would take Shakespeare another two years to find a way of reconciling himself to his tragic imagination also in respect of all tragic guilt that would be incurred from the impact human perversity could have—this in *The Winter's Tale*. Between Pericles and Leontes (the tragic protagonist of *The Winter's Tale*), we read allegorically the sum total of tragic consequence as Shakespeare had imagined this over the course of his entire tragic period. He is by the time of the ending of *The Winter's Tale*, however, transcendentally restored by the power of his own Muse, who has borne, as 'wife' and 'mother', all of that tragedy with him, having bestowed upon him the power of an enduring self through which he has come through, with which we associate the 'daughterly' force of Marina (in *Pericles*) and Perdita (in *The Winter's Tale*).

The Tempest itself builds on the whole massive structure and content of the psychological experience I have just described, referring us to Shakespeare more openly and fully than before. For the death of Prospero's wife we read the multiple form of death as borne over the course of Shakespeare's entire tragic period by Shakespeare's own Muse. In this sense Prospero repeats in his own loss the loss of every other

Shakespearean tragic hero that has gone before him (on which more below). By then, however, the force of enduring self Shakespeare's Muse has bestowed upon him has evolved, in the figure of Miranda, to the point of complete development—Miranda taking the power brought forth by Marina in a first stage and by Perdita in a second stage to the point of a third and final, fully formed achievement. How is that consummation of self-transcendent power achieved? By the final 'sacrifice' Shakespeare's Muse now performs, which seems to have taken the form of her actual 'death' in his life. In *Pericles* and *The Winter's Tale* both, wife and mother are returned from death—i.e., Shakespeare's Muse continues to support him and to bear him up in his struggle to recover. In *The Tempest* wife and mother are *not* returned—i.e., his Muse has passed beyond him. She has left him to fare for himself, though with the ultimate gift of consummate enduring power as reflected in the figure of Miranda who has been left behind. That ultimate gift Shakespeare's Muse brings about by her own final 'death' in his life. This further action of 'sacrifice' corresponds to the difference between Shakespeare bearing the forces of self-transformation as a principle of integration in his mind alone and his finally bearing that integration in his very self as the possession of his own individual person. That difference may be summed up as a difference between the power of his creative thought and such thought become an actuating power in the world. It is the latter development that is reflected back to us in the figure and actions of Prospero, who now works in a supreme power of continual self-transformation symbolically represented to us in the figure of his daughter, Miranda. From her Prospero cannot be dissociated in his essence, while in her *own* person she stands to offer, by her marriage to the world (as represented by Ferdinand), to perform infinitely more for our humanity in the future.

Whoever Shakespeare's Muse may have been, we must suppose that she had everything to do with driving him along the whole strenuous route that I have traced. His Muse drives Shakespeare along this route, initially at least, without either his will or his desire in the matter. From this extraordinary destiny we finally deduce purposes that are generally unknown today, inasmuch as a further *evolution* is supposed on the basis of the fullest possible engagement with the worst forces of our human nature. The challenge was laid down to Shakespeare to imagine the very worst of human nature, ultimately purely on behalf of our humanity and in an entirely experiential way. Thus 'Know thyself' acquires, as the behest to Shakespeare of his Muse, the most terrible of implications.

That the journey was worthwhile *The Tempest* will finally bear witness. Profoundly fitting it is that, when Prospero and Miranda finally do come forward, in their very first gesture, they should be looking out towards that whole destructive 'sea' of ultimate tragedy they themselves have successfully braved. We imagine Miranda, as she stands looking out with Prospero, literally gathered to his bosom, for in one function she stands there as the innermost power of his very self, the very fruit of the whole tragic journey Shakespeare has taken. Shakespeare could not have imagined anything greater or imagined her by any other route than the one he was compelled to take, and she has become, via the self-sacrificing action of the Muse in which he has shared, the greatest gift he could finally have bequeathed to humankind.

PART ONE

Otherworldly Hamlet, and The New Tragedy

Preface on *Hamlet* and Luther

One of Luther's editors has shown how in Luther's experience of faith:

> It is confessed that the mystery of God's act in all its priority incorporates and includes the re-direction of man's capacity of decision. Another way of putting this is to say that faith includes infinitely more than the deciding capacity of man.[1]

By the end of Shakespeare's play, Hamlet has undergone an experience of providential re-direction of his destiny that roughly suggests the Lutheran experience of faith.[2] It is fairly obvious, however, that the providential experience is far from being altogether satisfactory to Hamlet; it *remains*, in fact, painfully ironical for him to the bitter end. If so, this is precisely because of Hamlet's need to affirm his own 'deciding capacity' in his attempt to relate himself to his otherworldly experience, including his attempt to relate himself to that experience in his commitment to revenge. The standard conventional view of Hamlet as the hero of indecision, a man who suffers because 'he could not make up his mind', pales badly before the play's evidence of a tremendous affirmation on Hamlet's part that man *should* be able to decide the ultimate question of his destiny, especially as, in Hamlet's case, that destiny depends on an otherworldly experience that continues to elude him.

The contrast with Luther, in fact, is extensive, for Luther had *his* otherworldly experience, although he never went so far as to claim that he had actually been visited by a Ghost (though his father had, desperately, suspected that it was the Devil that had spoken to Luther all along). Years later, recalling that decisive experience that brought the new insight on which he was to build his entire mature Reformation faith, Luther said that, at the time he had the experience, he felt that he 'had entered paradise itself through open gates'.[3] His 'tower experience'— so called because it came to him while in the tower of the Augustinian monastery in Wittenberg—had brought to Luther his clearest vision of what 'the righteousness of God' entailed:

> There I began to understand that the righteousness of God is that by which the righteous lives by a gift of God, namely

> *by faith. And this is the meaning: the righteousness of God is*
> *revealed by the gospel, namely, the passive righteousness with*
> *which merciful God justifies us by faith ...*[4]

In the tower at Wittenberg, Luther had received ultimate confirmation, as Luther's editor puts it, that:

> *In faith, man stands before God in the light of grace. For him,*
> *even at his best, there is no other possibility ... aside from this,*
> *the actuality of his situation is that he is totally a sinner.*[5]

Himself fresh from Wittenberg, Hamlet comes away from *his* 'tower' experience with the Ghost (the encounter takes place in a remote area high up on the battlements of Elsinore castle) with a vision of human nature that, as I show, is fundamentally Lutheran in tendency. In the 'actuality of [their] situation'—in contradistinction to 'the imputation of righteousness'[6] that Hamlet receives from the otherworldly basis of his vision—men and women are, for Hamlet, totally sinners; all are damned in the experience of libido, which nothing can cure. It is crucial to note, however, how Hamlet's vision, as Hamlet comes away from the Ghost, is in direction in inverse relation to Luther's tower experience, which allowed Luther to admit himself a sinner only because, as revealed to him, there was now no longer any reason for despairing of salvation. Thus, a matter that did not concern Luther because of the thrust of his experience, but that does profoundly concern Hamlet, is the whole basis on which one could know that humankind was universally degenerate. Luther was in the end to elaborate his vision of human degeneracy, in contrast with the divine imputation of righteousness, on the basis of a clear understanding of the gospel, fully inspired into him during his tower experience—understanding that directly confirmed his own personal experience. Shakespeare, through Hamlet, raises the question of how the vision of degeneracy *itself* relates to a basis in immediate otherworldly revelation, for it is on the basis of the Ghost's account of himself, and only on that basis as I show, that Hamlet has come to understand that such degeneracy is indeed the case.

Scholars are not convinced that Luther was not in fact mistaken in his account of when the tower experience came to him. This attribution to Luther of a lapse in memory is a potentially dramatic indication that the meaning and value of Luther's experience as revelation were in a sense irrelevant to the vision of human nature that Luther propounded, that vision depending as it did in the end on a clear reading of the gospel. But the meaning of Hamlet's 'tower' experience with the Ghost, and especially its value as visionary objectification, are for Hamlet of the utmost concern. For without what I call the sustaining 'actuality and coherence' of immediate, otherworldly vision, there can be for Hamlet, from the time the Ghost disappears, no full certainty that the view of man and woman that lingers in him from that vision, and defines that vision for him, is sufficiently well-founded. Nor, consequently, can Hamlet's view of human degeneracy find a proper focus in relation to the cleansing act of revenge that has been required of him.

The inverted relation to Luther points to a relative emphasis in Shakespeare's presentation that is critical in understanding Shakespeare's own vision in his play. That vision is not simply Lutheran, nor is it at all a simple response to Luther. Luther's vision of man's degenerate condition and his vision of the role played by libido in that condition was, I believe, the most significant immediate influence on Shakespeare when Shakespeare was producing his play. From Hamlet's treatment of Gertrude and Ophelia, as well as from the way Hamlet looks upon himself, it would seem that Shakespeare in this play took Luther's negative vision of human libido very seriously indeed. But what of a continued, otherworldly justification for that vision, of no further account to Luther? Hamlet's vision of the degenerate tendency of human libido, otherwise known by him to be based in an objective presentation of the human condition, must appear to have implications all the more tragic and grave just because that vision, once the Ghost disappears, for the most part lacks a clear and sustained connection to its original justification in otherworldly revelation.

Another of the effects that Hamlet has in single-handedly seeking to impose his vision on his world is to highlight tragically what would have had to be surrendered to that vision at the time *Hamlet* was written—namely, the innocent, romantic view of love and of religion so characteristically Elizabethan. In fact, the impact of the Lutheran vision of human libido on Shakespeare would not have been nearly so tragic as it was, had Shakespeare, as a product of the Elizabethan age, not been himself so hopelessly romantic. Although I have said that I believe the Lutheran vision of human libido constituted the fresh influence on Shakespeare when he was writing *Hamlet,* a whole number of other influences continued to play into Shakespeare's representation. Another strong influence playing into Shakespeare's representation at this time was the whole disposition towards otherworldly vision stemming, as I show, from a continuous, native tradition going back through Thomas Kyd to Thomas Sackville. As the evidence of that literary tradition suggests—

especially the precedent set by Kyd—the question of continuing to base an account of the human condition in a direct otherworldly vision remained, right up to the time of *Hamlet,* a critical consideration. Within this tradition—and *Hamlet* cannot be separated from it—man's capacity for acting ethically at all depended on his being directly sustained by an ideal otherworldly relation. *Severed* from that ideal relation, Hamlet cannot, in fact, properly focus his revenge—otherwise heroically required of him to halt the course of evil in his world—in a manner satisfying 'perfect conscience'. Separation from an otherworldly experience is for Hamlet, as it was for Kyd's hero, Hieronimo, a matter consequently of very special concern and sorrow.

The question of what then becomes possible to Hamlet in his tragically dissociated condition receives further imaginative treatment in the play in the form of Hamlet's extended meditation on the possibilities of revenge implied throughout, of which I attempt a convenient outline in the section on Revenge. Herein we shall find some of the play's most dramatic pictorialized evidence of that identification with the 'deciding capacity of man' that I am claiming simply must follow from the condition that separates Hamlet from the otherworldly basis of his vision. Still more evidence of the identification with man's deciding capacity is to be found in the play's last movement that follows on Hamlet's failure to execute his revenge in the prayer scene. Indeed, in light of the play's insistent preoccupation with man's deciding capacity, right down to the play's very last sequence, the theme of the impending death of Hamlet, formally announced long before there can be any resolution of the question of vision, must appear to have an effect all the more tragically pathetic. The play's final effect of pathos is underlined in an especially striking way with reference to the painting by El Greco that Shakespeare's final action seems almost to invoke directly, but with which Shakespeare's action in the play as a whole, because of its underlying preoccupation with the tragic frustration of Hamlet's vision, must be seen as ultimately contrasting poignantly.

1

Sorrow

When Thomas Kyd preceded the play's events in *The Spanish Tragedy* with the Ghost of Andrea giving an account of his descent into hell, he was building on an innovation that Thomas Sackville had introduced years before in his contribution to the *Mirror for Magistrates.*[7]

When Sackville's *Induction* was first presented to the *Mirror*'s curiously sensitive, though always well-meaning body of distinguished compilers, the poem had roused them to wonder and consternation at the audacity of its invention. Radically unlike the other stories in the *Mirror*, the *Induction* was being made room for as a 'preface' to Sackville's less anomalous contribution of the story of Buckingham; as an artistic *cadre* for that story Sackville's *Induction* was unusual, for both its elaborate sophistication and audacious use of the vision-structure that the *Mirror* poets had been applying to the stories in the tradition of Boccaccio and Lydgate. Each story in the *Mirror* was narrated by the Ghost of its subject who was to be imagined appearing to the poets in a vision. With only one exception (the ghost of Richard of Gloucester was pictured 'howlinge from the deepe pit of hell'), the ghosts had been imagined by the *Mirror* poets as speaking either freshly dead or on the point of death (and thus as an 'Image of death'), or else 'newly crept out of the grave'. Sackville's *Induction* had disturbed this pattern by setting its speaking ghost among thousands of others in the depths of hell, after Sackville claims to have been led into hell on a journey by the Goddess Sorrow.

The fear of the *Mirror* poets was that Sackville's procedure was likely to be ill-taken, since the hell-setting implied a judgment on the statesmen ghosts, whereas it had been until then the general procedure of the *Mirror* poets to refrain cautiously from such judgments. Even worse, in its sympathetic qualities Sackville's judgment 'savoured' of Purgatory, thus catering to the papist misrepresentation of the otherworld. This fretfulness was allayed by the intervention of the *Mirror*'s less excitable voices. Falling back on Renaissance syncretic method, it was concluded that Sackville's hell was really no hell at all but in fact a symbol for the grave; and so it was that Sackville's subversive *Induction* was reconciled to *Mirror* procedure: even then, the syncretic solution was unnecessary since Sackville's Hell was merely 'a Poesie', relevant 'adornment' merely.

The decision of the *Mirror* poets to restrict their visions to the moment of death was not merely to be traced to their determination to eschew political and theological controversy. The extraordinary complacency with which some of the *Mirror* poets treat of the topical implications of the *Induction* show that. The procedure said a great deal rather about their basically rationalist assumptions about the nature and function of the creative imagination. In refraining (with the exception of Richard of Gloucester whose damnableness was obvious to all) from taking their ghosts beyond the brink of the grave, the *Mirror* poets were merely acting on their limited belief as to how far the creative imagination could go in developing a conceit that had in any case been adopted more from deference to tradition than from any real insight into its poetic function. Nor is this implication of *Mirror* procedure contradicted by one or two spectacular exceptions to the rule, most notably in the ghosts of York and Collingbourne who are imagined speaking one out of a headless trunk, the other with his heart in his hand, 'smoking forth the lively spirit'. In these cases, the *Mirror* poets were merely employing a sensationalistic rhetoric guided by a sense of the miraculous reality one might effectively project onto death for compulsive reading, for which the conceit, that is, served merely as conceit without any suggestion of a projection of literal reality. Not only were the ghosts kept scrupulously close to the grave, it was clearly established from the first that they were to be regarded as the creations of story-telling: at most, they could receive a sensationalistic representation from the influence of a fantastic ardour always rhetorical in purpose.

The basic procedure for telling the stories finally rationalized the appearance of the ghosts. But, in proceeding along the lines it did, the practice of the *Mirror* poets stood out in sharp contrast against the claim to visionary organization that even the *Mirror* poets acknowledged respectfully of their models, Boccaccio and Lydgate. This isn't to say, of course, that the *Mirror* poets did not believe in the power of creative imagination; indeed, the effectiveness of their stories depended on it. Thus, it is correct to say, with Alwin Thaler, that 'the *Mirror* group believed in true feigning, true imagining by poet and audience'.[8] It is an account, however, that obscures the actual position of the *Mirror* group for whom 'true feigning' consisted in seeing that 'imagining' was merely an effective means for conveying what was true, and not actually true in itself.

It was inevitable, therefore, that these poets should fail utterly to appreciate the extraordinary status of Sackville's *Induction* as vision. Significantly, the obvious function of Sackville's poem as vision led Baldwin, the *Mirror*'s chief editor, to associate it rather with the extraordinary creations of Lydgate and Boccaccio than with the more sensible fictions of the *Mirror* group. Yet, far from representing an effort at real understanding, Baldwin's gesture merely served to highlight the group's spectacular incomprehension, for the syncretic-rhetorical reduction showed how Sackville's visionary journey was finally to be taken. Sackville's vision was to be reduced to symbolic thought or to fiction: what the *Mirror* group had failed to see was that the journey Sackville described took reality precisely from the extraordinary developments by which mere thought had transformed itself into vision. The Goddess Sorrow, who serves as Sackville's guide for the journey into Hell, could not have put the import of Sackville's experience more unambiguously:

> ... *behold the thing that thou erewhile*
> *Saw only in thought* ...
> (ll's 530-531)

Sackville's *Induction* stands out from the other more modestly-shaped stories in the *Mirror* by virtue of its active belief in the transformational powers of the imagination. From that belief, it followed that what only appeared to be an outer shell for thought was to be taken in fact as literal vision. In presenting its vision, Sackville's poem drew on the conventional medieval form of the marvellous journey. In doing so, it had taken on the narrative form as literal fact. The power that had made the journey possible was the Goddess-guide Sorrow, who according to the pattern is more than merely a personification. She is the spiritual objectification of the poet's own grief, round whom the expanded vision of hell takes place: the visionary product of a 'busie minde' lost to its metaphorical 'musings' (ll.64,156).

In beginning *The Spanish Tragedy* with a descent into hell himself, Kyd could not have been unaware of Sackville's use of the marvellous journey as vision. Whether or not the intensity of the narrative actually justified the claim to vision is not the point, neither here nor in Sackville. Both accounts, unlike in the rest of the *Mirror*, acted on the assumption of the literal function of narrative, thus projecting, in contrast to the *Mirror*, an unlimited belief as to how far the imagination could develop the traditional conceit inherited from Boccaccio and Lydgate. In all cases, the conceit of the speaking ghost had been adopted to intensify the impact of the tragic events treated. That much is clear from the use made of the conceit by the *Mirror* poets. The capacity of the audience to imagine a speaking ghost, to lose themselves, as it were, to the fiction, accounted for the intensity with which the stories would be received. By filling out the fiction, the imagination of the audience built on the intensity that the poets likewise had brought to their story-telling by imagining themselves as speaking ghosts. However, the fact that the narrative could also serve, as in Boccaccio, to express a claim to literal vision ('As hym thoughte in the inward siht'[9]) could only have added to the psychological value of the narrative for both poet and audience. That value was likely to be intensified the more extraordinary and expansive the vision, so that Sackville and Kyd had everything to gain from linking a vision of the speaking ghost with an evocation of the otherworld, a larger vision of the descent into hell.

The full metaphysical significance of this linkage in Kyd can be best appreciated by first tracing what Sackville had done to Boccaccio. Boccaccio's vision had operated within the tradition of an artistic framework for the narrative of falls, which set the pattern for the later narrative tragedy of the *Mirror*. As Howard Baker points out, in his *Induction to Tragedy*: 'The ordinary procedure was to have the ghosts of the fallen Worthies appear successively as in a vision, before the poet ... The ghost ... was sometimes conducted from the infernal regions to the poet's chamber to the 'stage' by a guide.'[10] It was Sackville's daring innovation at this time to fix once again on the literal possibilities of the journey in Boccaccio's vision, building in part on the powerful precedent of epic tradition, including Dante, but, primarily, Virgil. The appearance of the ghost before the poet in Boccaccio already assumed a journey from the infernal regions to the poet's chamber. In that journey the ghost had been led by a guide. In his own development of the vision, Sackville had used the guide, inversely, to carry the poet from his chamber on a journey into the infernal regions where ghosts awaited him.

In a further development, Kyd had brought both models together. The drama of the Ghost's appearance in the Prologue ultimately emphasizes his immediate presence in the world: that is where the Ghost finds himself quite unexpectedly after the process of judgment in the underworld is mysteriously interrupted. There, Andrea performs the function of the ghost in Boccaccio, appearing before the audience on the stage as the ghost had appeared to the poet on his own 'stage' in the poet's chamber. This is a presence however that, unlike in Boccaccio, recreates as immediate background the marvellous journey into hell following Sackville:

> *When I was slain my soul descended straight*
> *To pass the flowing stream of Acheron:*
> *But churlish Charon, only boatman there,*
> *Said that my rites of burial not perform'd,*
> *I might not sit amongst his passengers.*
> *Ere Sol had slept three nights in Thetis' lap*
> *And slak'd his smoking Chariot in her flood,*
> *By Don Horatio, our Knight Marshal's son,*
> *My funerals and obsequies were done.*

Then was the ferryman of hell content
To pass me over to the slimy strond
That leads to fell Avernus' ugly waves:
There pleasing Cerebus with honey'd speech
I pass'd the perils of the foremost porch.
(I.i.18-31)[11]

Once again, it is necessary to insist that Kyd's narrative, like Sackville's, functions as literal vision. Though the narrative itself may suggest something still far removed from a totally convincing projection of an embodied vision, it is certainly more than merely a fiction: there is no basis for allegorizing the narrative or reducing it to something else, for not taking it exactly as it appears as itself.

Moreover, the function of the Ghost and his narrative as vision would have been immeasurably enhanced when the transposition from one 'stage' to the other had been fully grasped. For the whole power of the Prologue depends on seeing it as a dramatic development of narrative procedure. What this meant was that the total vision that we see and hear on the stage, in the form of the Ghost and his narrative, was to be taken as the direct transposition of the vision acted out before the poet on his own stage when writing the play out in his chamber. The transposition implied an analogy between the audience watching and listening to the Ghost on stage and the poet watching and listening to it in his chamber; indeed, on the analogy of the poet in his chamber, the audience was being compelled to respond to what was taking place before it as a vision of their own, in a final extraordinary merging of the poet's vision with the vision of the audience. Something of this complex, metaphysical relation, one assumes, survives in the presentation of the Ghost in *Hamlet*, and it may explain the portentous intensity that unites us with the Ghost in his account.

One can see from developments in narrative tragedy that a perception of visionary development was intimately associated in this literature with the immediate inspiration of the chamber or the study, the concentrated solitude of which it is easy to imagine offering the poet precisely that marvellous setting for dynamic thinking in the complex metaphysical representation of his experience that he would well have been seeking. Nowhere is the sensitivity to the inspiration of this setting reflected in more dramatic terms than in that great inward achievement in the drama of the Elizabethan Renaissance, *Dr. Faustus*. As Helen Gardner has noted 'the play begins and ends with the hero in his study'.[12] Moreover, in a central scene from (one version of)

that great play, the devious power of supersensible manifestation that
Faustus brings with him to the court of the Emperor Carolus is explicitly
projected by the Emperor as fulfilling that insistent identification with
the sensible realization of metaphorical thought brought into dynamic
focus in the concentrated solitude of the study—that intimate, yearning
preoccupation with supernatural vision—that one ought to look upon as
a typical experience in the Renaissance:

> *Then, Doctor Faustus, mark what I shall say.*
> **As I was sometime solitary set**
> **Within my closet, sundry thoughts arose**
> *About the honour of mine ancestors,*
> *How they had won by prowess such exploits,*
> *Got such riches, subdued so many kingdoms,*
> *As we that do succeed, or they that shall*
> *Hereafter possess our throne, shall,*
> *I fear me, never attain to that degree*
> *Of high renown and great authority;*
> *Amongst which kings is Alexander the Great,*
> *Chief spectacle of the world's pre-eminence,*
> *The bright shining of whose glorious acts*
> *Lightens the world with his reflecting beams,*
> *As when I hear but motion made of him*
> **It grieves my soul I never saw the man.**
> *If, therefore, thou, by cunning of thine art,*
> *Canst raise this man from hollow vaults below,*
> *Where lies entomb'd this famous conqueror,*
> *And bring with him his beauteous paramour,*
> *Both in their right shapes, gesture and attire*
> *They us'd to wear during their time of life,*
> *Thou shalt both satisfy my just desire*
> *And give me cause to praise thee whilst I live.*[13]

In terms that are in keeping with this whole background material,
the process of visionary engagement begins for Hamlet in a substantial
sense and, to a degree greatly understressed in one aspect of the criticism
of the play, in the experience of loss and division in the death of his
splendidly noble father. One will acknowledge here as motive force
initially the 'sorrowful imagination' of native narrative tradition with its
embodiment of the experience of loss or death, or evil—or the tradition
of the 'vision growing out of extreme sorrow' as Howard Baker accounts
for it in his *Induction to Tragedy*—a tradition one can trace not only in

the near-contemporary work of Sackville, as Baker does, but in as remote and individual a manifestation of that tradition as Chaucer's *Book of the Duchess*. In Hamlet's case, there is the added, complicating experience of subsequent disgrace and outrage:

> HAM. *Thrift, thrift, Horatio! The funeral bak'd-meats*
> *Did coldly furnish forth the marriage tables.*
> *Would I had met my dearest foe in heaven*
> *Or ever I had seen that day, Horatio!*
> *My father—methinks I see my father.*
> HOR. *Where, my lord?*
> HAM.   *In my mind's eye, Horatio!*
> HOR. *I saw him once; 'a was a goodly king.*
> HAM. *'A was a man, take him for all in all,*
> *I shall not look upon his like again.*
> (I.ii.180-188)[14]

Whether Hamlet's emotions are actually evolved enough in this early part of the play to render the visionary figure of the Ghost fully believable as the projection of Hamlet's identification with his father in death is a moot point, one about which one cay say at least that it is of no immediate concern to the play. It is sufficient for the play at this juncture that the relation is established within its own frank appropriation of the idea of the visionary possibility. Nor does this relation depend alone on the passage where Hamlet is shown claiming to 'see' his father 'in [his] mind's eye'. Powerful as such an evocation is already, it is rendered the more powerful when viewed as the surface expression of a crucial relation developed earlier when Hamlet is described 'seeking' with 'veiled lids' and 'eye' (I.ii.68-71) for his 'noble father in the dust'. One seeing is another. The play shows no embarrassment in associating the metaphorical import of Hamlet's mental 'seeing' as developed in the later passage with an even more literal relation in the earlier passage projecting vision as a miraculous extension of physical 'seeing'. Indeed, what is insistent about the initial action of this play is its status as a spectacular *fulfilment* of the rhetorical, wishing structure implicit in metaphorical vision:

> HAM. **Would I had met** *my dearest foe in heaven*
> *Or ever I had seen that day, Horatio!*
> *My father—***methinks I see** *my father.*
> HOR. *Where, my lord?*
> HAM.   **In my mind's eye,** *Horatio.*

The rhetorical structure, through the implicit operation of the earlier (wilful) relation, now turns dramatically into literally true development, projecting a faith in metaphysical possibility as extraordinary as anything in the age and characteristic of one aspect of it. This is the very development of literal fact that had escaped Richard II in his own quest for the visionary realization of an otherworldly power, greatly supporting and vindicating the common claim of these heroes to a knowledge of substantial reality in the experience of grief and outrage, in spite of the inevitable sceptical disbelief of their worlds. (so Hamlet: 'I have *that* within...'; so Richard: '*there* lies the substance').[15] Moreover, Hamlet's engagement in vision gains further (although perhaps too obviously) in intensity from its association, when Hamlet speaks his mind to Horatio, with Horatio's experience of having once 'seen' Hamlet's father in life. It is a dramatic collocation of different orders of 'seeing' characteristic of this age's bold consideration of an accommodation of visionary realization at the level of the 'real' world. One is especially struck by the effort in this context to suggest that the Ghost possesses a vividness of reality directly comparable to bodily actuality. This is the gist of Horatio's response to the Ghost, which he communicates at first to Marcellus and then to Hamlet:

> HOR. *Before my God, I might not this believe*
> *Without the sensible and true avouch*
> *Of mine own eyes.*
> MAR.   *Is it not like the King?*
> HOR. *As thou art to thyself.*
> (I.i.56-59)

> HOR.   *... each word made true and good,*
> *The apparition comes. I knew your father;*
> *These hands are not more like.*
> (I.ii.210-212)

The difficulty Hamlet faces in successfully grasping and retaining the complex substance of his experience at his meeting with the Ghost is immediately conveyed to us after the Ghost's disappearance. We may choose, following a main tradition, to attribute Hamlet's 'collapse' at this point to his tragic shock and accompanying infirmity over the extremity of the corruption and evil that have been revealed; for some, I believe wrongly, it is a shock that, in fact, precedes the revelation about the murder and that has thus already significantly incapacitated Hamlet by the time the murder is exposed. Such an emphasis on the extremity of the evil known is no doubt true, although it takes the rest of the play to make us aware of what this evil finally involves. For the emphasis *at this moment* points immediately for cause to a weakening in metaphysical intensity; as Roy Walker once noted, it is immediately the problem of paling vision:

> *Whether or not Hamlet will falter depends on his power to regain the stamp of this apocalyptic experience when the apparition is no longer before him but visible only to the inward eye ... the inward vision sinks below the level of consciousness.*[16]

The breakdown of consciousness that accompanies the Ghost's disappearance constitutes for Hamlet a descent back into the ordinary world of sensible experience where the Ghost no longer provides a coherent and objective focus for the multi-levelled revelation of Hamlet's vision and where inward reality thus lacks the intense actuality and coherence of visionary *objectification*. The significance of this breakdown in *Hamlet* may be gleaned from parallel developments in *The Spanish Tragedy*. For the truly significant development in Kyd's Prologue was the final placing of the vision. The immediate vision of the Ghost, as in Boccaccio, remained 'real' enough, but the vision of hell had shifted here from being the immediate vision of the poet himself, as in Sackville, to being the remote vision of the Ghost. The literal function of narrative already ensured that even a vision presented at second-hand would be experienced by the audience as literal vision, even as immediate vision, but when it becomes clear that the Ghost has actually been narrating his vision from this side of the world, the vision undergoes an extraordinary deflation. What had been experienced by the audience at first as immediate vision becomes a vision suddenly placed in time and space beyond the world: indeed, in the bafflement that we re-enact with the Ghost in finding ourselves with him on this side of the world, it is as if the vision had never taken place, having vanished 'in the twinkling of an eye' (I.i.85), as quickly as the Ghost had been transported back to the world. Our initial experience of vision has convinced us that the vision has been real, but it is no longer immediate, and there is a sense in which it has even become unreal.

This ambiguity in the status of the vision is clinched when Kyd has the Ghost remark that in being transported from one place to the other, he has passed 'through the gates of horn' (I.i.82). G. K. Hunter has seen Andrea's return through the gates 'as dramatic equivalents to the introductory sequences of medieval dream allegory'; from this, he concludes that 'the play may be viewed as what Andrea dreams'.[17] Yet this significance can hardly be obvious, for surely the use of the gates works the other way around: they confer the status of dream on Andrea's vision of the otherworld, not on the world to which he returns, which is the reality the dream-vision throws into relief.[18] That Andrea's dream is associated with the gates of horn suggests that Andrea's vision has been real, but once relegated to dream it becomes something less than itself— the memory of what has taken place on another plane. Nevertheless, we might add that Kyd's use of the dream-vision contrasts sharply in this respect with the mundane use made of it in the *Mirror*, as in Baldwin's dream of the Ghost of the Duke of York, which, though it puts the dream-vision into its traditional setting, presents something quite unlike the potently ambiguous reality of the dream-vision, since here the dream-vision amounts merely to 'fantasy' (1.59; p.181).[19]

By contrast, in his Prologue Kyd relies, as we have seen, on a more subtle use of the vision-structure for the creation of 'real' perspective. First, the abstraction of the Ghost is given its own forceful 'reality' in the play through the theatrical transposition by which the poet's vision merges into the vision of the audience. The problem of abstraction posed by the descent into hell was likewise obviated through recourse to a literal appropriation of narrative: the Ghost's vision of the otherworld was to be experienced for itself; as elaborated, it drew on the sense of immediate wonder one can easily imagine being associated with the marvellous journey into hell. That Andrea's vision in the underworld should then suddenly undergo deflation is all the more extraordinary considering the pains Kyd has taken in the Prologue for the creation of perspective. But the deflation would seem to be crucial to Kyd's theme. The same breakdown in reality, with its new, paradoxical awareness of limitation-*in*-reality, could be demonstrated in the progression of Hieronimo's speeches, making Kyd the first among Elizabethan dramatists to embody, to his own limited degree of realization, a new expression of the fortunes and significance of sorrowful imagination:

> Hier. *And art thou come, Horatio, from the depth,*
> *To ask for justice ...*
> ....
> *But let me look on my Horatio:*
> Senex. *Ah my good lord, I am not your young son.*
> Hier. *What, not my son? Thou, then, a fury art,*
> *Sent from the empty kingdom of black night*
> *To summon me to make appearance*

Before grim Minos and just Rhadamanth,
To plague Hieronimo that is remiss
And seeks not vengeance for Horatio's death.
SENEX. *I am a grieved man, and not a ghost,*
That came for justice for my murder'd son
HIER. *Ay, now I know thee, now thou nam'st thy son,*
Thou art the lively image of my grief.
....
And all this sorrow riseth for thy son:
And selfsame sorrow feel I for my son.
(III.xiii.133ff.)

And so we may imagine Hamlet saying: 'And selfsame sorrow feel I for my father': just when the self might have counted on its old capacity to crystallize an otherworldly vision, it finds itself suddenly tragically isolated, conscious of itself as possessed of an identity known in direct relation to its separation from such capacity. It would take an exposition far beyond the limited scope of this chapter to bring out the full significance of the dramatic breakdown in imaginative capacity to which the hero is now subjected. Yet, already one appreciates the picturesque pathos and gravity of the change that comes over this scene as the hero is suddenly jolted *out* of his full identity with an otherworldly reality and world-basis. Gone suddenly is the initial certitude of an original connection immediately linking the hero in his sorrow to its visionary correlative in the otherworld. In its stead is now the *isolated* human sorrow, more real certainly in 'our' sense of what is real, but emerging, as one can see, as the sorrowful separation into a consciousness of self whose identity is thus defined through the fact that it is known in direct relation to this tragedy of lost contact with an otherworldly reality and world-basis—a contact and capacity from which the human 'self' is distinguished by its separateness but from which it cannot originally be separately conceived; for the emergence of the human self represents in this manifestation pre-eminently a lament over the loss of such capacity.

Hamlet, it is true, breaks through to another, final 'vision' of the Ghost, in the play's so-called 'closet-scene' in III.iv. And what is emphasized at this difficult, extraordinary reunion of mother, son, and father, in states so hopelessly and irreversibly changed from the innocent condition in which they had known each other before the murder, is the tremendous pity of the family break-up and separation. The pity of that predicament is emphasized to us the more as a result of Hamlet's effort, as a consequence of this separation, to substantiate what must seem to

Hamlet and to us the only means left for these three to *justify* themselves again. That effort is to be seen where Hamlet desperately seeks to direct Gertrude's attention to the reality of his vision of his father's Ghost and what this portends of hope:

> QUEEN.   *Whereon do you look?*
> HAM. *On him, on him!* **Look** *you how pale he glares.*
> *His form and cause conjoin'd preaching to stones,*
> *Would make them capable.* **Do not look upon me,**—
> *Lest with this piteous action you convert*
> *My stern effects; then what I have to do*
> *Will want true color—tears perchance for blood.*
> QUEEN. *To whom do you speak this?*
> HAM.   *Do you see nothing there?*
> QUEEN. *Nothing at all; yet all that is I see.*
> HAM. *Nor did you nothing hear?*
> QUEEN.   *No, nothing but ourselves.*
> HAM. *Why,* **look** *you there.* **Look how** *it steals away.*
> *My father, in his habit as he liv'd!*
> **Look where he goes even now** *out at the portal.*
> (III.iv.124-136)

Hamlet's directing action with Gertrude is his latest and most poignant attempt to bridge that impenetrable gap between the *reality* of vision, on the one hand, and, on the other, the desperate insistence of a speech entirely given over, in its metaphysical reaches and at its metaphysical limits, to the expectation of such vision. But with this last experience of the ultimate elusiveness of the Ghost and his reality, an old possibility of experience passes away for good, having, with its disappearance, ushered in a new significance for sorrow.

We have seen, then, how *Hamlet,* and its predecessor *The Spanish Tragedy,* build on the entirely extraordinary faith of that age in a power of 'sorrowful imagination' as literally true development. Only a careful consideration of the complex developments from narrative to dramatic tragedy will allow us to appreciate clearly the extraordinary daring and depth of originality entailed in reviving a faith of that kind. Sackville, in breaking away from the highly conventionalized mode of the *Mirror,* was the first to restore vital power to an ancient and venerable visionary tradition. By the time *Hamlet* was being written, awareness of the possibilities of sorrowful imagination had become general, as is evidenced by the Emperor's speech from the 1604 A-text of *Dr. Faustus.* But in further adapting that tradition to the tragic self-consciousness of his own time, Kyd must be credited with having displayed quite as much daring as had Sackville, breaking with tradition while yet preserving a wonderfully comprehensive sense of continuity with the past. *Hamlet* brings both the tradition and the new tragic self-consciousness into a further relation of consummate power and poignancy. And in an age as sceptical as our own, when the question of our relation to the possibility of an otherworldly experience has all but ceased to possess any direct urgency for so many of us, one can only marvel at the profoundly searching spirit that could make a traditional power of otherworldly experience once again available to the Elizabethan imagination, as well as at the acute understanding that imagination reveals of one, peculiar dimension of the modern sorrowful self. That dimension both Shakespeare and Kyd would seem, as a consequence of their traditional power, to have been in an especially privileged position to see in terms of an otherworldly relation.

2
Sexuality

A consistently progressive view of Hamlet's overwhelming engagement in visionary destiny has been greatly undermined in the criticism of this play by a prominent opinion that has stressed Hamlet's revulsion at his mother's sexuality as the *exclusive*, fundamental motivation in Hamlet's experience. Such an opinion rests strongly, though not entirely, on a reading of Hamlet's emotions about his mother's marriage in his first soliloquy, which has been taken to express Hamlet's melancholic disgust, an emotion before whose intensity the revelation of the murder and the sense of horror it inspires have been felt to be secondary and superfluous. As a matter of fact, what is more properly described as Hamlet's outraged despair over his mother's marriage constitutes at the point of Hamlet's first soliloquy an entirely *new* emphasis in Hamlet's grief, for until then Hamlet's melancholic outburst is one we are bound to refer on the whole to Hamlet's grief over his father's loss and to the sorry state of affairs to which the 'world' has come since the death of his father. Hamlet begins his account of his feelings in his soliloquy with precisely this emphasis:

> *... That it should come to this!*
> *But two months dead! Nay, not so much, not two.*
> *So excellent a king that was to this*
> *Hyperion to a satyr; so loving to my mother,*

That he might not beteem the winds of heaven
Visit her face too roughly. Heaven and earth!
Must I remember? Why, she would hang on him
As if increase of appetite had grown
By what it fed on; and yet, within a month—
Let me not think on't. Frailty, thy name is woman!—
A little month, or ere those shoes were old
With which she followed my poor father's body,
Like Niobe, all tears—why she, even she—
O God! a beast that wants discourse of reason
Would have mourn'd longer—married with my uncle,
My father's brother; but no more like my father
Than I to Hercules.
(I.ii.137-153)

I see no evidence in Hamlet's soliloquy of an *active* disgust over his mother's sexuality, but rather profound outraged despair stemming, on the contrary, from active pride in the sexual splendour of his father, which is specifically what has made marriage to Claudius insupportable, the marriage being, as Hamlet sees it, an unbelievable display of womanly weakness and insensitivity. Thus, when it is revealed that what occupies Hamlet specifically is his mother's hastiness in marrying a second time, the revelation is one that is already deeply conditioned by our sense of the outrage it represents to the memory of Hamlet's father who projected in Hamlet's eyes a contrastingly noble condition. 'Let me not think on't': think on what? On Gertrude's marriage with Claudius. Yet the direction of the thought is predetermined by the earlier 'Must I remember?', where it is clear that Hamlet is *also* thinking on the splendid union between Gertrude and Hamlet's father now so pitifully outraged.

Nor is Hamlet's identification with his father in grief, subtle and profound as it is here in expression, restricted to these terms, for there is the further suggestion that the motive force in Hamlet's experience lies in his ultimate identification with his father in death and God's reality, including the implicit, favourable judgment assumed to have been bestowed on Hamlet's father, in contrast with the present ignoble life of his mother with Claudius:

O, that this too too solid flesh would melt,
Thaw, and resolve itself into a dew!
Or that the Everlasting had not fix'd
His canon 'gainst self-slaughter! **O God! God!**
How weary, stale, flat, and unprofitable,

> *Seem to me all the uses of this world!*
> *Fie on't! Ah, fie! 'tis an unweeded garden,*
> *That grows to seed; things rank and gross in nature*
> *Possess it merely. That it should come to this!*
> *But two months dead! Nay, not so much, not two.*
> *So excellent a king that was to this*
> *Hyperion to a satyr; so loving to my mother,*
> *That he might not beteem the winds of heaven*
> *Visit her face too roughly. Heaven and earth!*
> *Must I remember? Why, she would hang on him*
> *As if increase of appetite had grown*
> *By what it fed on; and yet, within a month—*
> ....
>   *... why she, even she—*
>
> **O God!** *...*
> ....
>   *... married with my uncle ...*
>
> (I.ii.129ff)

And so, when Horatio finally breaks the wondrous news of his father's visitation, the terms in which Hamlet expresses his impatience with Horatio to tell on are all in keeping with this fundamental motivating inspiration:

> *For God's love, let me hear.*
> (I.ii.195)

With the Ghost's account, however, comes a dramatic re-orientation in Hamlet's view. For from the moment the Ghost begins to reveal himself at the interview, it is established for a start that judgment on Hamlet's father has *not* been favourable as Hamlet has supposed, thus greatly complicating and intensifying the grieved pity Hamlet already feels over the loss of his father:

> *Thus was I, sleeping, by a brother's hand*
> *Of life, of crown, of queen, at once dispatch'd;*
> *Cut off even in the blossoms of my sin,*
> *Unhous'led, disappointed, unanel'd;*
> *No reck'ning made, but sent to my account*
> *With all my imperfections on my head.*
> *O, horrible! O, horrible! most horrible!*
> *If thou has nature in thee, bear it not ...*
> (I.v.74-81)

At the heart of the outrage to Hamlet's father is the suggestion of a horrible inhumanity represented by a murder whose significance for Hamlet's father is that he was 'Cut off in the blossoms of his sin'. It is a strange phrase, because of the violent juxtaposition we get of 'sin' with all the positive qualities invoked for us by the term 'blossoms'. Yet a somewhat complex adjustment on our part *will* allow us to penetrate the paradoxical and indeed quite terrible significance of the phrase. In our post-Romantic age, we will be inclined to overlook that 'nature' almost always automatically involved for the Elizabethans the *sexual* correlative; when we consider, furthermore, the overwhelming and contradicting influence of Luther and of Calvin at this time, we shall then be in a position to see in Shakespeare's use of the phrase the recognition of a power of judgment bearing down on the sexual optimism of the Elizabethans. What the phrase appears meant to convey, to the tragic confounding of Hamlet's aesthetic sense, is a judgment on the sinfulness of even the richest and noblest sexuality, what had formerly been assumed to be the expression of a noble beauty in nature fully embodied for Hamlet in the sexual splendour of his father as a man but which metaphysical events have now revealed to be finally punishable in the otherworld.

The objection will perhaps be raised that the Ghost at this very interview speaks of his 'love' as being 'of that dignity / That it went hand in hand even with the vow / I made to her in marriage', which would seem to suggest a 'love' that was sound. In fact, the Ghost is here referring to his faithfulness; faithfulness on his part does not imply soundness in the relationship; and we learn here there was Gertrude's adultery with Claudius, and that already implies a relationship between Gertrude and the elder Hamlet no longer sound. But in any case, for Luther as for Calvin, neither faithfulness nor marriage could *ever* ensure soundness in the sexual relationship; or as Luther puts it:

... nothing can cure libido, not even marriage ...[20]

And the Ghost's sudden revelation captures all that is most disturbing in the Protestant view, namely that such a significance for sexual love could not be known for certain except as a judgment in the otherworld. Such a reading of the Ghost's situation will explain what has long baffled critics, as to why Hamlet should treat the sexual problem as if it were a universal affliction. For the effect of this revelation on Hamlet, we must assume, must be to make of his father's fate a universal embodiment of the tragedy of sexuality.

The motivating force behind Gertrude's adultery and the murder it engenders is a judgment of the profoundest implication. It isn't merely that a bestial lust leads to (or is involved in) the inhumanity of murder; ultimately, the significance of such lust is to emphasize the lust in all love, involving a murder that is *itself* a violent arraignment of sexual love, leading to judgment in the otherworld for Hamlet's father. In this arraignment we find represented that darker Lutheran view which is now brought into further tension with another view that is yet reserved, more indulgent and typically Elizabethan, according to which sexual love is innocent and a normal indulgence of nature, to be atoned for and settled (in preparation for the otherworld) through the customary religious rites:

> Cut off even in the blossoms of my sin,
> **Unhous'led, disappointed, unanel'd;**
> **No reck'ning made,** but sent to my account
> With all my imperfections on my head.
> O, horrible! O, horrible! most horrible!

It is to the full implications of these most complex developments, in themselves extremely unwieldy, and not, as has been suggested, to some mysterious psychotic disturbance, that we must attribute Hamlet's later hysterical preoccupation with sexuality. It is how Hamlet's original sense of the moral-emotional outrage against his father is ultimately experienced. Such hysteria is not to be confused with the 'hysteria' over his mother's sexuality as displayed in the first soliloquy, which has been much exaggerated and, I believe, in any case, misinterpreted. The 'hysteria' expressed there measures the gap between his mother's lust for Claudius and the innocent intensity of her sexual love for Hamlet's father. This distinction is not merely intensified, it is tragically confounded by later revelations about the larger sexual implications surrounding his father's life and death—and no doubt the outrage is the greater for this. To this is added the horror of punishment in the otherworld, all of which calls for full and immediate revenge. Thus, in his preoccupation with sexuality, Hamlet is not giving vent to a disturbance independent of the play's pattern of crime and punishment, with implications strictly for Hamlet's character or his view of life.[21] On the contrary, he is coming to grips with a deep disturbance at the very heart of the play: with the horror of an act that, in exposing the inherent 'sinfulness' of sexuality as such, leads directly to punishment in the otherworld for Hamlet's father.[22]

And so we get that tortuously pained and tragic accusation, so complex, that Hamlet brings against Gertrude in the closet-scene:

> *... Such an act*
> *That blurs the grace and blush of modesty;*
> *Calls virtue hypocrite; takes off the rose*
> *From the fair forehead of an innocent love,*
> *And sets a blister there; makes marriage-vows*
> *As false as dicers' oaths. O, such a deed*
> *As from the body of contraction plucks*
> *The very soul, and sweet religion makes*
> *A rhapsody of words. Heaven's face does glow*
> *O'er this solidity and compound mass*
> *With heated visage, as against the doom—*
> *Is thought-sick at the act.*
> (III.iv.40-51)

One of the more significant features of Hamlet's complex accusation here is that it begins with an account of blighted love that would seem from the context to apply to the relationship between Hamlet's mother and father but that might equally apply to the relationship between Hamlet and Ophelia (it is not, as E. M. W. Tillyard claimed,[23] merely a reference to the latter). The ambiguity is significant and a clue to Hamlet's behaviour toward Ophelia in the nunnery-scene. Hamlet's behaviour there is not to be explained as a mysterious, fundamental disturbance regarding sexuality, one essentially *unrelated* to the murder; on the contrary, it is precisely Hamlet's disposition in this scene to view the nature of his relationship to Ophelia strictly in relation to the sexual implications of the murder, particularly its implications for the innocence of love. Thus, when Hamlet characterizes consummated love as something that would make of Ophelia a 'breeder of sinners' (by this, of course, Hamlet has specifically in mind a consummated love with him), Hamlet is acting on the assumption that all love is lust, when seen from the perspective of otherworldly judgment, as true of Hamlet and Ophelia as it was of his father and mother. The effect of this perspective on Hamlet is to persuade him that although he thinks himself 'indifferent honest' (III.i.122) and likely in the figure of Ophelia to be 'inoculated' by 'virtue' (117), he is inevitably bound to 'relish of it' (118). This is what Hamlet has now come to see, that:

> *... the power of beauty will sooner transform honesty from*
> *what it is to a bawd than the force of honesty can translate*
> *beauty into his likeness. This was sometime a paradox, but*
> *now the time gives it proof.*
> (III.i.111-115)

Yet such an account as I have given could not *alone* explain Hamlet's peculiar hysteria, either in the nunnery-scene or the closet-scene, which seems finally to emerge from the murder's full paradoxical implications for love. These set in tragic conflict alongside the otherworldly knowledge of love as lust a lingering sense of the fundamental innocence of love. Hamlet's behaviour in the nunnery-scene is ultimately explained by the knowledge that he could not from an otherworldly perspective have loved Ophelia with the innocence he supposed; yet, the knowledge itself is endowed with the full pain of a tragic discovery conflicting with the more immediate knowledge that he did and still does. And it is thus that we are given a sense of what has been lost, and must be abandoned: belief in a love that ennobles nature characterized in the play by the love between Hamlet and Ophelia and that originally assumed of Hamlet's father and mother, what the play elaborates as the 'rose' in love (III.iv.42-43) embodying 'rose of May' (IV.v.154)—contrasting with 'A took my father ... / with all his crimes broad blown, as flush as May' (III.iii.80-81)—that itself held the 'expectancy and rose of the fair state' (III.i.152), but that tragic events have revealed to be merely the 'primrose path' (I.iii.50)— consider 'the blossoms of my sin' (I.v.76)—to 'sulphurous and tormenting flames' (I.v.3).

Hamlet's behaviour towards Ophelia is thus finally bred of (and fully explained by) Hamlet's new tragic sense of the sexual paradox. In the context of this understanding, the further deduction is then made that there can no longer be any significance for the kind of compromise virtue, once treated as an absolute virtue till the Ghost's revelation exposed it as compromise, that once settled the sexual problem by properly subordinating sexual nature to the rites of religion, specifically to marriage. This bears out the second part of Luther's view, namely that 'not even marriage' can cure libido. Revelations about his fate made by Hamlet's father have also exposed, along the way, the limitations of marriage as a means of restraining and ordering the sexual drive. Given this additional implication, it seems inevitable that Hamlet should come to see Gertrude's marriage to Claudius as a living embodiment of all that marriage has been shown not to be, likewise inevitable that the question of an 'honest' love with Ophelia, which could only have been kept 'honest' by marriage, should drive Hamlet to say with special reference to the full abusive import of Gertrude's marriage to Claudius: 'I say we will have no moe marriage' (III.i.147). The tragic understanding underlying this climactic utterance is brought to full statement in the passage from the closet-scene already quoted (see p.56). There the suggestion is that the 'union' between Gertrude and Claudius (and the murder it involves) has implied a blighted love, not only between Gertrude and the elder Hamlet but also between Hamlet and Ophelia. This is so also in the sense that the union involves the falsification of marriage. Apart from the fact that it represents the degradation of one marriage by another, the full effect of this union has been to destroy the illusion that marriage actually sanctifies love or can really serve as a check on one's sexuality. What has been finally lost, in fact, is an innocent perspective on religion as a whole, what had formerly made it possible to indulge in sexual love and at the same time, and without contradiction, submit to the judgments and practices of religion: that 'sweet religion' ('sweet' in its seeming power to assuage guilt and anxiety) that tragic events have revealed to be merely a 'rhapsody of words'.

In the rest of the speech, Hamlet goes on to claim through some typical Shakespearean hyperbole, that the sexual outrage amongst them all is so monstrous and so appalling to Heaven, what it threatens is the break-up of the world itself, and the immediate precipitation of doom and judgment. This is more than mere hyperbole. In being represented as 'thought-sick', Heaven embodies Hamlet himself, the suggestion being that in his psychological experience of the outrage Hamlet has to a degree literally united himself with Heaven in the sense that he has come to possess as a result of his experience intimations of a visionary eruption in the world. The propelling force behind the anticipated eruption lies in Hamlet's profound experience of the outrage. From the representation of Heaven's face this is emphasized as a prodigious sense of shame, but a sense of shame represented significantly as the lust that has compelled it, as 'heated visage' suggests simultaneously the blush of modesty and sexual ardour. The ambiguity in the representation of Heaven's face would seem to be used by Shakespeare, finally, to build up the image of Heaven, on the verge of the Judgment, blushing over itself as a Great Whore. Whatever we may think of this as an intimation of the projected scope of judgment in this play, it seems clear that Shakespeare meant by it to project some sense of the ultimate implications of Hamlet's psychological experience, here specifically as it relates to his awareness of lust as a universal condition forecasting judgment for all in the otherworld.

To Gertrude's further exasperated appeal challenging an account of the intense accusation Hamlet brings against her—'Ay me, what act, / That roars so loud and thunders in the index?' (III.iv.51-52)—Hamlet replies, typically, not with any direct reply, but, as if to counteract Gertrude's contemptuous disbelief over his abstraction, by penetrating again to the contrast between his father and Claudius the wilful insistence on which in himself accounts initially for the process that leads to the appearance of the Ghost:

> Look here upon this picture and on this,
> Etc ...
> (III.iv.53ff)

One may look upon Hamlet's return to the contrast between his father and Claudius at this point merely as a regressive emphasis. As I understand this, it occasions in Hamlet rather some of the most intense, thinking penetration of that power of lust defying all reason that, whatever the precise causality in time, *remains*, on the level of significant metaphysical reality, not only the animating cause in the murder of Hamlet's father but the appalling occasion of Hamlet's revelation about a supernatural judgment testifying even more conclusively to that power's horror. When one bears in mind this further supernatural extension of the tragedy it becomes clear that the terms of Hamlet's penetration of the matter at this point are entirely essential, if pitifully inadequate and baffled:

> ... What devil was't
> That thus hath cozen'd you at hoodman-blind?
> (III.iv.76-77)

The outright hysteria that eventually emerges in Hamlet's baffled account only yields more point and penetration to his further effort from here to reach out (as with a searchlight) to the basis of a controlling and corrective good lying amidst such power of lust, which Hamlet desperately assumes must be there in one's being *in reality*, to be touched off, if good is to prevail:

> Eyes without feeling, feeling without sight,
> Ears without hands or eyes, smelling sans all,
> Or but a sickly part of one true sense
> Could not so mope. O shame! where is thy blush?
> (III.iv.78-81)

The power of the address to hell that follows comes thus from the literal object of Hamlet's thinking at this point:

> ... Rebellious hell,
> If thou can'st mutine in a matron's bones,
> To flaming youth let virtue be as wax
> And melt in her own fire ...
> (III.iv.82-85)

and at its climax gives ironic sign of the same desperate nihilism, the same utter lack of positive confidence about reality, if in a less advanced form, as will animate the later projections of Lear:

> ... *proclaim no shame*
> *When the compulsive ardour gives the charge,*
> *Since frost itself as actively doth burn*

finally invoking the ultimate horrible transformation and inversion:

> *And reason panders will.*
> (III.iv.85-88)

3
Revenge

Emphasis, in the meantime, on the questionableness to Hamlet of Ghost and revenge stems inevitably from an emphasis on a skeptical consciousness implicit in the play. The latter emphasis was developed, in the twentieth century, in several forms[24], each with its own distinctive moral-metaphysical perspective on the action and, in each, central reference is made to 'all those speculations about death and what comes after death'[25] that, in addition to the Ghost's ambiguous demands, would appear to have marked the play out as a tragedy of doubt and uncertainty in the most singular way. In this extended and highly flexible form, the skeptical viewpoint constitutes one of the major approaches to *Hamlet* in critical tradition. It is, in its main features, demonstrably a modern development of the nineteenth-century emphasis on the play as a tragedy of thought and irresolution[26], and, thus, the modern version of two major manifestations of the projection of Hamlet as the 'myth character of the doubting, self-contemplating intellectual'.[27] Since the larger critical tradition I have just outlined is one on which a good deal of attention has already been lavished, it would be supererogatory of me to attempt to represent it. My concern, rather, is with one, peripheral manifestation of this tradition as it bears on the authenticity and integrity of the Ghost. The Ghost's appearance and comportment, we are told, are such as to warrant intense doubt and self-questioning on Hamlet's part. On closer examination, this issue turns out to be one that many critics have felt to be, in fact, subsumed in the natural impression received from the play that the Ghost is genuinely the spirit of Hamlet's dead father.[28] Perplexing doubts, it is true, remain, for it is undeniable that both Horatio and Hamlet, when addressing themselves to the Ghost, act on the knowledge that the Ghost might possibly not be genuine. But in the structure of the exposition, such doubts are merely the measure of the Ghost's overwhelming power of engagement. For it is a fact of exposition that all doubts are ultimately subsumed in the larger emphasis on the wonder of the Ghost's *reality*, his pitiful majestic distress, and on his significance as the embodiment of a visionary revelation the determination of which must be extorted from him at all costs.[29]

The authenticity of the Ghost has also been questioned on the grounds that in the nature of its demands there exists a fundamental contradiction and an absence of integrity, an objection that centres around the command to revenge. This has been deemed questionable on the grounds that revenge is an unnatural and strictly barbarous principle inconsistent with and repugnant to the civilized-Christian viewpoint of the play. This is a reading that has had an extremely wide acceptance.[30] But implied in most criticisms of revenge as an unnatural and barbaric command is the idea of revenge as a physical act and punishment only, even though it is a crucial fact—one that could not, one feels, fail to be remarked, that revenge is enjoined not as a physical punishment primarily but as a metaphysical one designed to express Hamlet's complex relation to his father's murder and to pass divine judgment and, in this sense, enjoined as a sacred, heroic and creative act.[31] It is simply untrue and grossly unfair to the passionate majesty and visionary awesomeness[32] of the interview between Hamlet and the Ghost to say that the call for revenge is 'lugubrious'[33], or anything less than consummately engaging and extraordinary. It is precisely this aspect of the scene that lifts the Ghost's demands onto a higher *metaphysical* level of engagement, the moral unity of which we are not meant to doubt, remote and archaic as it may all appear to us to be today.

Nevertheless, this is not to deny questioning in the play at a more evolved stage, sometime after Hamlet's impression of the interview with the Ghost has faded, questioning that I should like to bring forward by focusing first on a significant ambiguity in the following passage:

> *I am myself indifferent honest, but yet **I could accuse me** of such things that it were better my mother had not borne me: I am very proud, revengeful, ambitious; with more **offences** at my beck than I have thoughts to put them in, imagination to give them shape, or time to act them in.*
> (III.i.122-127)

It is obvious that the passage, in context, is meant to be taken partly as self-dramatization craftily designed by Hamlet to reinforce (whether or not Hamlet assumes Polonius and the King to be immediately present) the erratic judgment of Hamlet's behaviour associated through Rosencrantz and Guildenstern with the King. The dramatization, however, is not entirely convincing, at least not to the King, who comes away as alarmed as ever, unconvinced that what obsesses Hamlet is either love or ambition. If this is so, it is partly because as with so much else in this scene, as with Hamlet's dealings with the Court generally, the passage constitutes, at the same time as it is meant to be evasively self-dramatizing, an alarmingly genuine if a typically enigmatic revelation about Hamlet's state of mind. To the King, on one level, it represents (and is meant to represent) a monstrous threat on his life judged to be of general 'danger' to him (III.i.167); to Hamlet (and to us) it is a suggestion of the projected 'revenge', on this level strangely exaggerated in part from genuine bafflement now about its import. The effect on Hamlet of his bafflement, strangely, is to suggest that *it is he himself who is monstrous*. The reason for this is provided through a highly significant ambiguity in Hamlet's use of 'offences' (III.i.12). This can be taken to mean either the 'offences' Hamlet threatens to inflict on Claudius or the 'offences' already inflicted by Claudius on Hamlet. Thus, a first suggestion is that one set of 'offences' is simultaneously the other; a second suggestion (drawn from what follows) is that both 'offences' are outside Hamlet's power of control and monstrous to Hamlet because of this. And so it is because Claudius' 'offences' cannot be properly controlled for purposes of revenge that Claudius' 'offences' become Hamlet's 'offences' in an *identical* sense, the latter representing, in fact, *the literal repetition of the former*.

The profound suggestion of literal identity emerges from another passage taking us back to Hamlet's disturbing projection of himself as Pyrrhus in the Player's speech about the slaughter of Priam, a passage unconsciously 'called for' by Hamlet. I am referring here to the section in the speech that depicts Pyrrhus in 'unequal' combat with Priam, particularly the point of hesitation as Pyrrhus is just about to descend on Priam:

> ... *his [Priam's] antique sword,*
> *Rebellious to his arm, lies where it falls,*
> *Repugnant to command. Unequal match'd,*
> *Pyrrhus at Priam drives, in rage strikes wide;*
> *But with the whiff and wind of his fell sword*
> *Th' unnerved father falls. Then senseless Ilium,*
> *Seeming to feel this blow, with flaming top*

> Stoops to his base, and with a hideous crash
> Takes prisoner Pyrrhus' ear. For, lo! his sword,
> Which was declining on the milky head
> Of reverend Priam, seem'd i' th' air to stick.
> So, as a painted tyrant, Pyrrhus stood
> And, like a neutral to his will and matter,
> Did nothing.
> (II.ii.463-476)

Once again there is a highly significant ambiguity, in the representation of Pyrrhus. It is obvious that as a 'painted tyrant' suspended over the helpless Priam, Pyrrhus is designed to suggest, in Kenneth Muir's words,[34] 'the ruthless king-killer Claudius'; less obvious is the fact that, hesitating in this fashion, 'like a neutral to his will and matter', Pyrrhus simultaneously suggests Hamlet. I believe Muir is wrong in claiming that insofar as it concerns Hamlet, the suggestion is that Pyrrhus is the 'ruthless avenger Hamlet wished to be himself'. In fact, the representation of hesitation and stagnancy so suggestive of Hamlet seems to point rather to the opposite conclusion: that Pyrrhus is precisely the 'ruthless avenger' Hamlet does not wish to be. The connection between revenge and murder, moreover, is more than a matter of common ruthlessness. If Pyrrhus' deed suggests both murder and revenge at once, as Pyrrhus suggests at once both Claudius and Hamlet, then up to a point revenge *is* murder, as Hamlet is Claudius; revenge is in some sense the *direct* expression of murder. This is so, I believe, in the sense that the energy and violence of Claudius' crime are *literally* the energy and violence of Hamlet's projected revenge—the two exist up to a point as *one* in Hamlet's mind, as Hamlet's psychological experience of the crime. However, if revenge and murder are one in the sense and to the extent I suggest, then the risk is that revenge will not emerge as itself, as an action taken to redress the violence of murder and, therefore, as an action morally different from murder, but as a literal *repetition* of the murder. Hence Hamlet's 'doubt', hence the hesitation.

By another ambiguity in the representation of Pyrrhus (one ultimately conveying profound pathos) Hamlet's 'scruple' in revenge is linked directly to the 'scruple' that in murder Claudius ought to have had but didn't, or the 'scruple' that he did have but chose to ignore. It is the scruple of conscience that could have averted the evil in the first place and, thus, spared Hamlet the anxiety of his own, the 'scruple-in-murder' that for a moment substitutes for the 'scruple-in-revenge' as the *other* countercheck to evil whose failure at the time is especially to be lamented now that it has made the operations of conscience in countering evil so much more complicated for Hamlet. And it is out of a sense of his burden in these terms that for a moment Hamlet (unconsciously) harks back to the thought of what he might have been spared had Claudius submitted to his 'scruple' when the moral conflict was clearer and easier, before the complications of murder rendered the operations of conscience so bafflingly problematic.

The point of the ambiguity is not to imply that Hamlet ought to act on his scruple as Claudius ought to have acted on his, anymore than the play assumes that revenge is, from a moral perspective, *necessarily* like murder. The play's meditation at this point stems rather from the fact that the evil set loose by murder, which conscience alone could not avert, makes the revenge required to restrain it tragically confounding, highlighting the problem of a violent action to be done in 'perfect conscience' (V.ii.67), perfect integrity of being and so raising the spectre of whether the act of revenge is 'to be or not to be'. Thus, when Hamlet, having just narrated the details of the sea-adventure to Horatio, later rationalizes the need for revenge by invoking the fullness of the evidence of Claudius' evil as well as the implicit evidence of a proliferating evil:

> ... *Is't not perfect conscience*
> *To quit him with this arm?*
> (V.ii.67-68)

he is (perhaps wilfully) obscuring for a moment the tragic complications inherent in countering evil with revenge. When he goes on to ask of himself if it is not:

> ... *to be damn'd*
> *To let this canker of our nature come*
> *In further evil?*
> (V.ii.68-70)

he suggests through this, by a significant *inversion* of the implications of revenge, which suggest that Hamlet's revenge is bound up with Claudius' damnation, that it is as much to be damned himself to let Claudius' evil rage unchecked as it is also to be damned, in a sense for the moment obscured by Hamlet, to counter evil with an improper revenge.

Thus, in Levin's phrase[35], the problem is 'how to know what to do', but not in Levin's sense—that the rational limits of human knowledge make it impossible for us or for Hamlet to understand the exact significance and purpose of the Ghost or if Hamlet is to accomplish his revenge.

Here the powers of human knowledge are adequate enough. It is rather that the normal, rational limits of human knowledge are inadequate to compel the tragic complexity of Hamlet's experience into the moral unity required by him to fulfil his purposes. These purposes demand, rather, the phenomenally integrating power of an original *visionary* knowledge that would seem to be irrecoverable. Thus, to the extent that the required revenge is unknown to Hamlet (in the visionary sense) and merely known (in the rational sense) it is tragically problematic, in the sense that there is a double danger of mistaking the known for the unknown and deferring to the lack of knowledge at the expense of the known, corresponding to the double fact that it is to be damned both to execute an improper revenge and not to execute a revenge at all. These dangers, together, measure what is right and what is possible: on the one hand, an *ideal* revenge representing a proportionate violence to be done in 'perfect conscience'; on the other, an *immediate* revenge to be measured according to its 'distance' from the other. Both considerations are crucial in helping us judge the complex effect of the prayer-scene, which seems to be precisely about the multiple ironies and complications connected with Hamlet's attempt to conceive of the required 'horridness' in revenge.

The conflicting judgments that have been brought to bear on Hamlet's behaviour in this scene make this, in Levin's phrase[36], the *vexata quaestio* in the critical interpretation of Shakespeare (second perhaps only to the ending of *King Lear*, and whether *Lear* is finally a pessimistic or optimistic play). It is a striking indication of the conflicting responses elicited by this scene that the 'reasons' given for Hamlet's delay have been traced to considerations of humaneness on the one hand, and hubris and monstrous inhumanity on the other. Thus, Helen Gardner (echoing G. Wilson Knight) argued that the scene appeals to our sense that we do not wish 'to see Hamlet stab a defenceless kneeling man'[37]. Similarly, Peter Alexander (echoing Bradley) brought attention to standards of humane conduct that keep Hamlet from 'stabbing a villain in the back'[38]. The purpose (and effect) of the scene, according to this position, is to create a set of conditions that, by appealing to considerations of humaneness, make revenge seem immediately inappropriate and ironic.

It is a glaring flaw in Alexander's argument, however, that he does not address the apparent monstrousness of the 'reasons' Hamlet actually gives. These cannot be explained merely with reference to the complementary virtue of 'toughness' in that general disposition of character in Hamlet whose heroic distinction for Alexander consists in being 'humane without loss of toughness'. The effect of Alexander's argument, in fact, is to suggest that the reasons given for Hamlet's delay (which Alexander draws, like Gardner, from the audience's sense of what is right and appropriate in the circumstances) are the explicit reasons Hamlet gives, another oversight that makes Alexander's interpretation of this scene finally unsatisfactory. Helen Gardner is herself more carefully explicit. She glosses the 'depth of hatred' to be found in the reasons Hamlet gives as an 'outlet' for 'baffled rage':

> *No.*
> *Up, sword, and know thou a more horrid hent.*
> *When he is drunk asleep, or in his rage;*
> *Or in th'incestuous pleasure of his bed;*
> *At game, a-swearing, or about some act*
> *That has no relish of salvation in't—*
> *Then trip him, that his heels may kick at heaven,*
> *And that his soul may be as damn'd and black*
> *As hell, whereto it goes.*
> (III. iii. 87-95)

On the other hand, for those for whom Hamlet's reasons given here are neither an expression of bafflement, nor insincere[39], in whom the inclination (following Waldock) is to assume that Hamlet 'means what he says'[40], the purpose of the scene is to draw attention to Hamlet's hubris, to show how in 'reaching out too far in his calculations'[41], Hamlet misses the 'perfect moment'[42] for revenge. Here emphasis has been given to Hamlet 'playing at God'[43]: 'the mere death of Claudius is not enough ... he will have him eternally damned as well, arrogating to himself a Judgment which should be left to Heaven'[44], or again '*he* it must be who decides the issue of Claudius' salvation, saving him for a more damnable occasion'[45]. It is a perspective accompanied appropriately by emphasis on the larger irony in the scene that shows Claudius to be not 'fit and seasoned for his passage' as he appears, but as suitable for damnation as ever.

Thus, while some have emphasized that revenge is inappropriate and ironic because inhumane in the circumstances, others have stressed that the circumstances are the fittest for revenge, making the opposite thought that revenge is inappropriate, because insufficiently horrid, ironic. With an acute power of synthesis, Harry Levin brings these conflicting, apparently irreconcilable interpretations together. He does this not without overlooking the fact that they imply opposite valuations (based on different levels of reasons) and lead to opposite conclusions about the immediate appropriateness of revenge. What permits him to overlook these, however, is his assumption that revenge is intrinsically inappropriate in any circumstances:

> *For all these criticisms, on varying levels, the common stumbling block is the code of revenge, the cult of blood for blood, the* **incongruity** *of a civilized man carrying out so barbaric an imperative, flouting the laws of God and man by taking his enemy's punishment into his own hands.*[46]

The convenience of Levin's synthesis for my purpose is that it shows what can become of the controversy attached to the prayer-scene when it is approached from a more comprehensive perspective. It should be clear from the point of view expressed in this study, however, that I believe Levin's perspective to be the wrong one. My own reading of the play leads me to approach the scene from the *opposite* perspective that revenge, in a strict sense, is entirely appropriate, that what is appropriate, in fact, is the right revenge. Ultimately, this leads me to see in this scene 'incongruity' of another order altogether.

To claim that Hamlet is overreaching himself and expressing hubris in the prayer-scene is to imply that Hamlet means what he says. However, it is precisely an indication of the complexity of the perspective in the scene that what Hamlet says is simultaneously a baffled substitute for what escapes him. This ambiguous quality in Hamlet's speech arises from the fact that the 'horridness' Hamlet projects is and is not the horridness Hamlet seeks, expressing Hamlet's double disposition towards an ideal and an immediate revenge. To the extent that the 'horridness' Hamlet projects aims genuinely at the horridness Hamlet seeks (from an immediate sense of the ideal) then Hamlet means what he says, and he is expressing hubris: he is, at least, prepared to *consider* acting on something so horribly imperfect. To the extent that the projected 'horridness' is obviously a *perversion* of the horridness sought (exposing the 'distance' of the immediate from the ideal) then Hamlet cannot mean what he says: Hamlet's projection is merely a baffled substitute for that right revenge that continues to elude him; it is clearly predicated on the knowledge that he is not *immediately* committed to act on what he says. To claim that Hamlet is not prepared to act on his projection of a more horrid fate for Claudius here might seem to be contradicted by evidence elsewhere that Hamlet *is* prepared to act on a possibility that is at least *not* the ideal act he seeks, as when Hamlet first enters in on Claudius. Yet here again Hamlet both is and is not prepared to execute his intention. To the extent that he seeks an immediate revenge, he is; to the extent that the revenge required is the ideal revenge, he is not. The emphasis when Hamlet enters, significantly, is on the nature of the possibility immediately presented as a finality ('*Now* might I do it pat, *now* 'a is a-praying; / And *now* I'll do't' (III.iii.73-74)), the question implied being: would such a revenge, seen as an accomplished act, serve?—'No', Hamlet concludes, for the complex 'reasons' Hamlet gives, and others.

Indeed, the profound ambiguity in Hamlet's disposition in this scene—an ambiguity rooted ultimately in the baffling *incongruity* of his situation—serves an impression that Shakespeare seems almost artificially to contrive to measure the problematic 'distance' from the ideal revenge of the revenge actually within Hamlet's grasp. It is an indication of the most complex purpose and meaning of the prayer-scene, precisely, that it has been almost artificially designed to exhibit the possibilities of revenge by deliberately keeping revenge *out* of Hamlet's reach. The reason for this, finally, seems to have been a tactical one. Had Claudius not appeared to be doing exactly what would keep Hamlet from revenge, had Claudius, that is, not been praying, or had Hamlet at least known that Claudius was praying unsuccessfully, Hamlet would have been forced to commit himself one way or the other, with the consequence that the problematic equilibrium established in the play between the double need for an immediate and for an ideal revenge would have been destroyed. As it is, Shakespeare gave himself the opportunity of capturing this equilibrium before the question was finally settled, as it is, in one intensely visual moment illuminating, as it were, the full import of Hamlet's predicament. As Peter Alexander once noted[47]: 'Here Shakespeare has reduced almost to visual terms the whole of Hamlet's problem'. I have claimed that there is something artificial about the *way* this equilibrium is framed. More important, I believe, is the naturalness of the action itself, which does not overwork the ideal revenge but makes the revenge ambiguously meditated an expression of the fact that Hamlet is merely in half-conscious possession of his designs, corresponding to the 'obliqueness' with which the play is finally forced to present the ideal revenge. Ultimately, this obliqueness serves to measure the immediate possibilities of revenge for Hamlet, specifically his problematic distance from an ideal that makes all revenge properly within his grasp ultimately merely the roughest expression of the right revenge.

4
Death

The perception of a complex operation of meaning is required to show how and in what sense the play's extended meditation on death serves in the last part of the play as a formal acknowledgment of human limitation before the mystery of visionary destiny. Here we may note to begin that the pattern of death so prominent in the last part of the play establishes itself by association with the failure of revenge, so that Hamlet's failure to act out his revenge between the prayer—and closet—scenes is immediately embodied in the death of Polonius, which may be taken in turn to stand effectively for the death of Hamlet, since the one leads directly to arrangements for (and formal announcement of) the other (see IV.iii.65).

It is the effect of Polonius' death, moreover, to shift the burden of a father's murder from Hamlet to Laertes and Ophelia who, in this way, become an immediate reflection of Hamlet's experience, but through a structure of association emphasizing Polonius' death as a literal *perpetuation* of the death of Hamlet's father, in the sense that one follows directly from the failure to revenge the other. The association of all three deaths (of Polonius' death with the imminent death of Hamlet on one level of suggestion, and of these with the elder Hamlet's on another) is developed in the following climactic passage where it is also connected with the frustration and neutralization of Hamlet's revenge brought about by his removal from the scene:

> *O Gertrude, Gertrude!*
> *When sorrows come, they come not single spies,*
> *But in battalions! First, her [Ophelia's] father slain;*
> *Next, your son gone, and he most violent author*
> *Of his own just remove; the people muddied,*
> *Thick and unwholesome in their thoughts and whispers*
> *For good Polonius' death; and we have done but greenly*
> *In hugger-mugger to inter him; poor Ophelia*
> *Divided from herself and her fair judgment,*
> *Without the which we are pictures, or mere beasts;*
> *Last, and as much containing as all these,*
> *Her brother is in secret come from France;*
> *Feeds on his wonder, keeps himself in clouds,*
> *And wants not buzzers to infect his ear*
> *With pestilent speeches of his father's death;*

> *Wherein necessity, of matter beggar'd,*
> *Will nothing stick our person to arraign*
> **In ear and ear.** *O my dear Gertrude, this,*
> *Like to **a murd'ring piece**, in many places*
> *Gives me superfluous death.*
> (IV.v.74-93)

The passage serves primarily to sum up for Claudius the full extent of the harm and confusion generated by Polonius' death, harm and confusion giving the sense of 'superfluous death'. But the terms of the account develop simultaneously a system of suggestions associating the 'hugger-mugger' of Polonius' death with the 'hugger-mugger' involved in the interment of the elder Hamlet, just as Laertes' clouded absorption in rumours is associated by implication with Hamlet's clouded absorption in the revelations of the Ghost, and the madness of Ophelia (most obviously) with Hamlet's own madness. Indeed, the full effect of the passage is to trace the developments associated with Polonius' death (developments that themselves involve the imminent death of Hamlet) implicitly back to their original source (and model)— to the developments associated with the death of the elder Hamlet. In the present passage, these developments appear primarily as an account of Hamlet's failure to revenge (traced here to conditions of clouded knowledge, self-division and errant violence) and, thus, as an account of the insidious sway and influence of 'superfluous death' in a sense unintended by Claudius, 'superfluous' in that what is involved are a superfluous number of deaths but due to an excess *unmasterableness* about the death of the elder Hamlet that makes death *intrinsically* 'superfluous'. The whole development leads to the terrible 'feast' of death at the end of the play (see V.ii.356-359) marking death's final triumph over all efforts to bring it within the possession of human power.

It is the express function of Ophelia within these larger concatenating developments to recapitulate Hamlet's experience in its aspect of grief: 'this is the poison of deep grief' (IV.v.72). At this point, the play harks back to its more esoteric speculations on the reaches of passion. Ophelia's disjointed speech in madness has the effect of highlighting a fundamental incongruity between experience and expression, one that in elaborating the play's equation of shapelessness with essence (as in Hamlet's depiction of the Player's emotional performance) re-invokes the sense of void at the heart of passion.[48] Yet this void paradoxically challenges, by its competing unintelligibility, the effort to give the essential passion shape and form, the futility of which is what can be said to account for the full pathos of the episode. Thus, 'Her speech is nothing' (IV.v.7), yet 'This nothing's more than matter' (IV.v.171), 'Though nothing sure, yet much unhappily' (IV.v.13).

In a later sequence, Laertes provides a fuller, psychological account of Ophelia's madness in grief:

> Nature is fine in love; and where 'tis fine
> It sends some precious instance of itself
> After the thing it loves.
> (IV.v.158-160)

The mental strain in Ophelia's passion is specifically characterized here as an imaginative compulsion to follow after her dead father, Ophelia's passion being thus made a feature of Ophelia's psychological attempt to 'pass from nature to eternity'. It is an account that for the moment counters the essential futility of such a compulsion, sensed elsewhere in the play, with an expression of confidence in the power of emotional subtlety. As such, it develops further the analogy with Hamlet whose own grief, like Ophelia's, is what led him at first to seek for *his* dead father, at first with an extraordinary success fully bearing out such confidence in emotional subtlety, only to find that the apparent success was really only an extension of failure since in successfully penetrating beyond the grave to the vision of his father's Ghost, Hamlet only makes us more intensely aware of the essential gap separating him from the otherworld and the actual basis of its reality, once that vision has faded.

By the time of the Ophelia episode, the metaphysical-psychological pattern in question has been significantly sentimentalized, even prettified, expressing the play's general modulation into pathos at this point. The sentimental reduction is explicitly acknowledged in another significant commentary of Laertes':

> Thought and affliction, passion, hell itself,
> She turns to favour and to prettiness.
> (IV.v.184-185)

Here, the sentimental reconciliation of psychological tension in Ophelia reflects pathetically Hamlet's larger heroic effort to breed order out of tragic passion. Such an effort has been elaborated by the play as the attempt to assert mastery over supernatural horror, and that feature is duly reflected in this passage in the association of afflicted passion with hell. The sentimental development is brought to a climax in the Queen's speech announcing Ophelia's death (IV.vii.167-185): at this point, it is elaborated for all it has and then deflated as Ophelia is described being 'Pull'd ... from her melodious lay / To muddy death.' The deflation does not, however, represent complete rejection, for while the weakness of the sentimental solution is duly acknowledged, it has served to symbolize movingly the play's contemplation of an ideal mastery over tragic passion.

Something of this purpose survives even the placing of the play's sentimentalism in the Clown's opening remarks in the churchyard-scene. Here, in a comic development fully expressing the play's resistance to sentimentalism, the moral incongruity of Ophelia's death is developed with all the tough impersonality of wit, as one Clown demands of the other:

> Is she to be buried in Christian burial when she wilfully
> seeks her own salvation?
> (V.i.1-3)

The full power of these lines lies in opposing moral incongruity to the suggestion of profounder imaginative purpose behind Ophelia's tragic sentimentalism, one ultimately linking it to Hamlet's tragic heroism; for if Ophelia can be said to have 'wilfully' sought 'salvation' through her death, it is not merely in a purely ironic sense emphasizing moral violation. The action symbolizes at the same time, through an equation of full metaphysical mastery with salvation, the imaginative effort to achieve full metaphysical mastery over tragic passion. Since it is in the nature of such passion in the play's terms to be subject to the dissociation of death (what separates 'nature' from 'eternity'), the effort of mastery is seen appropriately as a wilful precipitation into death.

Such an action can be said to constitute an effort towards 'salvation' in the psychological sense, but it is an action that also involves the risk of damnation in the moral sense. Thus, if Ophelia is said to 'seek' her own 'salvation', it is the 'salvation' that would come from a full reconciliation of moral conflict with psychological need, the basic incongruity of which is what the Clown's remarks finally serve to emphasize. Seen as such, Ophelia's fate measures Hamlet's own, fuller, psychological-heroic 'struggle' with death and damnation: the value of Ophelia's fate is that it confidently acts out on one level what Hamlet himself falls short of on another, due to his scepticism. That scepticism is also the play's, and it is expressed again with Ophelia through the Clown and then in the Priest's judgment over Ophelia's burial:

> *... Her death was doubtful;*
> *And, but that great command o'ersways the order,*
> *She should in ground unsanctified have lodg'd*
> *Till the last trumpet ...*
> (V.i.221-224)

Here, however, that scepticism is balanced with an expression of confidence in the integrity of Ophelia's purpose, and a claim to the reversibility of the moral judgment; thus Laertes:

> *... I tell thee, churlish priest,*
> *A minist'ring angel shall my sister be*
> *When thou liest howling ...*
> (V.i.234-236)

This brief account of the Ophelia episode should be enough to hint at the complexity of the dramatic developments in this part of the play. Our sense of the episode's dramatic power stems from our experience of the tension between levels of meaning, between what might be called the episode's sentimental and symbolical functions. A similarly rich suggestiveness is developed around the figure of Laertes, whose dramatic power in this part of the play stems likewise from a tension between functions, though here the application is different. In the Ophelia episode, the sentimental reduction is what paradoxically permits the full, unhampered symbolic exploration of visionary destiny. It is because the play already recognizes that the sentimental solution in Ophelia's experience could not by itself apply to Hamlet without serious reduction, that the play can permit itself a full exploration of the solution while avoiding inappropriate encroachment. By contrast, similar recognition of a fundamental reduction in the comparison of Laertes' experience with Hamlet's is what makes the unqualified encroachment on Hamlet of the *melodramatic* solution represented by Laertes maddeningly inappropriate, all the more so because the encroachment is so plausible and inevitable. The different application is used to different ends, expressing subtly varied perspectives on the control of visionary destiny. The purpose of the Ophelia episode is to outline, within a given recognition of failure, the possibility of success; the purpose of the Laertes episode to re-enact, within an outline of success, the full frustration of failure.

Laertes' encroachment on Hamlet is formally developed in IV.vii, where Claudius, showing a typical political cunning no less formidable for being coldly sinister, succeeds masterfully in absorbing Laertes' obsession with revenge into the swordfight-plot. He does this mainly by dwelling on the envy caused to Hamlet by the special praise given to Laertes for his qualities of swordsmanship by the mysterious Norman, Lamord. Claudius' carefully measured broaching of Laertes' reputation does not merely serve an ironic purpose: the extolment is not merely meant to point up, by contrast, all that makes Laertes' obviously shallow heroism so decidedly inferior to Hamlet's. The shallowness of this heroism is pronounced, and it is brought out marvellously through the skilful manner with which Claudius exploits Laertes' quiet but obvious vulnerability to praise, thus achieving the breakdown of Laertes' purpose. However, Claudius' extolment serves at the same time to build up the genuine encroachment of Laertes' heroism on Hamlet's, a development remarkable for taking place simultaneously with the breakdown and reduction just described. It is all the more remarkable as a development in being unaided by any previous suggestion, in being carried purely through the extolment itself, which succeeds due to the gratuitous prestige thrown over it by the mysterious associations of Lamord.

The purpose of Laertes' encroachment on Hamlet is to prepare for and build up a fundamental rivalry between the two, the significance of which is not made fully clear until the formal struggle between Laertes and Hamlet in Ophelia's grave, when encroachment and rivalry are brought to a climax couching the explanation. Of this confrontation Hamlet says later 'the bravery of his grief did put me / Into a tow'ring passion' (V.ii.79-80). The straightforwardness of this explanation in fact obscures the deeper import attached to it. Hamlet is stirred to outburst partly, as he remarks, over the offensiveness of Laertes' melodramatic heroism. What makes this heroism offensive is the ease with which it is in part assumed and aimed at Hamlet as a judgment on him for Ophelia's death. What it undermines is the crucial part played in this death by the larger struggle that has kept Hamlet from acting on such heroism in his own pursuit of revenge, precisely from his commitment to a deeper, genuinely visionary heroism. The deeper irony, however, is that the heroism that Laertes himself so uncritically assumes, the heroism for which Hamlet is shown elsewhere to have such inevitable contempt, is the only heroism of which Hamlet himself is ever seen to be *fully* capable. It is entirely to the point here that Hamlet should be driven by Laertes' heroism not to the expression of a more genuine heroism but merely to a more intense expression of the same, making us poignantly aware of the deeper, visionary heroism that has *escaped* Hamlet, our sense of which reduces his own immediate expression of heroism here to the level of 'rant' (V.i.278). The association of Hamlet's heroism with Laertes' is fully suggested at Hamlet's formal entrance onto the scene, in the ambiguity of his address, which leaves it unclear whether by the 'emphasis' of grief (V.i.249) Hamlet has in mind Laertes' expression or his own:

> ... What is he whose grief
> Bears such an emphasis, whose phrase of sorrow
> Conjures the wand'ring stars, and makes them stand
> Like wonder-wounded hearers? This is I,
> Hamlet the Dane.
> (V.i.248-249)

It is thus that the encroachment of Laertes on Hamlet is achieved. Hamlet's outrage stems from his sense of the fundamental reduction implied in the encroachment of Laertes' heroism on his own. That outrage is made all the more urgent and intense by the full plausibility of the encroachment, from the failure of heroism that has made a superficial comparison of Laertes with Hamlet inevitable. The effect of Laertes' encroachment is to re-enact for Hamlet the full frustration of failure: it is the occasion of a renewed struggle that is as much Hamlet's struggle to free himself from a real enslavement to a melodramatic heroism as it is his struggle to assert to the world that his own heroism is greater and harder than a purely melodramatic heroism. This 'struggle' takes place appropriately in the grave:

> ... Dost come here to whine?
> To outface me with leaping in her grave?
> Be buried quick with her, and so will I.
> (V.i.271-273)

thus bringing to dramatic definition the play's association of an incomplete mastery over visionary destiny with the impenetrability of death, in the play's larger terms ultimately a measure of its 'superfluity'. Hamlet's failure to revenge is to be traced ultimately to the impenetrability of his father's death, specifically to Hamlet's clouded knowledge of the otherworld that has made full mastery of visionary judgment impossible. Similarly, the incomplete mastery of such judgment, seen as an ironic struggle against the melodramatic reduction, is associated here with the *futility* of a literal confrontation with death (the melodramatic reduction being ultimately a measure of the limitations that prevent full power over death).

The limiting factor in Hamlet's experience, which we know elsewhere to be his inability to penetrate once again beyond the grave into a full vision of the otherworld, is thus seen to be the tyranny of the grave poignantly focused here in Ophelia's corpse, which is all that survives of her precipitation into death, just as all that can be said to survive of Hamlet's own penetration beyond death to the vision of his dead father is the vivid memory of his father's 'dead corse' (I.iv.52) 'cast up' (51) from the grave. The power Hamlet requires to achieve full mastery over his destiny is the power the play reserves for the mysterious Lamord who, as his name implies, is Death itself: the power to be 'incorps'd' (IV.vii.87), with all that this projects of full possession and knowledge of death and thus, in the play's terms, full possession and knowledge of the otherworld. It is a power that the play associates in the Lamord passage (IV.vii.84-92) with a power of metamorphosis, with a symbolical unification in horsemanship of horseman with horse, terms set by the ultimately chivalric import of Hamlet's struggle with Laertes (and all that he represents about Hamlet) in the face of Death. Whether or not Hamlet can be said in this struggle ultimately to attain to a full power over Death or a power approaching Death, or even to unite himself to Death, is a question that seems predetermined by the associations of futility attached to Hamlet's struggle in the grave. But all such associations are further subordinated to a significant reduction of the struggle involved in Hamlet's formal renunciation of the struggle later as implied in his apology to Laertes (see V.ii.218-236). The effect of this reduction is to turn the use the play makes of Lamord as a symbolical heightening of the struggle with Death into a purely isolated phenomenon that significantly the play ultimately fails to develop.

Yet, if the play cannot, in the end, permit itself any suggestion of full triumph over death, or even of a struggle challenging triumph, it seems eager to elaborate evidence of a 'return' from death, of providential immunity from the premature death that would mean complete frustration of revenge and the final perpetuation of injustice. Crucial to this development is the full import of Hamlet's experience at sea, which, as Hamlet's note to Claudius duly records, has been the 'occasion' of his 'sudden and more strange return' (IV.vii.46-47). Return from what, Hamlet's remarks in his letter to Horatio make clear: if Hamlet exhorts Horatio to 'repair' to him 'with as much speed as he wouldst fly death' (IV.vi.20-21), that is because Hamlet's experience has been for him a 'return' from death, the 'bore of the matter' (23) being that Hamlet is providentially snatched up just when death seemed inevitable (while, by contrast, Rosencrantz and Guildenstern themselves go to their own deaths when least expecting it, in the full irony of such ignorance as

Hamlet might have fallen victim to, himself). The pattern of 'return' that Hamlet's fate finally demonstrates is no isolated development: it represents the dramatic turning-point in the pattern of 'return' that the whole play can be said to enact in demonstrating how the final revenge is achieved through the succession of 'purposes mistook / Fall'n on th' inventors' heads' (V.ii.376-377). The significance of this very elaborate pattern is that it balances the play's portrayal of Hamlet's failure up to that point with the compensating perception of a guiding providence working directly through failure, indeed in the case of the conflict between Hamlet and Claudius, through different orders of limitations that ensure, by the 'return' from death that both experience, the inevitable and independent operation of divine justice.

Claudius is himself unable to profit fully from the death of the elder Hamlet, from limitations that ensure that murder shall always be exposed, even, if necessary, through extraordinary means, for example, through the revelation of a ghost; and just as Hamlet is unable for his part to arrange for the death of Claudius from the limitations that prevent him from framing Claudius' death within a totally actual realization of otherworldly judgment, so too Claudius in unable in his turn to arrange for the death of Hamlet, at first from the more mundane limitations that prevent him from pronouncing sentence on Hamlet for Polonius' death from fear of public outrage, limitations seen implicitly as an extension of the limitations besetting Hamlet ('And where 'tis so, the offender's scourge is weigh'd, / But never the offence', (IV.iii.6-7)), then from the limitations that prevent Claudius from securing Hamlet's death in England due to a 'shaping' divinity that represents as much a mockery of Hamlet's own ponderous plotting as it is more obviously a frustration of Claudius'.

It is the function of the play's catastrophe to bring to a dramatic climax Hamlet's hard-won faith in a guiding providence at work independently in developments in his world. It is indeed as the fruit and end-product of a very extensive effort to penetrate imaginatively to the inner determination of phenomenal developments in the world (a motivation that Hamlet's graveyard meditations suggest dies hard) that we view the suggestion to Horatio, after the adventure at sea, that behind the world's pattern of developments Hamlet has seen the operation of a 'shaping' hand working directly *through* frustration of the visionary struggle:

> ... *let us know,*
> *Our indiscretion sometimes serves us well,*

> *When our deep plots do pall; and that should learn us*
> *There's a divinity that shapes our ends,*
> *Rough-hew them how we will.*
> (V.ii.7-11)

It is the climax to that general condition in Hamlet throughout the play that shows him, despite the sincerity of his commitment to revenge, progressively absorbed in the drift of the world, involved through his dealings with the Court, apparently unnecessarily, at first with the Players, then with Fortinbras' army, and, later still, in the adventure at sea, and the swordfight with Laertes. The strength of Hamlet's perception with Horatio derives from the fact that it is rooted deeply in Hamlet's experience in this regard, when Hamlet's visionary struggle, having by the time of the sea adventure come to great impasse:

> *... in my heart there was a kind of fighting ...*
> (V.ii.4)

gives way, by a mysterious transformation, to the drive that lifts Hamlet providentially out of his despair. Despair of the visionary struggle is now compensated for by the self-transforming discovery of *integrity* in the disposition of events, saving Hamlet from premature death and returning him to Denmark. Although it is part of the effect of this discovery to leave Hamlet still buoyed in the confidence of an inevitable rendering of judgment, this judgment is now felt to be independent of his own determination; in fact, it is immediately accompanied by an *intensification* of the possible prospect of his own death and the related acceptance of the very large risk this prospect involves of a possible reprieve and lease on life for Claudius the malefactor.

Hamlet's discovery, paradoxically, is of *integrity* in this pattern. It is because the reversal at sea saves Hamlet from a course leading directly to his own death—because the reversal operates from deep within the pattern of failure—that an expectation of ultimate providence is engendered in Hamlet strong enough to justify renewed appearances of waywardness when Hamlet willingly submits later to suspicions of a new threat on his life and the renewed prospect of failure represented by the swordfight with Laertes. It is an expectation that comes to be linked with an attitude of resignation in Hamlet before an experience of Providence thought by some to represent a profound religious feeling, by others the fatalism of a *gran rifiuto*. It does not require an elaborate defense of structural complexity to realize that it is a measure of both. Hamlet's feeling is in fact the more intense for this—for, genuinely and profoundly religious as it is, Hamlet's feeling asserts itself in direct relation also to failure by the standards of the visionary struggle that has involved him throughout the play. Indeed, it is a feeling difficult for Hamlet to sustain in the balance of truth that yet continues to press in on him. Or at least a sense of reality at once larger and less assuring than the positive security of religious feeling must be invoked to account for the very complex mood ultimately associated with Hamlet's feeling, where strains of pathos and irony finally mingle uneasily with the faith expressed:

> HAM. *But thou wouldst not think how ill all's here about my*
> *heart; but it is no matter.*
> HOR. *Nay, good my lord—*
> HAM. *It is but foolery; but it is such a kind of gaingiving as*
> *would perhaps trouble a woman.*
> HOR. *If your mind dislike anything, obey it. I will forestall*
> *their repair hither, and say you are not fit.*
> HAM. *Not a whit, we defy augury: there is a special*
> *providence in the fall of a sparrow. If it be now, 'tis not to*
> *come; if it be not to come, it will be now; if it be not now,*
> *yet it will come—the readiness is all. Since no man owes of*
> *aught he leaves, what is't to leave betimes? Let be.*
> (V.ii.203ff)

Walker is no doubt right too in suggesting that we are ultimately meant to view the image of a divinity that shapes his ends in the way Hamlet's swordfight with Laertes finds resolution.[49] Yet we must bring to bear on this account a further crucial observation: the image we are left with in the end, an image otherwise associated with action built up on a tremendous scale, is an image nonetheless radically undeveloped as an elucidation of the workings of Providence. It recalls, in this respect, a similar absence of development of the Death-impinging qualities associated through Lamord with the chivalric struggle between Laertes and Hamlet. The reduction of theme both omissions imply can be seen operating in the reversal through which the resolution of the action is secured: 'Laertes wounds Hamlet: then in scuffling, they change rapiers, and Hamlet wounds Laertes.' That chivalry which in the Lamord passage had been transformed into the image of Death becomes in the collapse of struggle into scuffle, something considerably removed from such an image, being reduced to something far less than chivalry. The disposition of the outcome can be said to be achieved, likewise, through a reversal that substitutes, for the image of triumphant Providence one had been led to expect of such an action, merely the predominance of superior physical strength and energy. The treatment points to a deliberate reduction of theme that is total: human action is stripped of any of the larger, metaphysical associations that might be developed around it, as if Shakespeare had retreated from a final penetration of such associations.

The general reduction the action undergoes in the last part of the play is one also applied to the play's central focus on the possibility of visionary development. What we must recognize in considering the full significance of the play's final action is the overadded awareness we bring to the catastrophe from the play's previous visionary tenor, an awareness that compels us to see in the play's resolution merely the faintest echo of the elusive visionary resolution previously associated with the full implications of the action. E. E. Stoll has brought attention to the 'crowded and explosive' nature of the catastrophe, which finds its 'outward and sensuous emphasis' in the dramatic use of artillery:

> ... these thunders break out properly enough (on a stage where such portentous noise was not uncommon or illegitimate) not only to mark and distinguish the palpable hits in the fencing match, but, both there and after the eulogy, to signalize the importance of the scene as a whole. Where emotional effect is the chief concern, a greater weight of emphasis is, as in music, indispensable.[50]

Yet it seems obvious that no amount of emphasis *in this kind* could ever be powerful enough to distract us sufficiently from the full, metaphysical emphasis one *might* have expected of the catastrophe from major developments in the play. Here we may note specifically that no amount of thunderous 'bruiting' between the heavens and the earth (I.ii.127; V.ii.267-269) could ever substitute for the full visionary-judgmental thundering this may be taken to suggest, any more than the purely verbal intensity of Hamlet's emotional rant earlier could have been mistaken for the visionary 'horrid speech':

>   ... *What would he do,*
> *Had he the motive and the cue for passion*
> *That I have? He would drown the stage with tears,*
> *And cleave the general ear with horrid speech;*
> ....
>   *... amaze indeed*
> *The very faculties of eyes and ears.*
> ....

> ... *Bloody, bawdy villain!*
> *Remorseless, treacherous, lecherous, kindless villain!*
> *O, vengeance!*
> (II.ii.553ff)

And as with the general effect of the catastrophe, so too with Hamlet's moment of revenge:

> *Here, thou incestuous, murd'rous, damned Dane,*
> *Drink off this potion. Is thy union here?*
> *Follow my mother.*
> (V.ii.317-319)

Powerful as this expression is on its own level, it focuses the supernatural consequences of the union in the otherworld in such a manner as to suggest the dramatic borderline separating imminent judgment beyond death from the full, immediate vision of such judgment from this side of the world. The latter, I believe, is the kind of knowledge the play has envisaged for Hamlet from the first, yet it is the kind of knowledge that always remains significantly *beyond* the reach of the action. This is also part of the poignant effect of the vision of choiring angels that Horatio projects as attending the progress of Hamlet's soul beyond death, as if pointing again to that visionary realm lying just beyond the reach of this play's action:

> ... *Good night, sweet prince,*
> *And flights of angels sing thee to thy rest!*
> (V.ii.350-351)

The stringent exploration of visionary possibility provided over the course of this play will have persuaded us of a view too disturbingly problematic for us to be easily convinced of the immediate relevance to Hamlet's experience of such a visionary realization as Horatio innocently projects around Hamlet, in the spirit of *one* experience of the Renaissance visionary ideal as one finds this represented, for example, in El Greco.[51] And yet, it is equally true that one does not feel at the play's close that Horatio's eulogy might not still properly apply to Hamlet, even as we have known him implicated in tragedy. Indeed, one seems bound to acknowledge that it might yet be in the nature of the profoundly paradoxical development towards religious reconciliation in this last part of the play to admit of such a determination of fate for Hamlet in spite of the quite emphatically problematic value of Hamlet's action right up to the time of his death. In fact, I would go so far as to claim that the projection of a visionary destiny that is finally unproblematic is assumed in Hamlet all along as motivating inspiration and ideal. By the end this ideal has been very significantly confounded and undermined, but for all this, it is an ideal that we may *yet* be meant to suppose is maintained and observed in Hamlet, insofar as the psychological tragedy is consistently *resisted* in him, in spite of the many deaths he has caused by the end. The ideal is, in any case, boldly set off and released at the end as from a long and difficult gestation. And Hamlet might yet be allowed to die in an inheritance of it. But, if so, only by a difficult paradoxical determination over which Shakespeare has become by then himself problematically silent, having become in the end of *Hamlet* metaphysically disengaged.

Detail from *Burial of the Count Orgaz* [1586]
by El Greco, in S. Tomé, Toledo, Spain.

PART TWO

Othello's Sacrifice, and Romantic Tradition

On the Way of Negation

Thus far I have focused on Shakespeare's absorption in a pattern of tragic alienation from traditional otherworldly and salvational motives of action. In the next instance, I bring forward evidence of Shakespeare's absorption in a pattern of alienation also from romantic-transcendental and formal-aesthetic solutions to tragedy, two other popular 'saving' notions that remain strong with us to this day. The tendency to want to romanticize Shakespearean tragedy, as well as the tendency to suppose that, if anywhere, it is in Shakespeare that tragic passion is brought under control, will no doubt continue to remain with us. We will tend to these positions no doubt because we recognize that Shakespeare himself introduces these positions into his representations. The fact is, however, that Shakespeare had, from *Hamlet* onwards, come to understand, by a process very painful to himself, that love does not triumph over all only because we choose to continue to believe in the forms of love we have always known and wish to see it romanticized that way. Nor was there any hope in thinking that even his best art could bring the unconscious processes of tragedy into the complete light of day.

To put it in these terms is to paint a picture of the import of Shakespeare's development from a position well into his great tragic period. We need to recognize that Shakespeare had by then brought himself to the point of the complete negation of all saving notions in those familiar forms as they have come down to us to this day. Nor is it in the will of either the hero *or* the author to say how the renunciation will take place. It is also a case of seeing just how painfully tragic the process of renunciation is. It is a process that is being lived through immediately, and that we ourselves participate in directly. We do so by re-living the extraordinary way in which an attachment to these saving notions persists, even though the whole direction of experience is moving inexorably toward their negation.

Yet none of this explains how, or why, in Shakespeare's last phase, in spite of the great process of negation that has absorbed him down to that point, we suddenly get a miraculous recrudescence of otherworldly, salvific, and romantic terms. Here entirely unfamiliar forms demand from us an altogether new way of perceiving. Shakespeare's terms in the late romances also lie beyond the scope of formal representation. A further, evolutionary experience finally works directly *through* the tragedy that represents all life as death. And, as we shall see, that experience is only fully confirmed for us as experience in the end *outside* the sphere of literature, in what is known today as *Anthroposophy*, as that process of living further into the hidden 'wisdom' of 'man' that Rudolf Steiner succeeded at last in bringing within the reach of our developing understanding…

1
Othello's Sacrifice as Dialectic of Faith:
The Romantic-Transcendental Solution

It is great to give up what one wishes, but greater to hold fast to it after having given it up.

Should one perhaps not dare to speak about Abraham? I think one should. If I myself were to talk about him, I would first depict the pain of the trial.

What is left out of the Abraham story is the anguish.

Let us now have the knight make his appearance … he infinitely renounces the claim to the love which is the content of his life; he is reconciled in pain; but then comes the marvel, he makes one more movement, more wonderful than anything else, for he says, 'I nevertheless believe that I shall get her, namely on the strength of the absurd'.

Kierkegaard, *Fear and Trembling*[1]

The whole thrust and direction of Othello's speech that opens the fatal bedchamber scene in Act V brings Othello by degrees into a relation to Desdemona diametrically opposite to that envisaged of him in the following comment on the scene:

She has become the symbol of the irrationality that corrupts the world of his ideal …[2]

Expressed in this comment is the view of Desdemona that Othello elaborates rather in the second scene in Act IV, where, Othello, in terms strikingly reminiscent of Hamlet with Gertrude, carries on about Desdemona as a 'strumpet'. That view accounts, no doubt, for Othello's ultimate decision to kill Desdemona, but it is now directly contradicted by the whole spirit and thrust of Othello's approach in the later scene, where it is precisely the case that Desdemona revives for him in all her ideality:

> It is the cause, it is the cause, my soul.
> Let me not name it to you, you chaste stars:
> It is the cause. Yet I'll not shed her blood,
> Nor scar that whiter skin of hers than snow
> And smooth, as monumental alabaster.   5
> Yet she must die, else she'll betray more men.
> Put out the light, and then put out the light!
> If I quench thee, thou flaming minister,
> I can again thy former light restore,
> Should I repent me. But once put out thy light,   10
> Thou cunning'st pattern of excelling nature,
> I know not where is that Promethean heat
> That can thy light relume: when I have plucked the rose,
> I cannot give it vital growth again,
> It needs must wither. I'll smell thee on the tree;
> O balmy breath, that doth almost persuade
> Justice to break her sword! Once more, once more:
> Be thus, when thou art dead, and I will kill thee,
> And love thee after. Once more, and that's the last,
> So sweet was ne'er so fatal. I must weep,
> But they are cruel tears; this sorrow's heavenly,
> It strikes where it does love. She wakes.[3]

It would appear, indeed, that just *because* his decision to kill Desdemona has become irreversible and absolute, Othello cannot now stop himself from again valuing her with that characteristic total immediacy and completeness with which he had always valued her, before he began to see her differently. In fact, it would appear that any view of Othello's role that sees him in his resolution to kill Desdemona as ultimately separate from her in *any* sense, however favourably we may conceive of that relationship, is bound to distort the dreadful pathos of the tragedy—whether we think of Othello in 'the role of a god who chastises where he loves', or 'of a priest who must present a perfect victim'.[4] We must rather think of Othello as disposed to killing Desdemona, paradoxically, in tragically sublime identification with her life. *That* identification, reinforced as it is by his sensuous kissing of Desdemona three times, involves Othello ultimately in a tremendous intensification of anguish that, in the philosophical sense, we must term absurd, since it has no reasonable limit whatsoever. For at a certain point, Othello goes so far as to say, or desire to say, right *through* the resolution to kill Desdemona, which remains unshakeable, 'I nevertheless believe that I shall get her':

> *Be thus, when thou art dead, and I will kill thee,*
> *And love thee after.*

We may feel that all Othello is expressing here is an intense form of wish-fulfilment, basing his desire on the familiar conceit, suddenly given a spectacular poignancy and relevance in context, of sleep as the counterfeit of death, that he is not really thinking this thought through and could not begin to believe what he says. Othello is, of course, only too aware in this speech of the absolute finality of death, and thus of the incommensurability of death and sleep. But to say that he is only aware of this truth, or that it is something he simply accepts, is to fail to enter into the drama, to see what it must mean for Othello to have to deal death to Desdemona as he has known her. The intention attributed to Othello of seeking Desdemona's death 'to save her from herself, to restore meaning to her beauty'[5] grossly ignores the fact that, for Othello, Desdemona dead is meaningless. Othello's anguish is the more insufferable especially now that his love for Desdemona has once again been freed, just because the resolution to put her to death *settles* the problem of her 'guilt'. Condemned to death, Desdemona has now ceased to be guilty, and the further issue arises: 'how is Desdemona's death to be reconciled with that characteristically complete and immediate love that is now once again freed in Othello, a love by nature entirely bound up with Desdemona's life?' It is from this more evolved and transformed point of view that we finally enter, in imagination, into the dreadfulness of what Othello 'must' do, suddenly struck by the likeness of Othello's case to that of the sublime-pathetic figure of Abraham, especially as Kierkegaard interprets him for us:

> *If one hasn't the courage to think this thought through, to say that Abraham was a murderer, then surely it is better to acquire that courage than to waste time on undeserved speeches in his praise ...*
>
> *We let Isaac actually be sacrificed. Abraham had faith. His faith was not that he should be happy sometime in the hereafter, but that he should find blessed happiness here in this world. God could give him a new Isaac, bring the sacrificial*

offer back to life. He believed on the strength of the absurd, for all calculation had long since been suspended. That sorrow can make one demented may be granted and is hard enough; that there is a strength of will that hauls close enough to the wind to save the understanding, even if the strain turns one slightly odd, that too may be granted. I don't mean to decry that. But to be able to lose one's understanding and with it the whole of the finite world whose stockbroker it is, and then on the strength of the absurd get exactly the same finitude back again, that leaves me aghast. But I don't say on that account that it is of little worth; on the contrary it is the one and only marvel. It is commonly supposed that what faith produces is no work of art but a crude and vulgar effort only for clumsier natures, yet the truth is quite otherwise. The dialectic of faith is the most refined and most remarkable of all dialectics, it has an elevation that I can form a conception of but no more. [6]

It was Kierkegaard's mockingly triumphant view that the sublime dialectic of faith he had hit upon in the case of Abraham was the only paradox Shakespeare had never ventured to speak about:

Thanks to you, great Shakespeare! You who can say everything, everything, everything exactly as it is—and yet why was this torment one you never gave voice to? [7]

Yet here for once, Kierkegaard's judgment would seem to have proved wrong, for this dialectic would seem to be precisely the one Shakespeare glances at in *Othello*. Faced, on a new, transformed level, with the absolutely contradictory claims of death and life, Othello inherits a dilemma and an anguish that could only be resolved finally in the manner of Abraham with whom Othello appears to be conceptually linked:

The moment the knight resigned he was convinced of the impossibility, humanly speaking; that was a conclusion of the understanding, and he had energy enough to think it ... but ... on this the knight is just as clear: all that can save him is the absurd; and this he grasps by faith. Accordingly he admits the impossibility and at the same time believes the absurd; for were he to suppose that he had faith without recognizing the impossibility with all the passion of his soul and with all his heart, he would be deceiving himself, and his testimony would carry weight nowhere, since he would not even have come as far as infinite resignation. [8]

The sudden emergence of the Abraham-conception from the midst of Othello's tragic experience will be conditioned, of course, by our knowledge of the tragic irony of Othello's case; and it will remain to decide Othello's actual relation to this suddenly invoked likeness. But certainly we could hardly imagine a potentially more dramatic *coup de théâtre*. An invocation of the possibility of a turn of events such as that associated with the Abraham story would seem to be a measure of the power of re-awakened love that is now developing in Othello. Of course, there could be no question in the world of *Othello* of a direct intervention from heaven. But this circumstance would almost seem to cast the audience itself in the role of the angel of the Abraham story, the Abraham-conception appealing, as it does, to the condition we have borne throughout the play of hovering over these thwarted lovers with our superior knowledge. That we know we would not intervene could only heighten the psychological intensity of Othello's anguish for us; and that heightening, paradoxically, draws us into a still more immediate relation to the hope of an ultimate resolution, breeding in us a feeling that perhaps something might yet come to pass to interrupt the course of events, as Desdemona suddenly awakes from sleep and death.

It is an illuminating experience, if initially a somewhat oblique one, to look back over Othello's speech and except for the fact that Othello would kill Desdemona because he thinks she is guilty, except that is, for the one line (6) in which the fact is recorded, except also for the early reference to 'chaste', to see Othello as Abraham. Simply on the basis of that extraordinary note of sublime elevation sounded at the beginning, the Othello of the opening could hardly be thought unworthy of the comparison:

> It is the cause, it is the cause, my soul ...

The idea of a Promethean re-kindling of life (in l.12), which arises so naturally in this sublime context, would also be out of place, grandly expressive as *it* is of the Counter-Renaissance denial of limit or its 'metaphysical ache'.[9] But, however small, there are those intensely poetic touches—of 'rose' and 'tree'—that might well suggest the symbolic Biblical landscape of the Abraham story, containing in themselves as well that typological foreshadowing of Christ with whom, in line with Renaissance exegesis of the Bible, it would be only too easy to associate Isaac and Desdemona in their innocence. Even the possibility of comparison with the Abraham-Isaac story on a sensuous plane is an experience for which an Elizabethan audience would have had an immediate precedent. They would have been adequately prepared for that experience in the Brome representation of the sacrifice from among the great Mystery Plays that had, not so long before, been a current feature of the popular life. What this wonderfully humanized and in its own way intensely moving version would certainly have brought to the forefront in popular imagination of this story was a feeling for the pathos and the cost of the sacrifice, accentuated by Abraham's kissing Isaac clearly in the terms of sensuous life:

> A, Isaac, Isaac, up thow stond,
> Thy fayere swete mowthe that I may kis.
> A, Isaac, my owyn swete child,
> Yit kisse me agen upon this hill!![10]

Then there are the lines, to which I have given some attention, that clinch the comparison on the level of the story's dialectic:

> Be thus, when thou art dead, and I will kill thee
> And love thee after.

And as we absorb the end of Othello's speech, the likeness to what would have inspired Abraham's own feeling would seem to present no difficulty at all:

> So sweet was ne'er so fatal; I must weep,
> But they are cruel tears; this sorrow's heavenly,
> It strikes where it does love.

A case might indeed be made for Shakespeare's having perhaps deliberately woven the Abraham-conception into Othello's situation as an inevitable and irresistible development of the sublime pitch and direction of Othello's address to the sleeping Desdemona. What the implied likeness would seem to signify in the end (to draw on Kierkegaard's own terms) is a transcendental 'movement' of the spirit that appeals directly to the unhappy sense we have of the inevitability of Desdemona's death at this late point in the drama. Desdemona will die, but the hope continues that she will live in spite of this. This is the implicit, subtextual import to the intention, well-noted of Othello in this scene, of sublime 'sacrifice'. However, when Desdemona awakes eventually to deny any share of guilt, the tenuous framework of her recovered innocence on which Othello has been building, within his own specialized frame of reference, is suddenly and ironically threatened with being shattered. The drama at this point shifts drastically from one term into the other, that is, from a potential resolution by way of a dialectic of faith along Kierkegaardian lines (into which the scene originally modulates) into the now actual irony of the case. Caught as we are between these two terms over the course of a scene that Dr. Johnson thought too 'dreadful' to be 'endured',[11] we are hardly spared any measure of 'fear and trembling', both in Kierkegaard's sense, and also in a sense, beyond Kierkegaard, characteristic of Shakespearean tragedy. In sharpest contrast with the extraordinary hope that is so poignantly invoked, we are suddenly made aware of the brutally ironical paths along which even the most sublime efforts toward resolution are borne, when these run counter to the facts of the case. From the ultimate disposition of the play's events, it is clear that for Shakespeare, faced with the prospect of a transcendental resolution, it is the facts of human nature that take precedence: in this case, that dark, incriminating process between them over which Othello and Desdemona are unable to exercise control, and of which they fail to establish any conscious understanding. And indeed what we are made to witness in the end is the furthest thing from the Abraham-conception: brute 'murder' rather than 'sacrifice', the most horribly ironical of deaths experienced by one at the hands of the other in this most noble-minded of pairs:

> DES. *Alas, he is betrayed, and I undone.*
> OTH. *Out strumpet, weep'st thou for him to my face?*
> DES. *O, banish me, my lord, but kill me not!*
> OTH. *Down, strumpet!*
> DES. *Kill me tomorrow, let me live tonight!*
> OTH. *Nay, if you strive—*
> Des. *But half an hour!*
> OTH.   *Being done, there is no pause—*
> DES. *But while I say one prayer!*
> OTH.   *It is too late.*
> DES. *O Lord, Lord, Lord!*

2
Shakespearean Tragic Representation and the Formal-Aesthetic Solution

Again and again in the post-Romantic criticism of Shakespeare, one encounters a view that one suspects still haunts, in some repressed form or other, the minds of all students of the Bard who have known the temptation to Bardolatry. The view was expressed by Sidney Lanier, for instance, who helped to propagate it in *Shakespeare and His Forerunners*. There Lanier dug up the common ghost with an exuberance that became embarrassing to the twentieth-century reader: 'In Shakespeare,' Lanier intoned, 'passion is furnished with a tongue adequate to all its wants.'[12]

Bradley

After Lanier, passion was no longer regarded at least entirely as a question of character. For A. C. Bradley, who emerged directly out of the fashion that absorbed Lanier, 'the fundamental tragic trait' was indeed the 'tendency [in the hero] to identify the whole being with one interest, object, passion, or habit of mind'. But though this tendency illustrated 'the full power and reach of the soul', it linked up with the sense of an incomprehensible and uncontrollable 'force' (Bradley also called it 'fate')[13]. This force was not only not strictly a property of character, it also received representation outside the character of the hero in the rest of the play.

Hough

Yet, in spite of the development toward greater sophistication in the understanding of passion, *the claim of full articulacy* survived. One finds it, for example, in Graham Hough's '*A Preface to* The Faerie Queene'. In his treatment of the full scope and possibilities of allegory, Hough considers the significance of 'incarnational literature'. Hough presents it as 'the kind of literature best represented by the work of Shakespeare'; 'Incarnational literature' is that in which 'any 'abstract' content is completely absorbed in character and action and completely expressed by them.'[14] Whatever Hough may have meant by 'abstract content', it was not strictly equatable with character inasmuch as it also encompassed 'action'. Equatable with neither one nor the other, it necessarily transcended both. It pointed, in fact, to an identity with the play as a whole and with the creating dramatist who shaped it. 'Abstract content', Hough associated, in fact, with 'theme', 'the moral-metaphysical abstract element', as distinguished from 'image', 'the concrete characters, actions, or objects in which it is embodied.'[15] The sense of a consciously articulated and consciously elaborated 'theme' is enough to suggest that whatever Hough may have owed to Bradley for a perspective on drama that transcended character, he did not mean by 'abstract content' the sense of vast, unarticulated reserves of psychological-metaphysical energy evoked by Bradley's use of the word 'force'.

Leavis

By 'abstract content' Hough, it would seem, meant what F. R. Leavis meant when he said that 'the control over Shakespeare's words in *Macbeth* ...

is a complex dramatic theme vividly and profoundly realized'. For Leavis[16] its embodiment was, however, more narrowly a function of language, of 'the poetic use of language', or of 'poetry'. In Leavis, the emphasis was on 'poetry' as 'exploratory creation', or as Leavis' one-time associate, L. C. Knights develops it[17], on 'a poetry that is profoundly exploratory, that evokes what it seeks to define'. The emphasis on 'exploration' would seem at first to have encouraged a view that would see the chief value of the Shakespearean achievement in its tentative and, one presumes, by the way impressively successful, evocation of hitherto unarticulated areas of experience. In fact, the emphasis in both men tended to enunciate a claim of full articulacy. Knights may have put it in less absolute terms. He seems to show an awareness of range of possible achievement that Leavis, in his essay on *Macbeth* at least, doesn't reflect on. There seems little question, however, of where the achievement was thought to lie. We are dealing in Shakespeare, according to Knights, 'with a poetry… in which the implicit evaluation of experience is entirely dependent on the fullness of evocation'. Leavis puts it more strongly: 'Poetry as creating what it presents, and as presenting something that stands there to speak for itself, or rather that isn't a matter of saying, but of being and enacting…'

G. Wilson Knight

To these views we may add G. Wilson Knight's emphasis on 'the visionary whole'[18] of a Shakespeare play. The term seems to have included for Knight what 'image' included for Hough—all the characters, actions, and objects in which the theme of a play is 'completely absorbed' and 'completely expressed', or embodied. Whatever emphasis might be given to the aspect of suggestiveness in Shakespeare's achievement, and so, to a theme that remained finally indeterminate however fully evoked, the effect in all these cases was to treat the achievement as if it were a *full articulacy*. As the very epitome of 'incarnational literature', Shakespeare was said to proceed by a 'harmonious wholeness' between theme and image that Hough himself denied, for example, to the term 'symbolism' where theme and image 'assert their unity, but the unity is never achieved, or if it is, it is only a unity of tension'.[19]

Apart from the passages in which it is the poetry that was believed to hold forth a power of full articulation, equally popular with critics were those in which an inchoate verse was thought to do so: for example, in Lady Macbeth's sleep-walking scene, and in Lear's mad scenes. Alwin Thaler once claimed that whereas Richard II only talks about 'the unseen grief that swells with silence in the tortured soul':

> ... *Lady Macbeth ... really expresses it, in broken whispers which are the sighs of a soul unbosoming itself, at last, of long-repressed agonies.*[20]

Writing in the mid-nineteenth century, J. Wilson, in the *Dies Borealis*, once justified considering Lady Macbeth's passage as prose rather than as the alternative blank verse, in similar terms; it must be in prose

> ... *because these are the **ipsissima verba**, yea the escaping sighs and moans of the bared soul. There must be nothing, not even the thin and translucent veil of the verse, betwixt her soul showing itself, and yours beholding.*[21]

Wilson's argument about the greater spiritual transparency of prose here is a spurious one, for no amount of formal 're-shuffling' of the form of Lady Macbeth's lines will prevent her 'prose' from hitting our ears as rough blank verse. The idea of the bared soul is, as I argue below, especially misleading. Writing in the middle of the twentieth century, W. H. Clemen had roughly the same thing to propose about the 'bared mind' in the case of Lear:

> *The images of the next scenes [III.iv; III.vi] in which the King goes mad, are again illuminating for Lear's state of mind. The swiftly passing images, logically unconnected with each other, which we hear Lear utter, correspond to the abnormal state of the King; they are the adequate form of perception and expression of a lunatic. 'It is his mind which is laid bare,' Charles Lamb said as an interpretation of these strange speeches—especially in the fourth act. Lear's insanity should not be dismissed as simple craziness. It is rather another manner of perception, by means of which, however, Lear now sees and recognizes what formerly remained concealed to him, as long as he was sane. The images are the fragments of his inner visions, which have not yet attained to the form of thoughts; they have not yet been transformed, ordered and connected in logical sequence and in the service of clear statement.*[22]

The quotation from Lamb follows rather perilously on the point about Lear's lunacy. It suggests an identity between the bared mind and mental fragmentation even more extreme than the one actually implied by Clemen in the passage as a whole. Just what Clemen means by his quotation from Lamb takes some unravelling to say. But judging by the ring of his use of the words 'interpretation' and 'strange', he seems to suggest a measure of bafflement in himself that could not surround the sort of claim implied by his reference, for no one's mind could be laid bare to one to whom that mind remained in any way or to any degree unknown. Yet that Lear's 'fragments' remain to be logically connected or clearly stated establishes beyond doubt for Clemen that these 'visions' represent Lear's inner mind 'bared' to us. Yet one would think it obvious that no manner of mental fragmentation could ever be mistaken for the vision whose actualization is by these devious means being aimed at. What has been taken for positive vision in Lear is actually the radically ambiguous creation of a mind lost to the violent consequence of a 'mere' identification with vision that has in fact become *un*real. It is precisely because one is bound to posit a disastrous *unreality* at the basis of the imagination of so many of Shakespeare's characters, as I shall show, that to speak of a representation of complete value, in the sense attributed to the Shakespearean achievement by post-Romantic criticism, seems to be finally quite unfounded.

The great value of the work undertaken by the critics mentioned, as well as many others, lies in having brought the twentieth-century reader that much closer to what Coleridge described as Shakespeare's characteristic achievement of 'making everything present to imagination'. But in vindicating this claim, these critics also went too far. What is questionable is the *incarnational enthusiasm* that insinuates itself into what strikes one otherwise as a penetrating emphasis on the need for responding to the precise quality of the dramatic experience. The 'theme' of a Shakespearean drama cannot be grasped except as superb creation, but it is quite impossible to claim that the creation is brought to the point of an incarnational completeness. The formal representation of passion in Shakespeare offers ample evidence for this general moral. In what follows, I offer a detailed analysis merely of one portion of this massive testimony. It shows the significant use that might be made of what turns out to be the profoundly problematic tenor of Shakespeare's representational creation, *belying the post-Romantic claim of a full articulacy or representation of incarnational value.*

Among the literary conventions drawn upon for the formal representation of inward feeling, probably the most traditional and primitive but by no means the least effective, was the simple, straightforward statement testifying to feeling. The device took many forms and, as we shall see, came to acquire in Shakespeare a sophistication one would hardly have thought predictable from its apparent naivety as a representational formula. The device of using a character forthrightly to inform the audience of his/her inward state of mind came to express far-ranging evocative levels and a great variety of emotional nuances. In *self-exposition*, a character could resort to a technique by which he/she described the inward feeling more particularly and extensively, thus accounting for the essential movement of the mind. Alternatively, the character could also allude to the seat of passion, either by a localizing gesture directed to the breast or the head, or simply and more often, by open, verbal reference to the heart.

Not all references to inward feeling of this kind have, of course, representational significance. Many references appear too casually in the exposition or the dialogue to merit attention. Still more have a purely informative function. Kent's previous confrontation with Lear, and the possibility that Timon's steward has returned to his abandoned master because it has been rumoured that he is again wealthy, require that we know the genuineness of their intentions. When Kent returns to his own master, he is made to say 'So may it come, thy master, *whom thou lov'st,/* Shall find thee full of labors' (*Lear*, I.iv.6-7); likewise, Timon's steward: 'I will present / *My honest grief* unto him' (*Tim.*, IV.iii.469-470). Other references with some representational significance are, nevertheless, primarily designed either to define the emotional effect of a scene, as in Horatio's reaction to the Ghost in *Hamlet*: 'It [harrows] me with fear and wonder' (I.i.44), or to signal a momentary intensification of the action, as in Claudius' reaction to the murder of Polonius: 'O, come away! / My soul is full of discord and dismay' (IV.i.44-45). Others may be used to redress or re-adjust the point of view, as in Aufidius' sudden change of mind at the end of *Coriolanus*: 'My rage is gone, / And I am struck with sorrow' (V.vi.146-147).

Aufidius' sentiment signals and consolidates the larger structural effort at the end of the play to re-emphasize Coriolanus' essential nobility, after another, understandably ill-endured display of anger on Coriolanus' part has sparked his murder. With this we may compare Bolingbroke's protestations towards the end of *Richard II*, which are put to an analogous use: 'Lords, I protest my soul is full of woe / That blood should sprinkle me to make me grow' (V.vi.45-46). The judgment redressed here is a far more complex one: it includes Bolingbroke's own need to re-affirm himself as King in the face of the deeds committed. However, the more prominently psychological implications of Bolingbroke's lines,—his sense of guilt and dread—demonstrate how the more broadly dramatic function of self-exposition could merge into a more explicitly representational function. The lines Claudius speaks in *Hamlet* just prior to the nunnery-scene also have that double function. For the first time we learn from Claudius himself of his responsibility for the murder of Hamlet's father: 'O, 'tis too true! / How smart a lash that speech doth give my conscience!' (III.i.48-49). The lines reinforce the vital information we have about the murder, and they also represent Claudius' sudden inward qualm: they actually enact the inward motion the qualm entails—'smart', 'lash', and 'speech' providing us with a concrete representation in the motion and burning effect of the whiplash. The emotional process implied in Claudius' lines is a good indication of effective differences within the technique of self-exposition. These I shall get into later when I consider the question of different possible levels of evocative representation. In the meantime, the representational form of Bolingbroke's lines, to return to this, links them with a common self-expository device that consists in representing inward passion by the protestation or persuasion that it is being felt.

1. Protestation

The device is used again in the front end of the last scene of *Othello* when Desdemona suddenly realizes that Othello is serious about killing her: 'And yet I fear you... / ...Why I should fear I know not, / Since guiltiness I know not; but yet I feel I fear' (V.ii.37-39). It recurs in *Antony and Cleopatra* where it represents Enobarbus' crushing sense of remorse when his master, whom he has deserted, repays his treachery with a gesture of magnanimity: 'I am alone the villain of the earth, / And feel I am so most' (IV.vi.29-30). Now it is not at all unusual in Shakespeare, particularly not in the later tragedies, to find several things being underlined by one and the same passage. This is exemplified in Desdemona's case where the self-exposition, besides reflecting the tragic force and influence of Othello's personality, expresses the depth and power of Desdemona's intuition of tragic irony. The intuition is of an extraordinary kind, comparable to Hermione's in *The Winter's Tale* when, faced with analogously mad charges from Leontes, the Queen remarks: 'There's some ill-planet reigns; / I must be patient, till the heavens look / With an aspect more favorable' (II.i.105-107). What Desdemona intuits, less happily than Hermione, is not simply her own death but the whole fatal pattern behind it. This is a point made clear both to us and to herself in her reaction to Othello's disclosure of Cassio's supposed death a little later: 'O, my fear interprets' (V.ii.73). What the self-exposition serves to do in this case is to evoke deeper levels of emotional *engagement* in Desdemona, levels, moreover, that are indicated precisely *because* they arise mysteriously. It should be noted, too, that it is the mysteriousness of Desdemona's feeling that causes it to be ambiguously manifested to Othello as guilt, thus aggravating the tragic irony.

Emphasis on the tension between inward feeling and outward action and event seems to be the point consistently associated with protestation as a self-expository device, though the emphasis, as one would expect of Shakespeare, exists in different forms. In Bolingbroke's case, protestation measures the immediate inadequacy of his remorse as amends for Richard's murder. It is the magnitude of the crime that at once forces and invalidates the protestation. One would expect to find the same sort of relation between feeling and event in the case of Enobarbus whose situation is clearly analogous. But there the self-exposition seems rather to measure the inadequacy of all expression for a remorse that is absolutely final. In this effect, Enobarbus' case invites comparison with what is perhaps the most spectacular use in Shakespeare of this self-expository device. Towards the end of *Coriolanus*, Coriolanus' mother succeeds in breaking down Coriolanus' will outside the gates of Rome. She saves the city from his revenge but provokes from the hero the somewhat pathetic cry: 'But, for your son, believe it—O, believe it — / Most dangerously you have with him prevail'd, / If not most mortal to him' (V.iii.187-189).

Coriolanus' outcry here ends up being more, unconscious posturing from pride, designed, it seems, to deflect from the sense of shame over his submission to his mother. For far from being 'mortal' to him (except, of course, in the ironic sense in which it incites Aufidius to conspire his death), the significance of the submission is soon forgotten. Coriolanus returns to Corioli claiming to be 'No more infected with my country's love / Than when I parted hence...' (V.vi.71-72). Just the same, at the time it is spoken, Coriolanus' outcry expresses a perfectly genuine sense of shame. What it impresses upon us, as with Enobarbus, is the sense of an undemonstrably inward feeling. What it also impresses upon us is a sense of the general unruliness of inward feelings, for feelings mysteriously elude Coriolanus just as they compulsively overcome him. However, in the recourse to the protestation of feeling, Coriolanus' outcry typifies one of the possible, if always inadequate, means available to the character in his/her endeavour at inner representation. In the grapple with the knowledge and expression of inward forces (elusive, mysterious and extreme), he/she can, at least, emphasize or underline that they are there.

2. Inner Evocation

Extensive efforts *are* made to lend greater and greater inwardness of feeling to the self-expository technique. This is achieved particularly through verbal evocation. As a result of verbal nuance, even a relatively naive presentation of emotion can still project the suggestion of inward depth (in 'too *far* gone') in York's 'O Richard! York is too far gone with grief, / Or else he never would compare between' (*Rd.II*: II.i.184-185). We may cite a similar form of evocation in Leontes' 'Fie, fie, no thought of him; / The very thought of my revenges *that way* / Recoil upon me' (*The Winter's Tale*: II.iii.18-20). Expressed here is Leontes' frustrated desire to revenge himself on Polixenes for the effect on Mamillius (Leontes falsely supposes) of Hermione's 'dishonour'. Consider, also, Macbeth's 'Our fears in Banquo / Stick *deep*' (*Mac.* III.i.48-49). Verbal allusion to a *process, movement, or continuum of emotion* is, in fact, the secret to inner evocation in Shakespeare. It forms part of the basis for the uncanniness of such familiar lines as Banquo's 'Fears and scruples *shake* us' (*Mac.*, II.iii.129), or Angelo's 'And in my heart the strong and *swelling* evil / Of my conception' (*Meas.*, II.iv.6-7); Brabantio's 'Belief of it *oppresses* me already' (*Oth.*, I.i.143), or Lear's 'My wits *begin* to turn' (*Lr.*, III.ii.67).

The means by which an inward process is suggested are various and all the more fascinating for this. Brilliant effects are reaped from such small touches and familiar devices. In some cases, it implies the substitution of one part of speech for another: the substitution, for example, of the gerund for the noun, in the following line of the King's in *All's Well That Ends Well*: 'I am wrapp'd in dismal thinkings' (V.iii.128). The culminating exploitation of gerundial form (though here there is no alternative form of speech) is Cleopatra's sublime 'I have / Immortal longings in me' (*Ant.*, V.ii.280-281). Cleopatra's statement also benefits from the ambiguity of a more poetic phrasing in which 'immortal' is conducive at once to the meaning 'longings for immortality' and the more intense 'longings that are immortal'. In other cases, it is alliteration that is probed for effect. Antony's 'Love, I am full of lead' (*Ant.*, III.xi.72) manages to evoke with a brilliant concreteness the weight of Antony's despair simply by the sheer confluence of 'l' sounds towards the end of the line. It is by a similar touch, by a process of identity achieved in the verbal fusion of 'thought' and 'murther' in the 'th' sound, that Macbeth's thought of murder takes on a quality of reality, in the lines 'My thought, whose murther yet is but fantastical' (*Mac.*, I.iii.139). In Lear's 'Thou art a soul in bliss, But I am bound / Upon a wheel of fire' (*Lr.*, IV.vii.45-46), it is the vowel sounds that are exploited. The long 'e' and 'i' sounds, in 'wheel' and 'fire', following upon a series of short vowel sounds, manage to suggest the infinite reach of Lear's suffering. The horizontal and vertical movements, respectively of the 'e' and 'i' sounds, are clearly designed to suggest an experience spread out through all of space.

In still other instances, a process of emotion is suggested by devices that are either so hackneyed or so daring, it is a wonder they work so well. It is illuminating to remark how successfully Shakespeare redeems a device so parodiable in his own day as the antithesis, in the following lines from *Othello*: 'By the world, / I think my wife be honest, and think she is not; / I think that thou art just, and think thou art not' (III.iii.383-385). Part of the success of the use of antithesis here lies in transposing its application from the pretentiously high rhetorical sphere of the earlier dramatic verse of the period to one more conceivably real. Shakespeare motivates its use by a movingly pathetic desperation. Nonetheless, the vacillating motion of doubt that the antithesis enacts is successfully rendered, above all, by the frank simplicity of the antithetical terms. A comparably redeeming use of a naive rhetorical device is to be found in Macbeth's 'But now I am cabin'd, cribb'd, confin'd, bound in / To saucy doubts and fears' (*Mac.*, III.iv.23-24). Here redundancy is quite ingeniously made use of to suggest the unavailing inner struggle against inevitable spiritual circumscription. On the one hand, Shakespeare achieves inner evocation by an ingenious use of often hackneyed devices. On the other hand, he achieves this by a competent use of devices at once bold and imaginative—e.g., in Angelo's 'This deed *unshapes* me quite, makes me unpregnant / And dull to all proceedings' (*Meas.*, IV.iv.20-21), and Othello's 'I tremble at it. Nature would not invest herself in such *shadowing* passion without some instruction' (*Oth.*, IV.i.39-41). Here, Shakespeare combines with an inner emotional process by *verbs of action* the suggestion of a process quite properly and appropriately inchoate (through a dark movement in the words 'unshapes' and 'shadowing').

These instances bring us closer to the literal knowledge of a character's inward experience. In other instances, Shakespeare is more daring still. In the romances, inward feeling is often represented by sharp, single *nouns of sensation*. There is, for example, the following representation of despair in Imogen over Posthumus' enforced, violently sudden departure from court: 'There cannot be a *pinch* in death / More sharp than this is' (*Cym.*, I.i.130-131; following this, there is her half-conscious response to her father's vituperative anger: 'I am senseless of your wrath; a *touch* more rare / Subdues all pangs, all fears' (*Cym.*, I.i.135-136). We may compare with this Prospero's representation of Ariel's unnatural 'compassion' for Prospero's spell-bound victims: 'Hast thou, which art but air, a *touch*, a feeling / Of their afflictions' (*Tp.*, V.i.21-22), or the general representation in this play of conscience as inward 'pinching' (cf. V.i.74-77). It is a technique that can be ascribed to the characteristic presentation in the last plays of what have been called 'states of profound sensation'.[23] But the identification of inward passion with sensation is a technique discernible incidentally in earlier plays. There is, for example, Troilus' 'I am giddy; expectation whirls me round; / Th' imaginary relish is so sweet / That it enchants my sense' (*Troil.*, III. ii.18-20). Here, Shakespeare combines again with the evocation of an inner action, in 'whirls', the quite extraordinary device of invoking in the audience those concrete sensations that every lover has known at one time or another on the verge of an assignation. It is by the same appeal to familiar sensations that in the major scene of confrontation between Othello and Desdemona (IV.ii) we are brought one step closer to the direct knowledge of the rankling grief Othello experiences in his jealousy, in two of the most heart-wrenching lines in all of *Othello*: 'O thou weed! / Who art so lovely fair and smell'st so sweet / That the sense aches at thee, would thou hadst never been born!' (IV.ii.67-69).

In all the instances of self-exposition cited thus far, the underlying representational purpose is to fuse *explicitness of representation* on the one hand with *inward actuality* on the other. All of the instances are to varying degrees explicit and actual in these senses. But behind the effort at inner evocation lies the attempt (superior to the plain protestation of feeling) to attach to the formal representation of passion a greater and more tangible inward actuality. A third and more integrated device consists in attaching to the emotional actuality a more explicitly inward figure. Characters allude to the 'seat' of their passion by overt, verbal reference to the heart.

3. Overt Verbal Reference to the Heart

Reference to the heart as the seat of passion has more than a mere physical or physiological implication: it possesses simultaneously metaphorical and emotional implication; and it is all to the point that in this device the two are fused. The attempt at the direct, sensible representation of passion here takes the form of an effort to identify the two in the verbal figure, a very special one at that, one so ancient it has come to acquire a far greater inward concreteness for the human (and theatrical) imagination than the spoken word normally receives.

Instances of the use of verbal reference to the heart for purposes of the external representation of inward emotion abound. We shall only glance at a few cases that are particularly illuminating. These exploit the device's singular expressive potentiality, to suggest, at the same time, its inherent expressive limitations. An early and comparatively primitive recourse to the device is to be found in Bolingbroke's 'I have too few to take my leave of you, / When the tongue's office should be prodigal / To breathe th' abundant dolor of the heart' (*Rd.II*, I.iii. 255-257). Bolingbroke speaks this as he prepares for exile, in answer to Gaunt's reproach for failing to return his friends' salutations. What Bolingbroke is saying is that he feels he must keep his words to express the grief entailed in being parted from his father. But implied in Bolingbroke's lines is that words could not adequately express this grief, the intensity of which is best represented for the moment by the phrase itself: 'th' abundant dolor of the heart'. Recourse to verbal reference to the heart to express an emotion that could not otherwise be adequately represented is a recurrent representational focus. It crops up again in the following lines spoken by Richard where the phrase 'For on my heart they tread', apart from clarifying Richard's rhetorical figure, serves as a tentative reference acknowledging the representational inadequacy of a desperately fanciful verbosity:

> Or I'll be buried in the king's high way,
> Some way of common trade, where subjects' feet
> May hourly trample on their sovereign's head;
> For on my heart they tread now whilst I live,
> And buried once, why not upon my head?
> (III.iii.155-159)

This feature also recurs in Brutus' 'That every like is not the same, O Caesar, / The heart of Brutus earns to think upon!' (*Caes.*, II.ii.128-129). The device provides Brutus with a tentative representational solution for the problem that faces him (and his author) with regard to embodying his conflicting sympathies on the question of Caesar. And finally, we may see it again in Antony's 'Triple-turn'd whore! 'tis thou / Hast sold me to this novice, and my heart / Makes only wars on thee' (*Ant.*, IV.xii.13-15). Here the device temporarily answers Antony's immediately unsatisfiable and ultimately unrelieved rage over Cleopatra's third presumed piece of treachery.

A further aspect to the use of this device worth remarking on is the tendency, particularly in the later tragedies, to try to lend to it a greater naturalism and a deeper genuineness. An instance of this is to be found in Francisco's expression of melancholy at the beginning of *Hamlet*: 'For this relief much thanks. 'Tis bitter cold, / And I am sick at heart' (I.i.8-9). We may compare with this Macbeth's expression of despair and emptiness over the absence of love and loyalty in 'old age': 'Seyton!—I am sick at heart / When I behold—Seyton, I say!' (*Mac.*, V.iii.19-20). Here the naturalism, if far more hurried in its effect, is considerably deepened. Hamlet's famous profession of affection for Horatio is similarly a clear attempt to deepen the representational value of the ancient device: 'Give me that man / That is not passion's slave, and I will wear him / In my heart's core, ay, in my heart of heart, / As I do thee' (*Ham.*, III.ii.71-74). So too Desdemona's public profession of love for Othello: 'That I [did] love the Moor to live with him, / My downright violence, and storm of fortunes, / May trumpet to the world. My heart's subdu'd / Even to the very quality of my lord'(*Oth.*, I.iii.248-251). Yet, as with the tentative representational significance of the earlier examples, the effort to deepen here clearly betrays an underlying sense that the device has its inherent representational limitations. Other devices in the genre of self-exposition generally attach to themselves, as we shall see, a disturbed sense of the gap between the external representation of passion they provide and the actual inward nature and essence of the passion represented. However, this is entirely in accord with the constant sense that, however serviceable, all devices are ultimately inadequate. At best they provide only a partial or technical solution to the forbidding challenge actually posed by the ideal of a literal representation of passion.

The duality between outward and inward reality that Shakespeare inevitably came up against is reflected dramatically in a fourth self-expository technique through which characters are made to refer to the seat or center of their passions in this case along with an overt, localizing gesture.

4. Localizing Gestures to the Heart or the Head

It is a technique that, of course, might naturally accompany all references to the heart, or the head. But in certain cases this is an explicit feature of the reference; and its function then is clearly to suggest a physical or spatial locus for the inward passion.[24] In some such cases, the device has an entirely ironic value dramatically emphasizing a serious gap in men's knowledge of themselves. It is clearly in all ignorance of the questionability of his cause, and more immediately of his ambiguously self-seeking motives, that Cassius, with a typical, histrionic imagination, insinuates his conspiratorial plans to Brutus in *Julius Caesar*: 'Then, Brutus, I have much mistook your passion, / By means whereof this breast of mine hath buried / Thoughts of great value, worthy cogitations' (I.ii.48-50). It is in a somewhat lighter tone, but with implications no less serious for the matter of self-representation, that Troilus similarly, and with a comparable predilection for histrionics, aggrandizes his love-wounds in the opening scene of *Troilus and Cressida*: 'Call here my varlet, I'll unarm again. / Why should I war without the walls of Troy, / That find such cruel battle here within?' (I.i.1-3). In another case, the device, far from implicating human superficiality and emptiness, celebrates the inner-outer duality as the condition of human dignity. When facing Leontes' charges before an immediately acquiescent set of courtiers, cowed (or perhaps simply stunned for the moment) by his warnings against their intervention, Hermione disdains to express her grief outwardly:

> ... *Good my lords,*
> *I am not prone to weeping, as our sex*
> *Commonly are, the want of which vain dew*
> *Perchance shall dry your pities; but I have*
> *That honorable grief lodg'd here which burns*
> *Worse than tears drown. Beseech you all, my lords,*
> *With thoughts so qualified as your charities*
> *Shall best instruct you, measure me.*
> *(Wint.,* II.i.107-114).

The value attached to the duality here is typical of the return in the romances to a more discreet norm over the question of inward impenetrability. One resolves the problem of vindicating the reality of passion through a 'plain and holy innocence' (*Tp.* III.1.82).

But between the discreet resolution of the romances and the recognition of emptiness of the earlier plays stands the period of the later tragedies where the inner-outer duality and its immediate resolution are of the very highest concern. Instances in these plays measure at once the desire and effort to express, control or possess the inward passion in a literal sense, and at the same time the tragic helplessness of characters in this effort. In some of these instances, one feels that the desire is for a literal, physical possession of the inward passion. When Lear, for example, violently strikes his head on first explicitly recognizing his folly in dispossessing Cordelia ('O Lear, Lear, Lear! / Beat at this gate, that let thy folly in / And thy dear judgment out!' (*Lr.*, I.iv.270-272)), it is more than an irreversible error that Lear underlines by his gesture. It is the tragic gap between the inner and the outer Lear, specifically the inaccessibly inward unruliness and independency of his emotions. It is the very same gap—the *physical* distance between the inner and the outer man—that is resisted in a second such gesture by Lear in the storm: '[this] tempest in my mind / Doth from my senses take all feeling else, / Save what beats *there*—filial ingratitude!' (*Lr.*, III.iv.12-14).

In other instances, the technique clearly constitutes a pathetically desperate alternative to being unable to express an *inexpressibly intense* and (from the others' point of view) an impenetrably inward *emotion*. Consider, in this connection, Lear's complaint to Regan about Goneril's malice towards him: 'O Regan, she hath tied / Sharp-tooth'd unkindness, like a vulture, here. [*Points to his heart*] / I can scarce speak to thee; thou'lt not believe / With how deprav'd a quality' (*Lr.*, II.iv.134-137). Or Hamlet's movingly sudden, candid confiding to Horatio, on the verge of his duel with Laertes, of an innermost despair: 'Thou wouldst not think how ill all's here about my heart' (*Ham.*, V.ii.212-213). The helplessness of these characters before the control or possession of inward reality is perhaps most spectacularly demonstrated in another instance of the technique in *Othello*. In the process of bewailing the singular intolerability for him of suffering from betrayal, Othello suddenly points to Desdemona's breast as the locus of his suffering being, now entirely outside his control, in a most painfully tragic expression of the convention of the exchange of hearts:

> Yet could I bear that too, well, very well;
> But there, where I have garner'd up my heart,
> Where either I must live or bear no life;
> The fountain from the which my current runs,
> Or else dries up: to be discarded thence!
> Or keep it as a cistern for foul toads
> To knot and gender in! Turn thy complexion there,
> Patience, thou young and rose-lipp'd cherubin—
> I here look grim as hell!
> (IV.ii.56-65)[25]

Awkward, vexatious, is the transition from 'there' to 'here'. This can be explained, however, by the fact that in the interval Othello has moved towards Desdemona and is now face to face with her. Othello's tormented comments in the following lines about Desdemona's beauty and sweet smell clearly imply this (re: ll's 68-69). The stage action is itself representationally significant, a dramatically pathetic alternative to being unable to penetrate any further, ontologically—to Desdemona's heart.

Reflections of the inner-outer duality are likewise discernible in other instances of self-expository technique. In some cases, the suggestion of an inwardly withheld passion simply expresses a condition of social isolation in which the characters do not have or have not had the opportunity to express their emotions at all. Hence, Marina's necessarily private knowledge of grief over her lost parents and her persecution by Dionyza as well as her period of stay at the brothel, till her meeting with Pericles: 'She speaks, / My lord, that, may be, hath endur'd a grief / Might equal yours, if both were justly weigh'd' (*Per.*, V.i.86-88). Marina's purely expository account of her grief subsequently reflects once again the characteristically discreet resolution of duality in the romances. Nowhere is this more clearly evident than in other instances of self-exposition in *The Tempest*. When Miranda temporarily withholds expressing her love for Ferdinand at their betrothal,

> FERD.   *Wherefore weep you?*
> MIR. *At mine unworthiness, that dare not offer*
> *What I desire to give...*
> (III.i.76-78)

it is significant that the duality should be thought reproachable rather than agonizing. However, it is not only, as the cases of Miranda and Marina imply, that the romances return to standards of 'plain and holy innocence'. As the example of Hermione has testified, the privacy of inward life is here rendered a new respect and sanctity. This attitude is further reflected in Prospero's distant observation of the love between Ferdinand and Miranda: 'So glad of this as they I cannot be, / Who are surpris'd [withal]; but my rejoicing / At nothing can be more.' (III.i.92-94); also in the lengthy, silent, private self-communing permitted Gonzalo over the final reconciliations at the end of the play: 'I have inly wept, / Or should have spoke ere this' (V.i.200-201).

In the tragedies, however, the inner-outer duality remains consistently disturbing. It takes the form, in other cases of self-exposition, of self-representations that because of one form of pride or other, obscure, falsify or simply misrepresent the inward feelings that the characters are actually experiencing. In these cases, what the characters present as their inward feelings is clearly belied by what we know from hints in the action to be what they actually feel. This is clear, for example, when Alcibiades claims to pity Timon when they meet again in the woods, after Timon has rejected all human society—'I am thy friend, and pity thee, dear Timon' (*Tim.*, IV.iii.98). It is not Timon whom Alcibiades actually pities, but himself whose own fate he sees in Timon's: 'I have heard, and griev'd, / How cursed Athens, mindless of thy worth, / Forgetting thy great deeds when neighbor states, / But for thy sword and fortune, trod upon them ...' (*Tim.*, IV.iii.93-96). By similar but still more curious involutions of pride, Coriolanus on two separate occasions denies his inveterate envy of Aufidius and his equal hatred of the people and of the people's representatives. He does so by temporary reflexive, outward pretensions to indifference, as for example, when Coriolanus (then Marcius) first drops the name of Aufidius: 'I sin in envying his nobility;' (I.i.230). In the play's central confrontation between Coriolanus and the Tribunes in III.i, it is insinuated that he is dreadfully disturbed over the people: 'Choler? ... / Were I as patient as the midnight sleep, / By Jove, 'twould be my mind!' (*Cor.*, III.i.84-86). For her part, when Lady Macbeth bounces onto the stage while Macbeth is about the murder of Duncan, claiming, by rather uneasily proud antitheses, to have been made bold by drink—'That which hath made them drunk hath made me bold; / What hath quench'd them hath given me fire' (*Mac.*, II.ii.1-2)—it is clear from the terror and fear she evinces immediately after (in her nervous reaction to the hooting owl and to Macbeth's cry from within) that her boldness involves her unwittingly in horrible paradoxes. Neither Lady Macbeth nor Coriolanus nor Alcibiades on the occasions I have quoted can, of course, be said to be guilty of self-ignorance, of the kind demonstrated, for example, by Cassius or Troilus in earlier citations. The three can all be said to be aware, in some degree or other, of what they are actually feeling. But they are guilty of self-deception. Just what representational significance these many forms of duality possess must be seen to be 'ironic'. They are reflections of a concern with the problem of self-knowledge that antedates and postdates the *central concern with the problem of a literal representation of passion.*

If part of the problem connected with the literal representation of passion lay in the fact that characters could be too well aware of themselves, so to speak, it could only have been a pointed irony to Shakespeare that characters could also know themselves too little. In fact, the recognition of self-deception and self-ignorance, no less than the recognition of tragically helpless emotion (as in the cases of Othello and Lear above), constitutes, in relation to the central focus on a literal representation of passion, at once ethical incitement and philosophical brooding. We have already seen the overt representational significance of excessively and uncontrollably inward emotion in cases of self-reference in the tragedies. The same significance is implicit in other dramatically contrasting instances. Shakespeare appears to recognize as an obstacle to a literal representation of passion, on the one hand, human inability to sustain a certain level of intensity of passion, as in Cleopatra's remark about her fainting reaction to Antony's death: 'No more but [e'en] a woman, and commanded / By such poor passion as the maid that milks' (*Ant.*, IV.xv.73-74); and, on the other, the herculeanly-sustained experience of emotion so huge as to be unfathomable, as with Gloucester in *King Lear*: 'how stiff is my vild sense / That I stand up, and have ingenious feeling / Of my huge sorrows!' (IV.vi.279-281).

In instances of self-exposition involving verbal reference to the seat of passion, or of being, the same recognition of the gap possible between outward and inward reality is reflected in some cases again in the form of self-deception. A prime example of this is Othello's various pretensions to an untouchable emotional integrity whose tenuousness is spectacularly demonstrated when Othello contemptuously dismisses as preposterous the possibility of ever becoming jealous when, in fact, he is on the verge of the most serious doubts to the effect: 'Exchange me for a goat, / When I shall turn the business of my soul / To such [exsufflicate] and [blown] surmises, / Matching thy inference' (*Oth.*, III.iii.180-183). It is only somewhat less spectacularly that, at one point, Coriolanus represents his refusal to appease the people in his 'quarrel' with them as a high matter of integrity rather than as the matter of ambiguous pride that it actually is: 'Must I go show them my unbarb'd sconce? Must I / With my base tongue give to my noble heart / A lie that it must bear? Well, I will do't' (*Cor.*, III.ii.99-101). Integrity is indoubtedly a major and, indeed, a very noble concern of Coriolanus'. But rather than present Coriolanus as a man of positive integrity, most of the action seems clearly designed to express ambiguously, through the continual breakdown of his integrity and the effects on it of his self-deceiving involutions of pride: Coriolanus' illusion of it. The helpless recognition of the unrepresentably inward could not be applied more dramatically than in depicting the elaborate emotional ruses Cleopatra falls to using with Antony. At one point early in the play, after Antony has announced that he is leaving for Rome, Cleopatra counters Antony's disarmingly frank amazement at how far she can go. She makes the claim, clearly designed to confront us with the *paradox*, that her ruses are actually a genuine expression of her inward feeling: 'Tis sweating labor / To bear such idleness so near the heart / As Cleopatra this' (*Ant.*, I.iii.93-95).

One further aspect to the use of self-expository representational techniques remains to be noted. In the preceding pages, I have shown that in his use of self-expository techniques, Shakespeare shows a *motivating concern with the literal representation of passion*. Although Shakespeare achieves a partial success with these techniques, he inevitably recognizes their inherent *representational limitations*. This recognition largely takes the form of a contemplation of the inner-outer duality as this is reflected in many uses of the techniques, some of these strikingly dramatic. Now in other self-expository examples, Shakespeare demonstrates this representational concern and exploration more directly.

5. Tautology

All of the instances that I shall now proceed to cite have in common that they turn upon the inward experience with an intent to represent its essential nature or movement directly. However, this representational effort only brings out how rather dramatically inadequate is the language especially (since it seems most appropriately) chosen for the purpose. For instance, in the third scene of the first act of *Othello*, on arriving into the Senate council-chamber, Brabantio stops to justify his failure to address himself to Venice's crisis. He appeals to the indeferably inclusive urgency of his private grief over Desdemona's marriage: 'nor doth the general care / Take hold on me; for my particular grief / Is of so flood-gate and o'erbearing nature / That it engulfs and swallows other sorrows, / *And it is still itself*' (I.iii.54-58). To this category of representational technique also belongs the last part of Macbeth's 'Two truths are told' soliloquy, in which Macbeth describes the profoundly non-plussing effects and symptoms of the evil 'suggestion' to murder: 'My thought, whose murther yet is but fantastical / Shakes so my single state of man that function / Is smother'd in surmise, *and nothing is / But what is not*' (*Mac.*, I.iii.139-142). Still another occurence of the device, more difficult to detect principally because of the poetic density of the passage to which it belongs, is to be found in *Antony and Cleopatra*, at the point at which Antony despairs of life and of passion on falsely learning of Cleopatra's 'death': 'for now / All length is torture; since the torch is out, / Lie down and stray no farther. Now all labor / Mars what it does; yea, *very force entangles / Itself* with strength' (IV.xiv.45-49). The lines here are difficult and involved, but what Antony is saying is that, because of the inexhaustibly raging strength of his grief, all self-expression would be ineffectual and inadequate. Self-expression would be all the more frustrating because the passion (which would have been strong enough in any circumstances) is made all the stronger and more urgent by Antony's sense of the dishonour and baseness he has incurred by his furious, suspicious hatred of Cleopatra (just before the announcement of her 'death'). The sense of the inadequacy of self-expression is significant, for it reflects the very characteristic sense in *Antony and Cleopatra* of the great futility of self-expression, a futility felt in proportion to the great, changeable complexity of the passions.

Leontes in the heat of his jealousy in *The Winter's Tale* dramatizes similar expressive problems, even if he appears (far more tragically) to have greater facility of insight. He endeavours to trace his emotion to its source: 'Affection! thy intention stabs the center. / Thou dost make possible things not so held, / Communicat'st with dreams (how can this be?), / With what's unreal thou coactive art, / And fellow'st nothing' (I.ii.138-142). The fact that Leontes' passion is entirely unfounded (while this may at first sight appear to negate the significance of the effort) only makes it all the more tragically potent, for there seems to be a suggestion in the presentation of Leontes' passion that his conviction of Hermione's infidelity is in some sense visionary: he apprehends her faithlessness with the force of a sixth sense: 'Cease, no more. / You smell this business with a sense as cold / As is a dead man's nose; but I do see't, and feel't / As you feel doing thus [*grasps his arm*]—and see withal / The instruments that feel' (II.i.150-154). Although it would be useless to deny that Shakespeare thinks Leontes' passion an absolute error, nevertheless that it is sustained with a seemingly visionary intensity would appear to render it, for that very reason, all the more horribly mysterious. Hence the effort to capture it here despite the absolute irony, paradoxically of the most significant consequence.

In Antony's case, 'very force entangles / Itself with strength' constitutes a special expressive effort, one designed to capture the inward passion elementally, and such an effort is made out of a compelling sense that nothing less could be adequate. In Macbeth's case especially, 'nothing is but / What is not', one senses the great urgency of the expressive effort. Qualifying Macbeth's effort is a sense that the sphere it addresses might be more properly referred to the divine. But if the unique intensity and incomparable sophistication of Macbeth's effort are any indication, this only seems to have intensified the urgency and seriousness of *the essential problem common to passion and evil alike, which is the problem of inwardness.* Indeed, all of the instances from this last group without exception dramatize the knowledge or experience of an insight or intuition that it is impossible if imperative to communicate literally. If the terms of this effort are deliberately and appropriately abstract and, perhaps most curiously, tautological—Brabantio's 'And it is still itself'; Macbeth's 'nothing is / But what is not'—the essential impenetrability of these terms only underlines the serious extent of the challenge posed to language by the finally problematic nature of the inward passion.

3
The Coming of Rudolf Steiner
and Romantic Evolution

Swinburne's view of Othello as 'the noblest man of man's making' exerted in the post-Romantic age the most far-reaching influence.[26] If this is so, it is because in his *Shakespearean Tragedy* A.C. Bradley made of Swinburne's view the standard for an idealization of the Shakespearean hero that opened the door to a very extensive body of criticism intent, over many years, on carrying on with the justification of the hero at all costs. Years later, James Bulman, in *The Heroic Idiom in Shakespearean Tragedy*[27] felt called upon to restate the need for our continued familiarization with that heroic component in the tragic representation which, through our perception of the most horrible failure, generates and continues to sustain our *admiration of the hero* in his absolute dedication to high nobility as he sees it and his noble defiance of his fate. In giving expression to this view once again, Bulman was merely carrying on a very long line of commentary, certainly among *the* most characteristic forms of commentary of the twentieth century. The following critics may be seen as constituting our great exponents of the 'heroic' Shakespeare: Howard Baker, Willard Farnham, Moody Prior, Clifford Leech, D.G. James, Peter Alexander, Douglas Bush, Curtis Watson, William Rosen, Eugene Waith, Reuben Brower—the list is almost interminable.[28] And of course one thinks of Bradley, though from an older tradition, as illustriously spearheading this great line of masterful critics, though no one, as far as I know, has ever remarked upon the overwhelming influence on Bradley of Swinburne and his view of Othello.

Yet the influence of that view may be said to have been responsible for some of the most far-reaching criticism of Shakespeare over time—not only from Bradley who measured himself against Swinburne, but also from G. Wilson Knight who measured himself in turn against Bradley. Translating this influence into more modern terms, we might say that in each instance it is the case of the strong critic presuming to have out-wrestled his chief precursor and acknowledged master in heroic criticism. Thus Bradley perceived in the figure of Othello a form of nobility beyond even Swinburne's inspired ability to perceive:

> *This character is so noble, Othello's feelings and actions follow so inevitably from it ... that he stirs, I believe, in most readers a passion of mingled love and pity which they feel for no other hero in Shakespeare ... and to which not even Mr. Swinburne can do more than justice.*[29]

The extraordinary significance of Swinburne's influence on Bradley does not become fully apparent until we watch Bradley accomplishing the substitution of Lear for Othello as the figure in whom Shakespeare concentrates his very greatest achievement in high nobility:

> *There is nothing more noble and beautiful in literature than Shakespeare's exposition of the effect of suffering in reviving the greatness and eliciting the sweetness of Lear's nature ... There is no figure, surely, in the world of poetry at once so grand, so pathetic, and so beautiful as his ... in whom the rage of the storm awakes a power and a poetic grandeur surpassing even Othello's anguish.*[30]

How far Swinburne's influence extends cannot be entirely fathomed until we come to G. Wilson Knight and his still more remarkable attempt years later to establish the greater superiority of Timon over both Lear and Othello. Knight could speak now of the unsurpassably 'unswerving majesty' of Timon's passion:

> *which holds a grandeur beyond the barbaric fury of Othello [limited by the 'barbaric' element], or the faltering ire of Lear [equally limited in being 'faltering'] ... it is the recurrent and tormenting hate-theme of Shakespeare developed, raised to an infinite power, ... the onrush of a passion which sums in its torrential energy all the lesser passions of those protagonists foregone. Timon is the totality of all, his love more rich and oceanic than all of theirs ... he suffers that their pain may*

cease, and leaves the Shakespearean universe redeemed that
Cleopatra may win her Antony in death, and Thaisa be
restored to Pericles.[31]

Wilson Knight casts his own great shadow over the history of Shakespeare criticism. His successful appropriation of the tradition of heroic grandeur to his unrivalled treatment of the abysmal hate-theme in Shakespeare is especially to be noted. Thus Timon and his passion are made into the supreme Shakespearean tragic expression, the very noblest of all: the hero's self-expression in abysmal 'hate' and its truth 'really' represents his unsurpassed nobility and his 'love'. That manoeuvre back from 'hate' to 'love' is characteristic. Behind the great tradition of *the heroic criticism of Shakespeare* (behind the criticism of Swinburne, Bradley, Wilson Knight and many others), lies the seemingly irrepressible Romantic and post-Romantic assumption of man's innate grandeur and nobility through what might otherwise appear to us to be the most horribly abysmal and self-damning fate.

Swinburne himself owed his influential view of Othello to what Barbara Everett, writing on *King Lear*, once felicitously described as Romantic sympathy for, or participation in, the central character, involving a view of poetry that is plot-less, 'being, so to speak, rather than becoming'.[32] In this view, all disagreeables in the hero's fate could, and did, ultimately evaporate. And indeed the apotheosis of Lear as hero has the longest history in our post-Romantic age, dating as far back as Lamb:

> *... while we read it, we see not Lear, but we are Lear—we are*
> *in his mind, we are sustained by a grandeur which baffles the*
> *malice of daughters and storms ...*[33]

Part of the special distinction of Everett's essay is that it sought to counter the worst excesses of post-Romantic optimism, which had given us the transcendental, Christian Lear. Everett put forward another standard of Shakespearean heroic grandeur, one that allowed more scope for a more honest acknowledgment of the ironic disagreeables in Shakespeare's representation, on the model of Pascal rather than that of Romanticism:

> *... though Pascal was a man almost certainly wholly unlike*
> *Shakespeare in mind, temperament and way of life, his writing*
> *postulates a world in which it is still possible to think both*
> *seriously and ironically of 'la grandeur de l'homme'; and to see*
> *that the conditions on which such grandeur is based are close*
> *to those of tragic experience.*[34]

But whether Romantic, post-Romantic or Pascalian, the tradition of heroic grandeur lies in the mainstream of Western consciousness. It seems inevitable, then, that, with the perpetuation of that tradition into the twentieth century, there should have been added to it the masterly elucidations of the great twentieth-century scholar-critics who had arrived to prove, beyond trace of a doubt, that the vision of heroic grandeur of their own imagination was one also shared by the Renaissance in which Shakespeare wrote. To the overwhelming certainty of the Romantic imagination of man's innate grandeur, there could now be added the ascertainable authority of the influence on Shakespeare of medieval and classical precedent. Thus the tradition of heroic grandeur appeared to be put beyond the power of any criticism to attribute any other import to Shakespearean tragic representation.

And yet a criticism of that kind was for some time in the making in England. Its major value consisted precisely in the fact that it wrestled squarely with the overpowering tradition of heroic criticism. Indeed any criticism which sought to bypass confronting that tradition had inevitably to suffer judgment on its ineffectuality. That seems to have been the case, for instance, with Helen Gardner's retrospective article on *Othello*[35] in which she ventured to demur against what she recognized as that characteristic 'taste' of twentieth-century Shakespeare criticism for 'a giant art'. In raising to pre-eminence *Lear*, *Macbeth*, and *Timon*, such taste had unfairly relegated *Othello* to an inferior position as a play by comparison disappointingly lacking in grandeur. Gardner claimed that one ought rather to be able to value *Othello* as an extraordinary play in its own right, remarkable for the individuality of its characterization and the concentration of its plot. However, in the face of a tradition of such overpowering significance and authority, Gardner's case really amounted to an admission that *Othello is* a lesser play. It would rather have been incumbent on her to show how *Othello* relates to—takes its own distinctive place, as a first breakthrough, in—that unrivaled progress in heroic grandeur that undeniably defines Shakespeare's main achievement in this period.[36]

The paramount significance of the criticism I shall now proceed to cite is that it successfully related itself to the mainstream of Shakespearean tragic experience. It fully acknowledges all that heroic criticism of Shakespeare had sought to make of that experience. But it brings to light evidence of an embodiment of values in Shakespeare's representation which shows that he does not finally make of heroic grandeur what heroic criticism had us believing. Significantly, the stress of this criticism falls rather on that aspect of the representation that confronts us with all that is *not* in the possession of the hero in his awful pretension to such grandeur. In *Shakespeare and Tragedy*, John Bayley cites, among many other moments, the 'temple-haunting martlet' speech from *Macbeth* (I.vi.3ff) and the goings-on at the foot of Dover Cliff in *Lear* (IV.vi.11ff):

> *All ... in various ways, disclose kinds of existence outside the preoccupations of their tragic matter ... release us from the point of view, the preoccupation that, in rhetorical form, dominates tragedy ... It is a typical paradox that Shakespearean tragedy should consist so much of angelic moments ... which bring home the nature of the tragic, as his poetry gives it to us, more unmistakably than all its rhetoric of loss and darkness, misfortune and disaster. The art of Shakespeare draws our attention to how free we are from its own material and manipulation ... gives us a special awareness of such freedom; and it seems the same kind of awareness that tantalizes the consciousness of Lear and Macbeth, Hamlet and Othello. To be aware of it, and yet to be deprived of it, is for them the most absolute part of tragedy.*[37]

The first indications of this strong, *meta-heroic criticism*, if one may so designate it, were in fact first set down firmly by T. B. Tomlinson, in *A Study of Elizabethan and Jacobean Tragedy*.[38] We should turn especially to Tomlinson's opening remarks in his first chapter, 'The Elizabethan Tragic World' (to p.13), and to the chapter 'Shakespearean Tragedy'. Tomlinson's treatment of the import of heroic criticism for a later tradition that competes with it remains one of the most central statements. It is perhaps the most significant starting-point for the study of Shakespearean tragedy from this point of view. Its chief value at the time is that it built directly, critically, and fruitfully on the decisive historical contribution to Shakespeare studies of F. R. Leavis, in his *Education and the University* and L. C. Knights, in *Some Shakespearean Themes*.[39]

For Tomlinson, as for Bayley, the representational indications with the most decisive bearing on Shakespeare's tragic vision were also to be found in references such as 'the thick rotundity of the world' in *Lear*: 'We are conscious of suggestions of vitality springing from the very terms of tragic protest and tragic destruction':[40]

> *Blow, winds, and crack your cheeks! rage, blow!*

> *You cataracts and hurricanoes, spout*
> *Till you have drench'd our steeples, [drown'd] the cocks!*
> *You sulph'rous and thought-executing fires,*
> *Vaunt couriers of oak-cleaving thunderbolts,*
> *Singe my white head! And thou, all-shaking thunder,*
> *Strike flat the* **thick rotundity** *o' th' world!*
> (III.ii.1-7)

In pursuing this line, Tomlinson, faithfully, quotes F. R. Leavis on the Shakespearean tragic medium:

> *For Shakespeare's blank verse is a convention (so subtle that we forget it to be one) that enables him to play upon us, not merely through our sense of the character speaking, but also, and at the same time, directly; and the question how much of the one and how much of the other it may be in any particular case, does not arise.*

Tomlinson continues:

> *The Shakespearean tragic paradox includes a demonstration that nature, so far from being mere background or illustration of a morality or goodness truly grounded in man alone [in the face of an alien universe] is in itself an indispensable source of nourishment, the given body of experience and substance sustaining and supporting human life. The tragic hero often fails to see this, or sees it only imperfectly. But the plays see it, and consequently see human life as 'closely related to the wider setting of organic growth as indeed, in a quite concrete and practical way, directly based on man's dealings with the earth that nourishes him.'*[41]

Whether or not, as a final bearing, this *other* tradition satisfies our sense of Shakespeare's 'tragic progress' better (it opposes itself directly to the tradition of heroic criticism); in what sense, as *an alternative tradition*, it needs itself to be questioned, adjusted, challenged—I want to propose that these considerations should still properly be concerning and absorbing us today. For if not, the powerful and hallowed ghosts of Swinburne, of Bradley, and of G. Wilson Knight, to name only the seminal figures in the heroic criticism of Shakespeare, will otherwise have passed beyond our chance of ever laying them to rest.

*****

The problem we face in dealing with the overpowering tradition of the *post-Romantic heroic criticism* of Shakespeare is hardly settled by deciding that its great exponents were simply wrong or that we today, with our more learned and more practised forms of criticism, know better. It lies rather with us to strive to recognize and to come to terms with what was, in the hands of these exponents, a very powerful method of knowledge. That method must be seen as building on that of the Imagination, which Owen Barfield, writing in 1944 in *Romanticism Comes of Age*, went so far as to think a momentous advance in the evolution of human consciousness. He found some support for his view at the time in the writings of John Middleton Murry.[42] What Barfield had to say of critics after Schelling and Coleridge, in a re-issue of his book substantially amplified when it came out again in 1966, applies, I believe, to a pre-eminent degree in the case of the great post-Romantic Shakespeareans themselves, that is to say, to Swinburne, Bradley, and Wilson Knight among others:

> *Any number of critics following Schelling and Coleridge, have dealt with imagination as an ultimate mental activity that opposes and transmutes into a kind of aesthetic or mystical contemplation that absolute dichotomy between perceiving subject and perceived object on which our practical everyday experience (Coleridge's 'lethargy of custom') is necessarily based.*[43]

Post-Romantic Shakespearean criticism has, in it most vital and most powerful expressions, been entirely along the lines of the Imagination as set forth by Coleridge in the thirteenth chapter of the *Biographia Literaria*. In Coleridge's terms, 'elevating the thesis' [in our case, Shakespearean tragic experience] came from proceeding further 'from [the] notional to [the] actual'. That achievement Coleridge thought specifically made possible by 'contemplating the thesis intuitively ... in the living principle and in the process of our own self-consciousness'.[44] It is unlikely, therefore, that we shall ever come to terms with the full import of Shakespearean criticism since Coleridge without having first penetrated the profound method so memorably captured in these terms. Contemporary criticism, however, is almost brazenly *anti*-Romantic; in practice though especially by profession, it is marked by a contemptuous disbelief that there could ever have been a time when one could say that one believed in nothing so much as the truth of the Imagination. The irony of that predicament is that if our anti-Romantic critics lord it over us today, this is only by the allowance of a profound failure *within Romanticism* itself, a failure which it was Owen Barfield's remarkable achievement to have strenuously uncovered. It was of course Keats who said: 'I am certain of nothing but the holiness of the heart's affections, and the truth of the Imagination.' 'No,' says Barfield:

> *Today, we must know in what way the imagination is true. Otherwise we cannot feel its truth.*[45]

It was, as Barfield indicates, a matter of grasping 'the true nature of certainty':

> *And the first step towards the solution of this problem is the grasping of a right theory of knowledge.*[46]

I invoke Barfield's point of view because by no other shall we find our bearings with respect to *the profound impasse into which post-Romantic Shakespearean criticism has fallen* over the course of time. Because the entire criticism I have cited builds on a method of Imagination in fact *un*elaborated, without that further, certain basis that a right theory of knowledge would have provided, it has for long been easy to dismiss the vision of the hero's grandeur championed centrally by Swinburne, Bradley, Wilson Knight and others, just as it became easy to dismiss Leavis' controverting vision of 'Life':

> *either you felt Life or you did not. Great literature was a literature reverently open to Life, and what Life was could be demonstrated by great literature. The case was circular, intuitive, and proof against all argument, reflecting the enclosed coterie of the Leavisites themselves.*[47]

Leavis, as we have seen, ushered in a new phase in the history of Shakespeare criticism. He would certainly have thought of himself as standing over and against the Romantic legacy in Shakespeare criticism. But he falls himself within the pale of its tragedy. It says everything about the far-reaching influence of Romanticism, and of its tragedy, that Leavis' final formulation of 'the living principle'[48] should directly echo Coleridge. The phrase is from that very theory of the Imagination from the *Biographia* to the dramatic *discontinuation* of which Owen Barfield specifically laid down the tragedy. The tragedy is one that was mediated by the great post-Romantic Shakespeareans themselves. Having entered into a vision of the method of the Imagination, they supposed the vision *in itself* sufficient and complete, the Imagination 'true' without feeling the need to pursue the further question 'In what *way* is Imagination true?'[49]

Post-Romantic Shakespearean criticism today awaits an account that would make the necessary connections allowing us to relate an original term of *heroic grandeur* (re-discovered for us in such powerful form by our post-Romantic heroic Shakespeareans) to that opposing term (to which F. R. Leavis first introduced us) of *a meta-heroic life* established in direct opposition to the value of the hero. Between these polar positions (heroic grandeur vs. meta-heroic life) lies the all-determining area of 'abysmal' fate into which the hero is plummeted. The assumption of the complete sufficiency of their vision of the Imagination is what led many of our post-Romantic critics to dwell in the end almost exclusively in its dimension, and to ascribe, *by projection*, a corresponding integrity either to the hero, as in the case of our heroic critics, or, among those of Leavis' following, to Shakespeare himself as poet. What is left unapprehended, by heroic and meta-heroic critics alike, is precisely that 'abysmal' dimension opened up to us by the hero's tragic passion. The final import of this awful 'fall', as a reflection on heroic capacity, has yet to be fully accounted for on the basis of that 'right theory of knowledge' that would include a fully elaborated theory of the Imagination. Without our penetrating to such an account, there is no likelihood that the post-Romantic heroic criticism of Shakespeare will survive in our estimation as part of a continuous history. But if not, the life of the Shakespeare critic practising today and tomorrow will have become that much the poorer. It will become a haunted life— pursued by the shadow of ghosts who will remain unappeased; though it is still not too late in the day.

*****

Rudolf Steiner is the man Barfield acknowledged to be not only the outstanding influence behind his own work but the great world-historic figure who had come to *supply* what the Romantic Movement itself could not provide.[50] That Steiner was to remain virtually unknown in the literary and academic worlds even to this day is a phenomenon that Barfield could already see developing at the time he was writing. This fact constituted for him the deepest of disappointments. To witness the spectacle of Barfield's frustrated crusade on Steiner's behalf is to see how Barfield as philosopher-critic—though not as a disciple of Steiner—falls victim himself to the tragedy of the Romantic Movement. But by far the greatest part of the tragedy is that Steiner remains unknown to this day. And at the risk of following in the wake of Barfield's fate as a critic,

I myself would wish to insist on the desperate need in our own time to re-affirm the inevitability of Barfield's choice of champion. To the unanswered problem that the Romantic Movement in literature raised— 'In what way is Imagination true?'—the solution lay in grasping 'a right theory of knowledge'. Barfield has filled out the rest of the story for us:

> Now the Romantic Movement never properly crystallized into a theory of knowledge. In this country—apart from Coleridge— there was hardly even the desire for such a theory. But in Central Europe it was somewhat different. Apart from the group of Romantic philosophers, Goethe, with such conceptions as that of the 'exact percipient fancy' and with all his scientific work, brought an initial confidence in the truth of imagination at any rate to the verge of a theory of knowledge. And Steiner, in his 'Philosophy of Freedom', carried it over that verge and established it firmly in the promised land of philosophy.[51]

If, as Barfield has put it, 'the true *differentia* of imagination is that the subject should be somehow merged or resolved into the object'[52] then, as he points out:

> Only Steiner ... has clearly apprehended this activity as part, and but the first part, of a long, sober process of cognition [emphasis mine] that may end in a man's actually overcoming the dichotomy ...[53]

Only in the *continuation of the story,* then—as 'Romanticism comes of age'—do we finally find justification for the supreme value Barfield continued to ascribe in the history of the evolution of consciousness to the activity of Imagination. In Steiner's case, it was a matter of having to build on 'exact results with the help of a perceptive faculty developed through *controlled* imagination...'[54] From Steiner we learn that the method was one that Goethe had already understood and practised, though he left it undeveloped.[55] The key word here is 'controlled', for the ground-breaking value of Steiner's development of the method is that it is 'in its essence, *systematic imagination*'.[56] As Barfield explains:

> the 'Intuition', in which his method culminates, is to be reached by way of two preliminary stages, the first of which he terms Imagination and the second Inspiration. It is only at the second of the three stages, that of Inspiration, that the perceptive faculty is enhanced in a way that begins to have objective value for cognition.[57]

There have been intimations of the 'truth' of the Imagination as early as a hundred years before. But Steiner reveals, in his own comprehensive account of World-evolution, that it develops as the activity of Imaginative *cognition* only in the latter part of the nineteenth century. To associate Rudolf Steiner with a unique phenomenon of the late nineteenth and early twentieth centuries is another way of saying that one cannot approach him separately from the *Anthroposophical* Movement which he not so much founded as mediated.

Here I might add, by way of an autobiographical preliminary, that my own association with this Movement is the result of a combination of events that I should like to think frees me from the need for special pleading on behalf of the approach I will be proposing. I came to the Anthroposophical Movement along two routes—at once from the side of Anthroposophy *and* of Literature. My membership in this Movement is primarily, of course, my own choice of life; it is also, partly and crucially, the eventual result of the influence of personal associations in my life who were themselves associated with the Movement from an early age (for Anthroposophy—about twenty-eight; I speak of a full intellectual association, for Anthroposophical *culture*, of course, extends to every phase of life, as witnessed in the Waldorf schools founded on the basis of its principles). However, Anthroposophy was 'in my life' long before I myself found a personal relation to it. In the meantime, my research (for my doctoral dissertation) into the relationship between metaphorical language and an otherworldly reality led me by a natural course of discovery, and along an entirely independent route, to Owen Barfield's *Poetic Diction*. In a later edition of this work, Barfield formally acknowledges his debt to Rudolf Steiner. Barfield's association with Anthroposophy was, until then, unknown to me. And as I came to him then, so I come to him again now, though conscious now of a relation that I bear myself to Rudolf Steiner from my own place within the Anthroposophical Movement.

The task facing a Shakespeare critic who is also an Anthroposophist is beset with the greatest difficulty. The history of the Anthroposophical Movement itself testifies to the tragedy of misguided attempts to apply the results of Anthroposophical research directly to non-Anthroposophical areas of life. Anthroposophy became drastically changed in the process: to see the tragedy from the *other* side. But the obverse may also be true— namely, that it is impossible to approach the concepts that Anthroposophy yields without finally making the leap into Anthroposophy itself. What this means is that a Shakespeare critic who is also an Anthroposophist will always be conscious that his concepts are derived from within another experience: the *first-hand* experience of Anthroposophy. With Rudolf Steiner, the idea of the 'wisdom of man', or *Anthropos-Sophia*, is suddenly greatly extended. It is accompanied by a fully developed account of how, 'in the process of our own self-consciousness', we work our way cognitively into the World-process, in Imagination, Inspiration, and Intuition. Concepts are yielded that even critics who are not Anthroposophists will acknowledge fit the case of Shakespeare in a way that will appear inevitable. This is a direct consequence of the astonishing comprehensiveness of the vision of World-evolution Steiner acquired on the basis of the higher cognitive powers. Nowhere, for instance, but in Steiner shall we find a fully developed account of that tremendous otherworldly experience from which modern man has become tragically alienated, bearing out the view that 'from the fifteenth century onwards humanity has been gradually forsaken by the Gods'.[58] My own record of that process of alienation as presented in Part One above, written during a period of my life *before* my allegiance to Anthroposophy, by comparison has the value of a distant intuition, though it would appear that I *was* feeling my way in the right direction.[59] Just how far the process of alienation was meant to go for Shakespeare, or why it had to go that far, likewise cannot be grasped without the benefit of Anthroposophy. This is the view I will be highlighting in this chapter.

I know of no account that does more justice to the comprehensive nature of Shakespeare's progressive experience in tragedy than the account of *what Anthroposophy calls the 'Consciousness Soul'-experience* put forward by Barfield himself with special reference to Shakespeare as its most representative instance:

> *Seek death! Yes, know yourself and the world! Do not merely believe in the old way, substituting one creed for another. Rather live in the breakdown of all belief. Even encourage your own opposition, as men do in games. Immerse in the destructive element! And so learn to tear your true self free from all thought and all feeling in which the senses echo.*[60]

Experience cannot be pure, or complete, unless a renunciation has first been made. A life of thought and feeling given over to the world of the senses Steiner saw as the characteristic experience of the *Sentient Soul*. Where thought and feeling combine in the act of faith, we have the characteristic experience of the *Intellectual or Mind Soul*. The experience of the *Consciousness Soul*—of the self alone—falls in between these two Soul-experiences, in absolute separation from them both. The world of Shakespeare's tragedies marks the point where the Consciousness Soul-experience is brought to bear on inherited forms of faith and of sensual engagement that, for reasons that cannot be grasped at that time, have now to be renounced. The renunciation itself is a profoundly tragic experience. A perversely hopeful notion continues to be entertained at this time as to what it is that can be had in the way of 'faith' or a 'life of the senses'.[61]

Characteristically, a great power of 'faith' is being brought to bear on an experience of 'love' in sensual terms. And that is precisely what has become *unreal* as experience. An element of absolute freedom from these terms must first be introduced, before a right relation to them can be restored. It is precisely Shakespeare's great achievement at this time that *he* unconsciously supplies the mediating role. He embodies in himself the standard of true consciousness by which the attitudes of his characters, in respect of faith and of love, are judged wanting. Shakespeare's own role in this regard is far from being an indifferent one, as indicated in Barfield's point that he was 'only unconsciously the bearer of—consciousness'.[62] It is as if Shakespeare could not himself accept the profound failure implied in the self's tragic dissociation from any sure basis in faith and in love. The extent of his identification with the situations of his characters is reflected dramatically in that characteristic impulse to provide, as we have seen, a complete representation for his characters in their aims, even where these aims have become perverse (see p.107ff). The attempt itself may appear to us perverse, though to see it that way would be wrongly to dissociate ourselves from the profound evolution in experience Shakespeare was himself living through at the time, if only as creative genius.

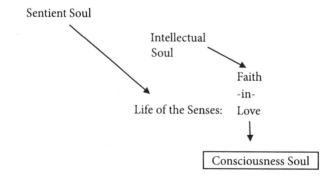

One main line of development in Shakespeare's 'tragic progress' traces the route that would have to be taken, if an experience of faith and of love were pursued without regard to the further evolution now necessitated. Wilson Knight's comprehensive tracing of the abysmal hate-theme in Shakespeare's tragedies remains, from this point of view, of tremendous critical value.[63] 'Hate' is the name Knight gave to an extreme form of violent cynicism about 'love' that overtakes many of Shakespeare's heroes from the time their own deepest aspirations regarding love are confounded. They themselves are thrown into utter confusion. But that such 'hate' in the last analysis denotes the final negation of love in all the forms Shakespeare's characters present love to us — here is a further view that no critic has been ready to embrace, it would appear in the absence of concepts that would account for such radical developments. Knight's own approach to Hamlet is a case in point. Knight acknowledges that what now absorbs Hamlet as experience implies not less than 'the negation of any passion whatsoever'.[64] Hamlet, Knight tells us, 'has seen through the tinsel of life and love'. Hamlet is 'right' —his 'philosophy' is 'inevitable, blameless, and irrefutable'.[65] But, in spite of Knight's acknowledgment that this is true, we find him strangely backtracking, appealing finally to the 'intuitive faith, or love, or purpose, by which we must live if we are to remain sane'.[66] And so, on the basis of this view, Knight finally rejects Hamlet's experience, for 'it is the negation of life. It is death.'[67]

Yet, as we have seen—'Seek death!'; 'Immerse in the destructive element!'—these are the great *dicta* of the Consciousness Soul-experience, though they are to be known in Imagination only, as Barfield's account implies. Hamlet we must see merely as the vehicle for Shakespeare's own evolution in consciousness. There can be no question, consequently, of a direct application of Hamlet's attitudes to life. This is part of the confusion that will be found to underlie Knight's view (notwithstanding his championing of a new form of 'imaginative' criticism at the time he wrote). That one can embrace a concept of destruction and death without this bearing at all outwardly in the circumstances of life is a crucial consideration that would appear to be beyond the understanding of a certain kind of criticism. However, it explains why Shakespeare himself could entertain such violent concepts in his plays with no corresponding manifestation to show in the outer circumstances of his own life (unlike in the case of Marlowe). Any confusion between the sphere of the Imagination and the sphere of Life understandably concerns criticism, and such concern reflects on what would appear to be a very real risk involved in entertaining such concepts. The danger is amply illustrated, for example, in the horrible atrocities that accompanied Martin Luther's exhortations to the people of his day to know themselves better as sinners.[68]

Luther's *desiderata* had, astonishingly, been taken literally as attitudes to be embodied in life, and Luther was, of course, horrified. He knew only too well that such knowledge was to be had strictly as an experience of the soul. But perhaps because the act of Imagination would have to bear fruit as a real or *objective* process in the soul, Luther may be said to have been guilty of roiling the waters? At any rate, from the import of his approach, it is easy to see how his auditors would have been misled:

> *Come, accept. Be a sinner! 'Esto peccator!' And don't do the thing by halves; sin squarely and with gusto, 'pecca fortiter!' Not just playful sins. No, but real, substantial, tremendous sins!*[69]

Luther himself may have been guilty of excess in his approach to it, but the process of Imagination he espouses is the same. 'Seek death': Luther's is, also, an account of the Consciousness Soul-experience, though he gives it to us unconsciously, inasmuch as the experience is still being expressed in traditional terms, as a concept of 'sin'. Yet Luther was also capable of an approach to the experience in non-traditional terms, as evidenced in his remarkable statement that 'nothing can cure libido' (see above p.15 and p.54). And in spite of Shakespeare's own adoption of the traditional language of devilry, sin and so on, his own approach is initially through a concept of 'libido', or 'lust' (in *Hamlet*). Primarily, it is a concept of 'evil' (evident from *Hamlet* onwards) and especially a concept of the overpowering *violence* of evil. Before the power of that violence and the hero's conception of that violence, all faith in love would wither, and it is not difficult to see what horrible uncertainty must attend on such an experience. Being primarily given to such faith, the Shakespearean hero is very far from ready for the experience. And where such faith most clearly takes on heroic proportions—from *Othello* onwards, where full expression in the 'Intellectual or Mind Soul' continues in the old way—the bewilderment and disillusion would have to be very great. The spectacle of the hero's tragic fall into abysmal hatred becomes, consequently, a very awful one to behold.[70]

The great service performed by our post-Romantic heroic critics of Shakespeare lay in the attempt to re-discover and preserve a proper sense of the full grandeur and scope of the Shakespearean tragic spectacle.

Lacking the insight and vision of Anthroposophy, however, they were finally without the conception of a further evolutionary relation to evil implied in Shakespeare's own creative relationship to this material. That they would not have derived that conception for themselves can be deduced from the nature of the material. The spectacle of evil in Shakespeare's tragedies is so very sinister and finally so overpoweringly violent, it is easy to see why these critics would have reverted to the original spirit of heroic faith for an establishing of 'values'. For them, 'morality or goodness [is] truly grounded in man alone [in the face of an alien universe]'. It is true that the evil finally overpowers the hero from without. Though it works into him inwardly, the hero himself is tragically helpless before that evil. *The evil is*, that is to say, *elusively and uncontrollably inward*; and this would appear finally to exonerate the hero, so that it is easy to see how in a certain case identification with the hero would continue. But this is finally to overlook the hero's own radical implication in this evil—among other things, his own abysmal fall into hatred, from which he never fully recovers. Thus, Hamlet might say:

> *If Hamlet from himself be ta'en away,*
> ....
> *Then Hamlet does it not, Hamlet denies it*
> (V.ii.234ff),

likewise Othello:

> *That's he that was Othello; here I am.*
> (V.ii.284)

Shakespeare's heroes in this way dissociate themselves from what has tragically taken place. But, by then, Ophelia and Desdemona, both, lie dead. One thinks also of Cordelia dead in Lear's arms. And in all these cases, the hero's fall into hatred has very substantially contributed to the deaths.

The spectacle of evil in Shakespeare finally transmutes into the spectacle of violent death via the hero's hatred, itself the involuntary and bitter negation of faith in love. That hatred is also by implication—in the violence of its effect—*negation of the heroic*. In fact, any view that continues to espouse the nobility of the hero in the face of the spectacle of evil Shakespeare offers us must eventually founder against the final emphasis on the violent death of a loved one, for which the hero has become (in a sense that is new in terms of the heroic) hopelessly responsible. No idea of expression in heroic spirit can be finally reconciled to that aspect of the spectacle. Before these deaths Shakespeare's heroes stand, whether consciously or unconsciously, at an absolute loss. They are, moreover, in a substantial sense that is pointless to deny, guilty of them. Nor can they make amends. On the other hand, it is no more possible to reserve from this aspect of the spectacle the idea of some greater Life that remains intact from the debacle. Here also it is the case of a tradition of critics who found themselves either indisposed or unable to allow for the value of a spectacle so overwhelmingly violent. To that other idealization of 'nature' (as 'the given body of experience and substance sustaining and supporting human life'—see p.119), we may oppose the following emphasis from the ending of *King Lear*:

> *I know when one is dead, and when one lives;*
> *She's dead as earth.*
> (V.iii.261-262)
>
>   *... No, no, no life*
> *Why should a dog, a horse, a rat, have life,*
> *And thou no breath at all? Thou'lt come no more,*
> *Never, never, never, never, never.*
> (V.iii.306-309)

That Shakespeare through his verse works directly on us, as Leavis insisted, to suggest other experiences that are possible, beyond the immediate tragic spectacle we are offered, will be readily admitted. It is on this basis that Bayley himself makes a point of the fact that 'the art of Shakespeare draws our attention to how free we are from its own material and manipulation, gives us a special awareness of such freedom'. But this is to say no more but that the process of Life continued for Shakespeare alongside the process of tragic representation that absorbed him as creative genius. By the time we get to the ending of *King Lear*, the process of '*Life*' *itself* is being *re-valued*, in the face of a more absorbing concern with the all-levelling power that evil could have in Shakespeare's Imagination. We may suppose that what added to the difficulty of seeing just where the spectacle of evil might lead is the fact that Shakespeare does not appear to have himself known what value there could be to the spectacle, except that submission to it appeared to him to be the truest experience in consciousness. In Anthroposophy, one would say that it is in the nature of the Consciousness Soul-experience that one cannot know or understand.

The overriding focus that I am saying finally crystallizes the essence of Shakespearean tragedy is not brought to complete expression until the ending of *King Lear*. It is already, however, anticipated in the ending of *Othello*, which suggests that Shakespeare was working his way progressively *toward* that later point. Othello, unlike Lear, cannot find words to express it, but his own fate comes around to the same obsessive focus:

> *O Desdemon! dead, Desdemon! dead!*
> *O, O!*
> (V.ii.281-282)

In spite of the sublime expression in romantic-transcendental faith we are given at the beginning of this scene (see above, p.88ff.) there is no altering the course events are taking. In the end, Othello simply does not get Desdemona back, though Shakespeare continues to tempt us in our hopes that Desdemona may yet escape death, as she recovers breath twice in this scene, speaking on one occasion:

> OTHELLO: *Not dead? not yet quite dead?*
> (V.ii.86)

> EMILIA: *O, who hath done this deed?*
> DESDEMONA: *Nobody; I myself.*
> (V.ii.123-124)

Ever since Johnson first declared the ending of *King Lear* itself a scene not to be 'endured', echoing with this comment his similar comment on the ending of *Othello*, critics have striven, in every manner and form, to circumvent the impression of all-leveling hopelessness on which the later scene especially appears to insist.[71] Only Nicholas Brooke in our time has sought strenuously to keep us to the way Shakespeare insists on our seeing it:

> *We are driven to see, not only the very human pain of Lear's end with Cordelia in his arms, but also the absolute negation of all forms of hope.*
> *Her death kills all life.*[72]

There is, at the last, no getting around, or away from, certainly the ending of *King Lear*. Shakespeare may have had to continue to trace the course of the hero's hatred through, as Wilson Knight proposed, if only to ensure that the hatred would be finally purged. He would have had to take us, that is to say, as far as *Timon of Athens*, taking up again a play he had already commenced. And along with *Timon*, he would have also had to give us *Antony and Cleopatra* and *Coriolanus*, simply because an attachment to heroic faith would not die so easily. This is apart from the fact that Shakespeare, as a member of his age, was more or less bound to continue working in the 'heroic idiom', at least for a time longer.[73] It would take much to break the illusion of the value of heroic spirit; it may be that it is never really and finally broken even in Shakespeare, as far as the outward evidence will say. But certainly *with the ending of* King Lear, *there is no further way to go*. Either there *is* no hope, as the ending suggests, and we *are* deluded about the surviving value of love, faith and all systems of life in the familiar forms we know—we are deluded, also, about the value of the heroic—or it may be that there is a further purpose to an enforced renunciation of these forms.

Brooke himself could offer no notion of any further purpose to Shakespeare's final focus as given to us in that ending. Such a focus might well appear to us pointless. But here again it is Steiner who, speaking out of the Anthroposophical Movement, provides the necessary vision:

> At this point a possibility comes in which may prove terrible. A man may lose his sensations and feelings of outer reality without finding a new reality opening up before him. He then feels himself as if suspended in the void. He feels bereft of all life. The old values are gone and no new ones have arisen in their place. The world and man no longer exist for him. Now, this is by no means a mere possibility. It happens at one time or another to everyone who seeks higher knowledge. He comes to a point at which the spirit represents all life to him as death.
>
> We understand this when we know from experience the point of transition from lower to higher knowledge. We ourselves had felt as if all solid matter and things of sense had dissolved into water, and as if the ground were cut away from under our feet. Everything which we had previously felt to be alive had been killed. The spirit had passed through the life of the senses like a sword piercing a warm body, we had seen the blood of sensuality flow.[74]

At a certain point we shall be unable to follow Shakespeare any further in his progress in tragic vision without referring ourselves to an account of the path to higher knowledge, along the lines of the one Steiner himself provided as the path appropriate for our time. Insofar as we approach this 'path' from the side of Literature—embracing Shakespeare's experience as reflected to us in the literature he left us—it is a question of seeing that no study of the tragedies can be really thorough that does not finally set them in direct relation to the higher processes of the later romances. The renunciation of all systems of life to which the tragedies bear such tremendous witness as a whole has its justification, finally, only in the higher life that emerges from that renunciation, corresponding to the experience as given in the romances. An idea of 'tragic progress', in this context, necessarily presupposes a further evolutionary relation to a triumphing evil, even in the overwhelmingly final form we get in the ending of *King Lear*. The key lies in the transition from *King Lear* to *Pericles*. Crucial to our understanding of this transition is an implied shift in focus away from the experience of the tragic hero to the transfigured mind of Shakespeare himself. A new life has already appeared, and the process by which it has come about is now to be outlined for us in a new form of 'allegorical' representation richly suggestive of the experience that lies behind, that is Shakespeare's own.

*****

The distinguishing characteristic of Shakespeare's representation in the tragedies may be said to lie in his progressive accentuation of the literal status of the tragedy, culminating in the ending of *King Lear*. It would be grossly to misconceive the very different approach taken to the representation of action in *Pericles* to suppose that the characters of Thaisa or Pericles, or Marina, or the tragedy that befalls them, are invested with anything like the same literal status. We have, with *Pericles*, moved far beyond an art that holds the mirror up to nature, where evil and death literally prevail. We are on firm ground with the action of *Pericles* when we see it rather as mirroring allegorically what evil and death have finally made and are making of themselves in Shakespeare's own mind. This would seem to be already evident from the obituary Pericles pronounces over Thaisa who is dead before we have known her:

> ... *Most wretched queen!*
> ....
> *A terrible child-bed hast thou had, my dear,*
> *No light, no fire. Th' unfriendly elements*
> *Forgot thee utterly, nor have I time*
> *To give thee hallow'd to thy grave, but straight*
> *Must cast thee, scarcely coffin'd, in [the ooze],*
> *Where, for a monument upon thy bones,*
> *The [e'er]-remaining lamps, the belching whale,*

And humming water must o'erwhelm thy corpse,
Lying with simple shells.
(III.i.54-64)

'Lying with simple shells' reflects back to us a kind of assimilation of a loved one's death inconceivable to one who has just been through the tragedy. Already, we are alerted to the fact that Pericles cannot be viewed as a character who is literally undergoing tragedy here, any more than we have a conception of Thaisa herself as a character. I do not want to deny, on the other hand, that a literal death has taken place—quite the contrary. It is precisely what makes the 'allegorical' form of representation in which Shakespeare had now chosen to work so amenable to his purpose that a death has certainly occurred, and it is irreversible. We are on firm ground with Pericles' speech, however, only when we see it as representing the effect that the death of a loved one has had over time. The death percolates down, as it were, to the bottom of the mind (represented here as the sea-floor) to become there the simple event it could never have been when it actually happened. It is from such a point in the mind—Shakespeare's own—that Thaisa is then 'returned' from death, by no means as a literal personage.

Approached in this way, Pericles is nothing in himself. He is everything when seen as echoing in himself the Shakespearean tragic hero's experience as this continues to reverberate in Shakespeare's own mind in the extreme and final form to which it had come. Addressing himself to the death that has occurred, Pericles remarks of his loved one, with a truth that fits the case literally: 'Th' unfriendly elements / Forgot thee *utterly*.' Earlier he had said: 'I do not fear the flaw, / It hath done to me the *worst*' (III.i.39-40). Awareness of the extremity of the evil undergone is also reflected in the words Pericles pronounces over the 'child' that is born with, and of, destruction and death:

... a more blusterous birth had never babe.
....
Thou art the rudeliest welcome to this world
That ever was prince's child.
(III.i.28;31-32)

Focus is *on the death that ends all life,* and all corresponding attachments to life. It cannot, therefore, appear how any future or ongoing life can contain anything within itself to compensate for the destruction:

Even at the first thy loss is more than can

Thy portage quit.
(III.i.34-35)

And yet, already a new life has appeared, though Pericles does not himself as yet bear any consciousness of this. That he does *not* testifies to the lingering power of the tragic experience in Shakespeare's mind, though the circumstances in which Pericles finds himself already imply an evolution out of that experience.

From this point, it no longer suffices to think in terms of an experience in the Consciousness Soul alone, which we have as a universal possession in our own day. We have the experience, and yet, if the course Shakespeare took in his tragedies is any indication, we seem unable to follow the full process of that experience through. We live, for the most part today, in the Consciousness Soul. We are otherwise happily or not so happily related in what are, in fact, remnants of the Sentient Soul and Intellectual or Mind Soul experiences; while more and more in critical trends today—by which I mean post-structuralist, post-modern, anti-Romantic—the pretension is to make a principle of the Consciousness Soul alone, as if there never were or could be any other Soul-experiences. And so do critics today deny in their criticism (and to their students) what they themselves could never do without in their own lives, even as remnants. For the Consciousness Soul-experience has no meaning alone—in itself it is death—and the superior value of the critics I have enumerated who were working in the shadow of Romantic tradition lies precisely in their (at least unconscious) admission of other Soul-experiences that are possible, where meaning actually resides. From Anthroposophy we learn that it was in the 'Egypto-Chaldean Age' (around 2800-700 B.C.) that the Sentient Soul received its full development; in the 'Graeco-Roman Age' (700 B.C.-1400 A.D.) that the Intellectual or Mind Soul received development. The Consciousness Soul is in process of being developed today, and will continue to develop, the 'Consciousness Soul Age' extending from approximately 1400 A.D. to 3500 A.D. The 'Imaginative Soul', as the first fruit of the Consciousness Soul experience, emerges around the beginning of the nineteenth century. A further development in Imagination, Inspiration, and Intuition takes place with Steiner in the late nineteenth and early twentieth centuries. All three additional Soul powers will not, however, become the common possession of whole groups of humanity until much later on, in Ages to come; and we are meant to see each new Soul faculty as emerging in turn out of the others.

Barfield, in *Romanticism*, describes the entire evolution as follows:

> *We may very well compare the self of man to a seed. Formerly, what is now seed was a member of the whole plant, and, as such, was wholly informed with a life not wholly its own. But now the pod or capsule has split open, and the dry seed has been ejected. It has attained to a separate existence. Henceforth one of two things may happen to it: either it may abide alone, isolated from the rest of the earth, growing dryer and dryer, until it withers up altogether; or, by uniting with the earth, it may blossom into a fresh life of its own. Thus it is with the Consciousness Soul. Either it may lose itself in the arid subtleties of a logistic intellectualism, which no longer has any life, though it once had—preoccupying itself with a nice balancing and pruning of dogma, theory and memory—or, by uniting itself with the Spirit of the Earth, with the Word, it may blossom into the Imaginative Soul, and live ...*

> *It will be easiest to plunge 'in medias res' and to inquire precisely what Steiner said of the further development of the human Ego beyond this stage of the consciousness soul. We have arrived, then, at the point of development at which the macrocosm is so to speak focused to an invisible point in the isolated Ego. What next? The answer of anthroposophy is that there are two alternatives open to it: ultimate death or nonentity on the one hand, and on the other the first step towards an expansion outward again to the macrocosm—an expansion of such nature that the center and source of life is henceforward within instead of without ...*

> *Let us, for the moment, express the whole course of human evolution in the following diagram:*

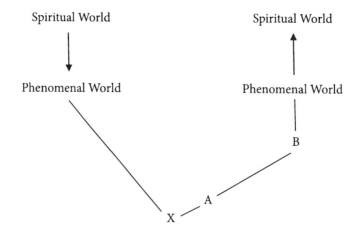

Then, if the point A is the consciousness soul, B represents the developed consciousness soul, the consciousness soul on its way to becoming what Dr. Steiner once called the 'Imaginative Soul'. And at X, which marks the intellectual soul, we have, says anthroposophy, the human nadir, the true mystery of the resurrection, the mystery of the New Man from the Old. Let us look at it historically:

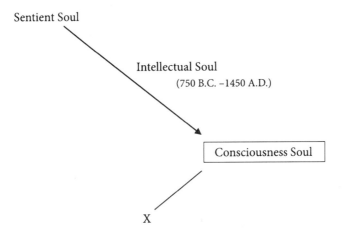

The result is that one begins to assert with confidence, and out of one's own experience, that some remarkable event must have taken place at X, some gift of power to arise from the depths, some passing over of life and meaning from the macrocosm to the microcosm, some mystery, let us say, of resurrection.[75]

Unable to see their way through to the evolutionary relation among these experiences, Romantic and post-Romantic critics were unable to see precisely how the process of meaning is established. These critics could not see how at their best they themselves were profiting from a heightened form of consciousness that was the direct result of this process of meaning being established as historical process.

Here is another of those tremendous insights that Anthroposophy has to offer. It would appear that Shakespeare was someone who went through this historical process directly. *Born as the first fruit of the process of the Consciousness Soul-experience is what*, in one form of denomination, *Anthroposophy calls the 'Imaginative Soul'.* This is, in its first full-fledged, historical manifestation, none other than what Coleridge and other Romantics would identify as the 'Imagination'—

that new, expansive Soul-power proceeding from and in 'the process of self-consciousness' that, for Middleton Murry, also represented a fundamental evolution in human consciousness. Romantic, as well as post-Romantic, critics were thus among the first to be aware of this new Soul-power, in their approach to Shakespeare as in other matters. But the Imaginative Soul does not, in fact, fully objectify itself in Shakespeare until well after the process of the Consciousness Soul-experience has run its course. It is from this point that Romantic and post-Romantic critics alike, operating without the benefit of Anthroposophy, neglected to understand how the full process of the Imagination sees itself through. They were not able to see that a fully effective Imagination stands in an essential and continuous relationship with the Consciousness-Soul experience.

From the side of Literature, we may say that *a first objectification of the Imaginative Soul in Shakespeare* coincides with his presentation of the birth of Marina. But not until Marina's 'coming of age', and Pericles' later 'recognition' of her, is the vision of this Soul power first brought to fully conscious expression. Anthroposophy speaks of the Imaginative Soul in association also with the Spirit Self or Higher Ego. This last term reminds us that the evolution in question emerges fundamentally as a further development of Ego-consciousness. In the structure of this evolution, Marina objectifies that new, higher power in the Ego, expressing itself in the Imaginative Soul. This power is then shown slowly lifting the Ego in its suffering aspect, represented by Pericles, out of its experience of death in the Consciousness Soul. We come by this route, then, to one of the most sublime moments in Shakespeare—the so-called recognition-scene between Pericles and Marina. At this stage of the 'progress', the suffering Ego has recognized, and is uniting with, a higher aspect in itself which, though perfectly sensitive to suffering, is yet insusceptible to despair. Pericles himself notes of Marina:

> ... yet thou dost look
> Like Patience gazing on kings' graves, and smiling
> Extremity out of act.
> (V.i.138-140)

What union with a higher power of Ego now opens up is, in fact, the prospect of a new 'life' in which *the Ego* can be fully *reconciled to tragedy.* Shakespeare's symbol of an extreme, destructive evil (the sea) converts in this context into the symbol of new joy:

PERICLES. *O Helicanus, strike me honored sir,*
Give me a gash, put me to present pain,
Lest this great sea of joys rushing upon me
O'erbear the shores of my mortality,
And drown me with their sweetness [to Marina]
                    O, come hither,
Thou that beget'st him that did thee beget ...
(V.i.190-195)

Opening out on the vision of Diana (V.i.240ff), new joy now leads Pericles back to Thaisa who is herself an other-than-literal personage. She is not the loved one who has been lost to death, but, rather, all that was lost as a consequence of that death: a 'lost connection to the world' following on 'lost faith' in all systems of life. That connection and that faith are what are now restored to the Ego. Restoration itself is the consequence of acts of preservation as well as of guidance (as in the case of the vision of Diana) that open out on still other mysteries that concerned Shakespeare at this time, for the allegorical implications of the action in Shakespeare's romances are extensive, indeed vast. However, the Ego's *restoration to the world*, in faith and in love as well as to the senses, represents, at this stage, an altogether different experience from what connection to the world was before. The whole experience takes place now on a higher plane. Shakespeare's experience in this regard is only partially reflected to us in that additional, ethereal Soul-quality in the verse that every commentator on the romances recognizes is new and is first sighted in this play (though its significance has never before been defined in terms of a consistent theory of meaning). We understand Shakespeare's experience primarily through an allegorical structure that he has built into the qualitative representation, from which we gather the greater development or progress that now engages him far beyond the confines of this (or any other) single play. The development or progress in question extends over both *Pericles* and *The Winter's Tale*. We find the same fundamental experience at the basis of the action in the later play, with Leontes substituting for Pericles, Perdita for Marina, and Hermione for Thaisa. But with this new addition: that the whole is approached, in this instance, from the point of view of the Ego's guilt or direct responsibility for tragedy. Thus *Pericles* gives us the experience from the point of view of the Ego's innocence in tragedy, *The Winter's Tale* from the point of view of the Ego's guilt. And only in the combined effect of both plays, as the expression of what is taking place in Shakespeare's own mind, do we find the evolution that corresponds fully to the experience of Shakespeare's tragic hero who is himself, of course, both innocent and guilty.

In light of what has been said thus far, we will not be surprised to find *The Tempest* extending representation of the fundamental experience still further. Here, however, we have a momentous 'return' to the literal level and well-rounded characterization of the tragedies, reflected in a dramatic foregrounding of the principal characters, Prospero and Miranda.[76] Here, again, there is the case of a loved 'wife' who is lost to death, coinciding with the birth of a 'daughter'. Miranda, we are told, is 'not / Out three years old' (I.ii.40-41), when she and Prospero are put out to sea. The mother is, thus, only recently dead, and not so long before that we cannot see her death as coinciding with Prospero's renunciation of state and devotion to study, or, for that matter, with Miranda's birth. The whole action is an integrated one. Prospero's decision to 'neglect' all 'worldly ends, all dedicated / To closeness and the bettering of my mind' (I.ii.89-90) may be directly referred to Shakespeare's own evolution, from the time the 'death' of a loved one became, for him, his one, essential tragic preoccupation.

Prospero incurs further consequences for his 'decision' being, along with Miranda, ambushed and driven out to 'sea' in what presents itself as yet another marvelous transfiguration of the essential tragic sorrow:

> ... *There they hoist us,*
> *To cry to th' **sea**, that roar'd to us; to sigh*
> *To th' winds, whose pity, sighing back again,*
> *Did us but loving wrong.*
> Miranda.   *Alack, what trouble*
> *Was I then to you!*
> Prospero.   *O, a cherubin*
> *Thou wast that did preserve me. Thou didst smile,*
> *Infused with a fortitude from heaven,*
> **When I have deck'd the sea with drops full salt,**
> *Under my burthen groan'd, which rais'd in me*
> *An undergoing stomach, to bear up*
> *Against what should ensue.*
> (I.ii.148-158)

It is the 'whole' sorrow that comes to expression once again here, the death of a loved one being at the center of it. The supporting power is, likewise, bestowed by Miranda as higher power, according to the pattern already described. We may take it as an implicit understanding that the whole evolution Shakespeare has reflected to us in the romances is here climactically embodied—insofar as literature can embody this—in Prospero and Miranda as literal inheritors of that evolution. That we have 'returned' to the literal level in this play will also explain, among other things, why in this instance Prospero's 'wife' is *not* restored, for there can be no question of restoration at this level.

Variations on the extraordinary experience that underlies these plays will, of course, also be observed, notably the fact that in *The Winter's Tale* the loved one is 'kept' alive rather than submitting to a formal 'death' as in the case of Thaisa (Hermione is otherwise *thought* to be dead, also by the audience). I would suggest that this latest representational gambit was conceived with the intention of intensifying comparison between the allegorical order of the representation characteristic of the last plays and our imagination of what a literal restoration of the loved one might be like. But the comparison works in a way opposite to what we might think. The purpose is to suggest that the experience of being restored to the world has *the same value as* a literal restoration of the loved one. There is, also, the additional effect: as though of some further meeting with the loved one beyond death; the Hermione who speaks at the end speaks in the *tones* of one who is dead, like a revenant. Certainly the idea that the loved one would have stayed alive and silent over sixteen years is not to be literally credited, would put too great a strain on credibility in literal terms. It is rather that Shakespeare arbitrarily 'keeps' Hermione alive because he saw that he could, by this gambit, reach out to a number of other effects that greatly intensify the fundamentally allegorical import of his action (there is, of course, the further effect achieved with reference to that magical life-likeness of art that can potentially suggest a living reality, when Hermione finally comes forth from herself as a statue).

With each new play, a new element or aspect of Shakespeare's experience is revealed. Concentration in *Pericles* lies with the emergence and recognition of a higher power of Ego (Marina) expressing itself freely in the Imagination beyond tragedy. On the plane of innocence, a higher power of Ego is clearly in itself sufficient to lift the Ego out of tragedy. Hence, that peculiar limitation to the quality of the representation in *Pericles*, as if the whole drama were taking place inside the Mind, with no further substantial connection to Nature. The case is different with *The Winter's Tale*. Here the greater problem of the Ego's guilt is addressed, the different concern corresponding to a significant extension of focus beyond the Ego into the realm of Nature. In keeping with the evolution I have been tracing, the saving power in this instance depends crucially on a relation to Nature established in the higher Ego (through Perdita). Concentration here, however, is not on the higher Ego itself so much as on a still greater ordering Power in Nature outside the Ego that the higher Ego yet mediates.

Beyond an experience in the Consciousness Soul, Anthroposophy also speaks of an experience of Imagination, of Inspiration, and of Intuition, with one experience leading into the other. Conforming with that evolution, we notice, with new developments in *The Winter's Tale*, a corresponding *extension of the operation of the Imaginative Soul* to a point inside 'great creating Nature' (IV.iv.88) where a great *Inspirational* order is now revealed. Here we reach the realm of *systematic* Imagination—of regenerative, evolutionary creation —where a higher life is constantly being re-created out of death. It is Perdita who expresses this (it is Florizel who signals her value to us in these terms):

> ... *What you do*
> *Still betters what is done. When you speak, sweet,*
> *I'd have you do it ever; when you sing,*
> *I'd have you buy and sell so; so give alms;*
> *Pray so; and for the ord'ring your affairs,*
> *To sing them too. When you dance, I wish you*
> *A wave o' th' sea, that you might ever do*
> *Nothing but that; move still, still so—*
> *And own no other function. Each your doing*
> *(So singular in each particular)*
> *Crowns what you are doing in the present deeds,*
> *That all your acts are queens.*
> (IV.iv.135-146)

We remark about this representation, especially, its powerful suggestion of a greater order or system, in progressive motion, *behind* the re-creative power attributed to Perdita as higher Ego. And it is only on being taken up into this order, active from a realm deep within Nature, that the suffering Ego (represented by Leontes) can hope to find again the integration that, insofar as it is guilty and hopeless, the Ego cannot itself bring about. On the other hand, the Ego reserves, over time, a direct link and claim to that order's saving power, by virtue of its shame and constant devotion to the memory of the harm that was done, as represented in Leontes:

> *... Whilest I remember*
> *Her and her virtues, I cannot forget*
> *My blemishes in them, and so still think of*
> *The wrong I did myself ...*
> (V.i.6-9)

That a higher power of Ego can still be positively active here might be taken as an indication that the Ego, in spite of its guilt, still retains a measure of innocence at some level. In a sense this must be true since, from the point of view Shakespeare has established on approaching this play, it is really a matter of a complementary division of the Ego's functions, in innocence and in guilt, enacted between *Pericles* and *The Winter's Tale*. And so, in going from one play to the other, we imagine what the Ego has already achieved. In its innocence it links up, beyond tragedy, to a higher power in itself. This achievement is now brought to bear on the Ego's guilty part. The Ego in its higher power has in the meantime tapped into a still greater Power in Nature, which is the principal saving agent here. By the time we reach the end of *The Winter's Tale*, we may confidently assume, then, a pattern of experience that points to a complete re-integration of the Ego beyond tragedy. That re-integration is the consequence of the activity of a higher power of Ego as well as of Nature, corresponding to an extension of the Consciousness Soul in Imagination and in Inspiration.

In *The Tempest* the pattern is brought to fruition in an experience of Intuition. The whole evolution in Imagination and in Inspiration finds a final focus here literally in Prospero's own person who is in some sense, then, Shakespeare himself, since it is his experience that is reflected to us in the progression of these plays. As Steiner reminds us, Intuition means 'dwelling in God'.[77] Hence the focus here on a concentration of power in the individual 'I' insofar as it finally comes to dwell within the 'I' of God. Consider Prospero's words to Miranda:

> *... who*
> *Art ignorant of what thou art, nought knowing*
> *Of whence I am, nor that I am more better*
> *Than Prospero ...*
> (I.ii.17-20)

They mediate the words in which God declares Himself (in *Exodus*):

> *I am that I am ...*

We thus reach the point where the individual 'I', far beyond the higher relation it has found within itself and within Nature, finally consummates its identity in the God Who dwells within it all:

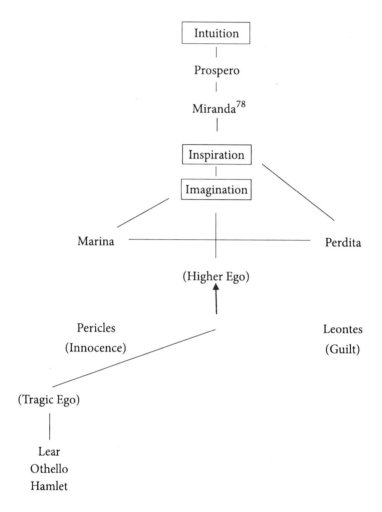

It was John Middleton Murry who saw in *The Tempest* 'the most perfect prophetic achievement of the Western mind'. 'It stands', he said, 'on the very verge of a condition that still lies far before the human soul.'[79] But it was typical of the kind of Romantic criticism Murry himself practised that he could have an apprehension of these matters also without any full theory to account for them, or, in his case, any theory at all. Murry's concern rested strictly with *The Tempest* as achievement rather than with the process that produced it. For him, Shakespeare finally gathered his strength in *The Tempest* 'after playing [only] half-wistfully with the figures of his imagination in *The Winter's Tale* [and *Pericles*].'[80] Murry could also recognize 'that there are greater and smaller fulfillments', Shakespeare being the greater fulfillment to Romanticism's smaller one.[81] But no more than any other critic working in the Romantic tradition could Murry say precisely how or in what way this was true. Murry could not see—what, with the benefit of Anthroposophy, it is possible to see: if it is true, this is because Shakespeare had already taken the evolution of the Imagination further—in Inspiration and in Intuition, as far as this was possible in his own time.

It is both ironic and significant that at the time Murry was formulating these views, Steiner had just about completed his great life's work. In him we find a full experience and understanding of the Imagination, Inspiration, and Intuition of which Shakespeare had had his own kind of prophetic experience. What we have in Shakespeare in outline, as it were, and by suggestion for the most part, is in Steiner for the first time fully presented and accounted for. Precisely how the Imagination unfolds itself, how it leads on into Inspiration and Intuition, and all that this reveals along the way of a great World-order or system in evolution from ages past down to our own day and beyond into the future—we shall find all duly elaborated upon by Steiner in full and concrete detail. And this is what the 'wisdom' of Anthroposophy represents as a specific content finally accessible to the thinking 'I', apart from the 'wisdom' implied in the process of thinking itself—the two are one for Anthroposophy.[82] *Taking the line that Anthroposophy represents, our approach will be conditioned*, at every stage, *by awareness of an astonishingly complex historical evolution.* Thus, among innumerable accounts of that evolution in Anthroposophy, we find the following aimed at substantiating what is happening in the Renaissance (it is one of many accounts of that period). Steiner cites a 'power' at that time that

> *wants to keep [man], with his consciousness, in spiritual realms that were adapted for him in ancient times. It wants to prevent pure thinking, directed towards the understanding of physical existence, from flowing into his dream-like, imaginative conception of the world. It is able to hold back, in the wrong way, man's power of perception from the physical world. It is not, however, able to maintain in the right way the experience of the old Imaginations. And so it makes man reflect imaginatively, and yet at the same time he is not able to transplant his soul completely into the world in which the Imaginations have their full value.*[83]

Not until the ending of *King Lear* is the process of 'pure thinking' of which Steiner speaks here brought to completion in Shakespeare, to such form of completion as was possible for that time. Before that point, Shakespeare's hero continues to be enmeshed in his 'dream-like, imaginative conception of the world'. Though he is without the right experience of 'the old Imaginations' (for the time for these had passed), nevertheless Shakespeare's hero acts as if he might still be able 'to transplant his soul completely into the world in which the Imaginations have their full value'.

Heroic criticism takes its whole tone and import precisely from awareness of the persistence of an idea of this prospect right through the age in which Shakespeare wrote. Only in *Hamlet*, however, does the hero, in the process of his 'dream-like, imaginative experience', succeed in transplanting himself for a time, and only partially, into that [other] world 'in which the Imaginations have their full value'. Hamlet's vision of the Ghost of his father, in which others also share (namely Marcellus, Bernardo, and Horatio), is precisely such a visually crystallized and objective Imagination. But this vision, which Hamlet is having in the Intellectual or Mind Soul, should be seen as itself signifying merely the latest remnant vision, and among the last, from an earlier time when very much more of an otherworldly nature was revealed. Anthroposophy will indeed confirm that there once was an otherworldly experience of the very greatest diversification the further back in time we go, and that not so very long ago (in evolutionary terms)—at the time of the Renaissance, identification with the idea of the possibility of an otherworldly experience was still great. Among other things, it was my own purpose to show that this was so in Part One of this book. But the Consciousness Soul-experience is at that time in process of accomplishing through itself a major re-orientation in relation to that idea, preparing for the accommodation of that new element of intellectuality or pure thinking with which all otherworldly experience would, in future, have to contend.

Hamlet marks that point in Shakespeare's imagination where an otherworldly experience continues to declare itself in the Intellectual or Mind Soul just as the Consciousness Soul is coming to birth, so that it *appears* as if an otherworldly experience can immediately be had again in the Consciousness Soul—though this was not to be for some time yet. By this I mean that Hamlet anticipates a form of otherworldly vision that is not just the given or involuntary experience of the Ghost's earlier and later appearances—the product, that is, of a relatively 'naïve', though supernaturally potent, thought-life in the Intellectual or Mind Soul. There is the suggestion that Hamlet also expects a form of vision that would represent his own individual, fully voluntary possession. This anticipates the production of a far more developed and higher *Imaginative* thought-life, proceeding out of the Consciousness-Soul, of the kind that the later Romantics would themselves come by. *Hamlet* stands half-way between the earlier and the later forms of thought-life, in an unstable relationship to them both. In fact, it is impossible, at a certain point, to dissociate Hamlet's anticipation of one form of vision from an anticipation of the other. The play's ambiguous position in this respect will perhaps justify the approach I make to Hamlet's 'visionary heroism' in Part One of this book, which represents my own contribution to post-Romantic heroic criticism.

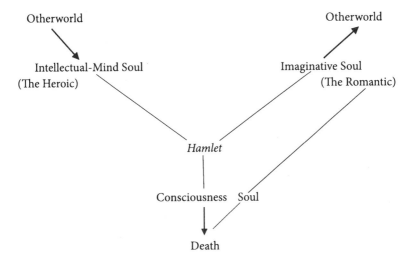

But, in spite of the links between the two in respect of their otherworldly tenor and import, *the 'heroic' and the 'Romantic'* represent substantially different modes, *separated by a major evolution in consciousness.* At least two hundred years of further evolution in the Consciousness Soul stand between Hamlet's own kind of 'Romantic' expectation and that of the later Romantics. Much, much more would have first to be undergone as regards the consciousness of death. A whole process of alienation would have first to be passed through, in order to effect the right kind of separation from an earlier, otherworldly experience. The consequence of alienation would be: metaphysical disengagement both from the traditional areas of faith (including the area of heroic faith) as well as from more recent, romantic-sensual forms of love (the new 'faith-in-love'—see above, pp.126-127). It is precisely this extraordinary 'rite of passage', through what we might call the great 'needle's eye' of the Consciousness Soul-experience, that we find already being enacted through and beyond the ending of *King Lear*. Astonishingly, because the full process would not be historically consummated until much later, with the coming of Anthroposophy. Yet it would appear that Brooke was on the right track where he says that to 'stare at the end of the play and nod assent ... would be to imagine one's own death'—though Brooke confesses that no more 'than anyone else' could he expect to be able to do this himself.[84] But again, it is a question of the way in which imagination is true ('imagining' one's own death), that is to say, the way in which 'thinking' is true, for the experience could hardly be referred to just any kind of cognition or idea of thinking. It is precisely here that Anthroposophy opens up the way, with the kind of elaborate preparation it offers us in the understanding and experience of thinking. It takes us *through* to the point of that decisive experience where 'the pupil ... will need all that presence of mind and faith in the reliability of his path of knowledge which he has had ample opportunity to acquire in the course of his training'.[85]

Coming around to that point, Steiner offers us his own dramatic transposition of the experience, which, by analogy, I am proposing Shakespeare in his own way passed through, with and beyond the ending of *King Lear*. We need to recall that it was for Shakespeare a matter of his assuming, at this point, direct responsibility for the tragedy he had imagined, both from the point of view of innocence and of guilt—a matter, that is to say, of bearing the full burden of tragedy himself. A further meeting with what Anthroposophy calls 'the Guardian of the Threshold' now takes place, Steiner dramatizing as follows the substance and effect that the Guardian would have in his sudden appearance in Imagination:

> *Now all the good and all the bad aspects of your bygone lives are to be revealed to you. Until now they were woven into your own being; they were within you and you could not see them even as with physical eyes you cannot see your brain. But now these aspects release themselves from you; they emerge from your personality. They assume an independent form which you can see, just as you see the stones and plants of the outer world. And I ... am that very Being who has formed a body out of your noble and ignoble doings ...*

My Threshold is built out of every feeling of fear remaining in you, out of every shrinking from the power to assume full responsibility for all your deeds and thoughts. As long as you still have any trace of fear of becoming the director of your own destiny, for just so long does this Threshold lack something that must be built into it. And as long as a single stone is found missing, you must remain at a standstill on this Threshold, as though transfixed; or else you must stumble ...

Visible do I stand before you today, as I have ever stood invisible beside you in the hour of death. When you have crossed my Threshold you will enter those kingdoms to which otherwise you had access only after physical death. You now enter them with full knowledge, and henceforth as you move, outwardly visible, about the Earth, you will at the same time move in the kingdom of death ... Through me you will die while still living in the body, in order to be reborn into indestructible existence.[86]

At a certain point in the experience of negation, the possibility is given of 'passing' onwards into a new Imaginative life. An otherworldly experience once again takes shape from that same point strictly and entirely as an accomplishment of the Ego-consciousness in thinking. The Ego now builds its own 'threshold' for reaching into that world. It is the purpose and the task of Anthroposophy precisely to provide for the requisite maturing and strengthening of the Ego-consciousness in thinking to ensure that 'passage' into that otherworld is fully and properly accomplished.

In Shakespeare that 'passage' is reflected to us in the first instance as the Imagination of an indestructible existence for the Ego. That existence represents the Ego's new life—which we have in the form of the figures of Marina, Perdita, and Miranda. For it is the peculiarity of this new world of Imagination that all that is of an inner nature immediately arises in independent, outer form. Hence, the 'allegorical' mode of representation in which the higher experience is given in Shakespeare's romances. But the experience is far from being as straightforward as it appears. From what Anthroposophy has to say, it assumes the pupil's continual struggle with the Guardian (otherwise known as his *doppelganger* or double) even after this Being gives way to Another Who reveals Himself as the informing and all-controlling Power within these worlds. From here, it is a matter of the student's making himself progressively more familiar with the further experiences in Imagination, Inspiration, and Intuition to be known through the help and mediation of the Christ as the great primordial Initiator in the 'passage' from death to new life.

That initiation is made possible today by a certain way of living into one's thinking—amounting to a vocation—that a devoted study of Anthroposophy provides. We have seen how Shakespeare was led in his own thinking, insofar as the last plays reflect that further evolution to us. What we make of the terms and conditions of these plays will be determined in the end precisely by the extent to which we succeed in *identifying* the kind of initiation-process Shakespeare was passing through at that time. However, it is not my purpose here nor could it be—within the limited scope of this account—to expound any further on the process of initiation. That is a task we would have to undertake along with Steiner, through the leap into Anthroposophy itself. A full exposition in these terms must await another and fuller approach to the subject, and another day (hopefully in the not too distant future).

It has been my aim here merely to point a path. My intention was to indicate the continuity and the unity for which we should be looking not only in the development of Shakespeare's own work but in that whole history of the evolution of consciousness in which Shakespeare and the Romantic Movement have played a major role. What I have been seeking in these pages with reference to Anthroposophy, finally, is the vindication of Romantic tradition. Without suggesting that we can or should be satisfied with its achievements or with its modes of comprehension until now, it has seemed to me better to understand how that tradition has evolved and where it was leading, than to seek simply to excise it from our cultural consciousness altogether, as some of our contemporary ideologues suppose they have done already. The point is not that we have seen the end of Romantic tradition, but that it is only just beginning—though the extreme exclusivity and intolerance of an academic culture that today pretends to egalitarianism in theory may well see to it that a continuation is never made.

Uniformity, rather than a diversification of choices—or a dialogue of options—is what today dictates the content of the approach being made to literature at our universities, so that it is unlikely that we shall see for some time yet an approach to literature that would make room for a program of studies on 'Shakespeare and Anthroposophy'. But while we wait, nothing will happen, for it is unlikely that the really new Shakespeare criticism we so desperately need to effect the necessary changes in this direction will come out of the ranks of Anthroposophists themselves, for the Anthroposophical Movement has no special need of it. The project I propose could only be realized, in fact, if our university doors could open *to* Anthroposophy from without, though the challenge in doing so is also great. For we could only undertake this project with the right intention if, as I have said, we approach the concepts that Anthroposophy yields, prepared at some point to make the further leap into Anthroposophy itself. Anything less than this would mean to allow the tragedy that I spoke of earlier to continue to make headway with us.

PART THREE

Prospero's Powers:
Shakespeare's Last Phase

1

The Relation to *Pericles* and *The Winter's Tale*

Prospero's 'secret studies' are not just another, independent part of the story that ranges from his wife's death through his later abduction. These 'studies' constitute, in fact, an altogether intrinsic part of the same story. Beginning with Miranda who, when the abduction takes place, is 'not / Out three years old' (I.ii.40-41)[1], we are reminded of the mother who in this period has died. We then hear of Prospero's reputation in the liberal arts, which now become '*all* [his] study' (74), to the point of a temporary renunciation of state. From here Prospero grows all the 'stranger' (76) to his state, as he finds himself further 'transported / And rapt in secret studies' (76-77). It is all too easy to overlook, in this fast-concatenating story, the role that Prospero's intensifying 'studies' have played *as a direct response to the mother's death*. It is the very effort from which Prospero is separated when Antonio casts him out to 'sea' where Prospero must again live out the great sorrow of loss and dispossession that, over a great many years, had continued to engage Shakespeare himself, up to this point:

> *There they hoist us*
> **To cry to th' sea that roared to us,** *to sigh*
> *To th' winds, whose pity, sighing back again,*
> *Did us but loving wrong.*
> MIRANDA.   *Alack, what trouble*
> *Was I then to you?*
> PROSPERO.   *O, a cherubin*
> *Thou wast that did preserve me. Thou didst smile,*
> *Infused with a fortitude from heaven,*
> **When I have decked the sea with drops full salt,**
> **Under my burden groaned**
> (I.ii.148-156)

Prospero's experience, in this climactic 'sea'-passage, has the effect of some great tunnicular vision. For one last time, we look back down the dark tunnel of Shakespeare's harrowing emergence through the tragedies, as Prospero is forced to live out again the great 'sea-sorrow' (170) of *that* momentous progression. Here Prospero gives no overt sign of effective power over that 'sorrow', although Shakespeare himself had passed through a great transformation over that entire time. At a certain point, all had come to a head for him in a great symbolic end-point in which the very worst of tragedy finds representation as the death of the mother of all faith, love, and life.[2] This is what Shakespeare's repeated representations of the death of a loved one had come to mean for him. It is how we are asked to see the deaths of Thaisa and Hermione that follow (respectively in *Pericles* and *The Winter's Tale*): as a great ongoing symbolic event of that extraordinary magnitude working itself out further in Shakespeare's own mind. On one level, the death of Prospero's wife clearly repeats and adds to this event. It distinguishes itself from these representations in being also a literal action now projected outside Shakespeare's own mental preoccupations—which is to say fully dramatized anew. Like Shakespeare's great tragic heroes before him (Hamlet, Othello, Lear), Prospero undergoes the death of a loved one literally, although unlike them he is not guilty of this death. Nor, unimaginably great as this death is, is he unprepared for it. Standing there as the dramatized reflection of Shakespeare, Prospero has the advantage of having, in the meantime, passed through all that Shakespeare himself passed through in living out the consequences of the many earlier deaths as the expression of the great symbolic event of the death of the mother.

For one thing, by now, that death has come to be linked further with the symbolic birth of the daughter—in this case, Miranda, who has her own extraordinary lineage in the anterior figures of Marina and Perdita, both likewise born of the death of the mother (respectively in *Pericles* and *The Winter's Tale*). Miranda, in the 'sea'-passage I quoted above is, indeed, the very power that bears Prospero up from within the dire maelstrom of the symbolic event:

> *... a cherubin*
> **Thou wast that did preserve me. Thou didst smile,**
> **Infused with a fortitude from heaven,**
> When I have decked the sea with drops full salt,
> Under my burden groaned, **which raised in me**
> **An undergoing stomach to bear up,**
> **Against what should ensue.**
> (I.ii.152-158)

Out of the tragic Ego's experience as borne by Shakespeare himself across his last plays, there emerges over time, precisely through the death of the mother, a saving power of higher Ego of new, indefatigable quality, represented in the birth of the daughter. This new power Shakespeare extracts from his own psychological experience, allegorically dramatized between *Pericles* and *The Winter's Tale*. From there, he will go on to bestow his own experience dramatically upon Prospero. This is to suggest that Prospero contains in himself the entire drama that precedes him: not only those newly allegorized abstractions of the tragic Ego as given to us in Pericles and Leontes—respectively the tragic Ego in its aspects of innocence and guilt—but also the power of the suffering mother in her own correspondingly different aspects as Thaisa and Hermione; likewise, the new power of higher Ego that emerges *from* the death of the mother, which undergoes its own further evolution as saving power.

Prospero and Miranda together take the whole previous experience still further. Miranda, as higher power, represents yet another, still more evolved aspect of Prospero's now all-encompassing Ego. She is herself a literal embodiment of this higher power, who 'profits' in turn from an education at Prospero's hands, is 'given' to Ferdinand—the panorama is endless. From these structural developments, it follows also that Prospero's wife—as the mother—is likewise both a power that he incorporates and herself (more remarkably still) a literal embodiment of this power. *Her death is the actual sacrifice without which the rest of power would not follow.* Clearly Prospero is not alone in facing this death. However, it is precisely what gives Prospero's fate its sublime pathos that he must (in extended form) undergo this representative death again. On the other hand, he is borne up by powers of which we can barely have an idea unless we make ourselves fully acquainted first with the more recent lives/dramas that Prospero interiorizes. These are given to us in the action of both *Pericles* and *The Winter's Tale*. This is another way of saying that we first approach Prospero, in fact, coming away from those earlier plays, in relation to which Prospero assumes the function of Presenter as his very first role.[3] Prospero's 'studies', as we shall see, coincide directly with the development of those powers that lie dormant in him from his association with his previous 'lives' in *Pericles* and *The Winter's Tale*. Prospero does not come into full possession of these powers, however, until the full significance of his wife's 'death' comes 'home' to him—that is, not until he is cast out to 'sea', where his whole 'sorrow' awakens and is consciously given full scope, and he *now* experiences his wife's death *as* the 'death of the mother'. Then it is that there revives within him all that has lain dormant from his *past* 'experiences' of this 'death' in his earlier 'lives' (in *Pericles* and *The Winter's Tale*). In relation to this decisive 'experience' Prospero's 'studies' have been a *preparation*, and they now bear fruit as a direct experience of those higher powers reserved for Prospero from his 'past'/the very powers he has unconsciously been cultivating in himself in the course of his 'studies' (the two developments are one).

2
Study of the Liberal Arts

To get to the bottom of these developments, we shall have to assume quite another attitude than the purely external one taken by the most recent Oxford editor of the play, for whom there is nothing 'inherently mysterious about the[se] studies themselves (they were, after all, the 'liberal arts').'[4] On the contrary, these studies were hedged round with very great 'mysteries', as we learn from more authoritative sources. Rene Querido[5] has shown that in the School of Chartres, study of the liberal arts served as the basis for the accomplishment of a very grand goal:

> On the cathedral [at Chartres] they placed the seven liberal arts around the Virgin Mother and Christ Child to indicate the goal of their striving: **the virgin-like soul and the birth of the higher self** ...

Querido explains further that:

> This inner birth occurs through man's own efforts ...[by] working on his soul with the seven liberal arts.[6]

A fuller account follows:

> For the masters and their pupils, the seven liberal arts were more than disciplines; they were beings. The study of an art was an approach to a being. The mastery of an art was a connection with a being who, belonging to the spiritual hierarchies, would then inspire one as the priestess or guardian of that particular art. Each of the seven guardians had her 'place' in the spiritual world, which was one of the planetary spheres ...[7]

The main steps of the process are in this way opened out to us:

> [1] Man's soul, they taught, was influenced by the activities of the seven planets ...
>
> [2] Thus, following the path of the liberal arts was bringing one's soul into the right relationship with the planetary system...

> *[3] ... [eventually] reformation, or purification, would result in*
> *the virginity of the soul, which could then bear the child of the*
> *true self, or divine ego ...*[8]

As I have argued, it is Prospero who, as the hero who represents Shakespeare, incorporates this entire development in the higher Ego. Prospero incorporates all the powers separately represented by Marina, Perdita and Miranda, after himself experiencing purification through death, or the worst of tragedy (in Shakespeare's sense), and along a route on which *he* was at one time a master of the liberal arts ('in the liberal arts without a parallel'). What Shakespeare, through Prospero, consciously *recovers* in his own time are powers that were largely *given* within the possibility that the Masters of Chartres conceived of. In connection with the latter, Rudolf Steiner speaks of 'a true inspiration of ideas', though the 'old teachings ... were well-nigh shadowed-down to concepts and ideas'[9]. However, Steiner also gives us a full account of what 'until the 7th or 8th century'—'in the last relics of the ancient Mysteries'—it was still possible for some to attain *as direct experience*:

> *... above all there appeared to them as a living Being ... the*
> *Goddess Natura ... the ever-creating Goddess with whom he*
> *who would seek for knowledge must in a certain way unite*
> *himself ... And when the seeker after knowledge had been*
> *sufficiently instructed by the Goddess ... the teachers saw to it*
> *that their disciples should gain a feeling, an idea of this living*
> *intercourse with Nature ... Then ... they were introduced to the*
> *planetary system. They learnt how with the knowledge of the*
> *planetary system there arises at the same time the knowledge of*
> *the human soul. 'Learn to know how the wandering stars hold*
> *sway in the heavens, and thou shalt know how thine own soul*
> *works and weaves and lives within thee.' This was placed before*
> *the pupils. And at length they were led to approach what was*
> *called 'The Great Ocean'—but it was the Cosmic Ocean, which*
> *leads from the planets, from the wandering stars, to the fixed*
> *stars. Thus at length they penetrated **into the secrets of the I**,*
> *by learning the secrets of the universe of the fixed stars.*[10]

Steiner speaks also of the extraordinary experience to be reserved for Brunetto Latini in the age that immediately follows that of Chartres, Latini's experience being among the very last of this kind:

> *Then he saw what man could see **under the influence of the***
> ***living principle of knowledge**: He saw a mountain mightily*

*arising with all that lived and sprang forth from it, minerals,
plants, and animals, and there appeared to him the Goddess
Natura, there appeared the Elements, there appeared the
Planets, there appeared the Goddesses of the Seven Liberal
Arts, and at length Ovid as his guide and teacher. Here once
again there stood before a human soul the mighty vision that
had stood before the souls of men so often in the first centuries
of Christianity.*[11]

Shakespeare's own extraordinary transformation, as reflected
in his last plays, would appear to represent another crystallization of
this fundamental experience, in a later and rather different age. In *The
Winter's Tale*, it is Perdita who reflects (in the power of Inspiration) this
newly found, higher relationship to Nature as well as to the still greater
planetary world that Nature mediates. In *The Tempest*, it is Miranda who
reflects (in the power of Intuition) that supreme relationship to the secrets
of the fixed stars (the secrets of the I).[12] Both relationships are present, as
we have seen, in Prospero himself. Behind the entire development is the
birth of the higher Ego first represented (as Imagination) by Marina in
Pericles and continuously *extended* in the figures of Perdita and Miranda.
This birth of the higher Ego—as we learn from Steiner[13]—takes place
out of that sphere where the planetary world opens out on the world
of the fixed stars—the sphere of the 'Great Ocean' in Steiner's present
account[14], the higher Ego coming to fuller and fuller expression first
through a development of the relationship to Nature, to the planetary
world and so on.

Rudolf Steiner also testifies that, among those who carried the
knowledge forward from the Masters of Chartres, the Rosicrucians too
could claim:

*We have been among the stars and among the Spirits of the
stars, and have found the old teachers of the occult knowledge.*[15]

But the route of the Rosicrucians to 'Star Knowledge' would come,
rather, by the *suppression* of the Intelligence, which had by then already
become too gross for Revelation of this kind, not having as yet undergone
purification. The Rosicrucians would have to heed the momentous
words of their Master, who was Christian Rosenkreutz himself—as
Steiner dramatizes these:

*'I am come to reveal to you that the inner being of man
remains unchanged, that the inner being of man, if it bears*

itself aright, can yet find the way to divine-spiritual existence. For a certain period of time, however, the human intellect and understanding will be so constituted that they will have to be suppressed in order for that which is of the Spirit to be able to speak to the human soul.[16]

Indeed the full recovery of such Revelation, through the faculty of the human Intelligence, would have to wait for Steiner himself. For the moment, the Rosicrucians would have to *give up* their 'Star Knowledge', in the form of a rite. So, the Rosicrucians could tell themselves:

in order that man ... may be able to find for himself of his own free will what in earlier times the Gods have tried to find for and with him, let now the higher knowledge be offered up for a season ...[17]

What Shakespeare comes by later, in his own degree, represents in fact something of a return *already* of such 'Star Knowledge', sometime after the act of Sacrifice is accomplished by the Rosicrucians:

Whatever in the years that followed showed itself to be of a truly spiritual nature was a kind of echo sounding on of this creative working from out of unknown spiritual worlds. Side by side with the external materialism that developed in the succeeding centuries, we can always find here and there individuals who are living under the influence of that renunciation of higher knowledge ... / [K]nowledge was communicated ... we cannot quite say, without words, but without ideas, although not on that account without content.[18]

3
The Freeing of Ariel

The great repository of such higher knowledge *today* are the works of Rudolf Steiner, who has put the task of understanding for our time in the following terms: 'in what natural science gives us we must find something which stimulates us inwardly *toward* Imagination, Inspiration, and Intuition. In this way we acquire', Steiner informs us, 'the help of Christ within'[19], and through this help we find once again that '*inner astronomy* that will show us the universe proceeding from and working out of the spirit ... the rediscovered power of Isis, which is now the power of the divine Sophia ...'[20]. What this 'something' is I shall expound upon in the next section[21]; here I only want to point out that Steiner bases his own great power of development in supersensible vision on the very achievement that Valentin Andreae depicted in *The Chymical Wedding of Christian Rosenkreutz*, the famous text that first appeared in Shakespeare's own time.[22] Commenting on this text, Steiner points out that:

> For his contemporaries Andreae wishes to portray the foremost spiritual investigator of a declining epoch, one who perceives in the spiritual world the death of that epoch and the birth of a new one ... Andreae wished to say to [his contemporaries]: Your path is fruitless; the greatest who has most recently followed it, has seen how useless it is: realize what he has perceived and you will develop a feeling for a new path ... **The present-day scientist of the spirit**, if he understands the signs of the times, **still** finds himself continuing the effort that originated with Johann Valentin Andreae.[23]

One way of having 'Star Knowledge' (i.e., one form of the higher wisdom) had necessarily to give way to another, and Rudolf Steiner has accounted for that difference: in lieu of a 'spiritual *instinctive* understanding rooted in man's heart and mind'—in what Steiner generally refers to as the 'Intellectual or Mind Soul', there now arose spiritual knowledge based on 'understanding which, *liberated* from the instinctive forces, worked in the light of full consciousness of self'—in the 'Consciousness Soul'.[24] Christian Rosenkreutz was to be the one who would bear the *new* form of knowledge into the modern age. Steiner, in another context, refers to this great event as 'the passage of the Sophia through man'.[25] *Shakespeare himself reflects that event* to us in his great theme of the death of the mother of all faith, love and life in those now *outdated* forms that had come down to him in his day.[26]

Prospero's tremendous experience of this 'death', as the prototypic experience of Shakespeare's last phase, further awakens *in him*, as I have argued, altogether new powers of Imagination, Inspiration, as well as Intuition in nascent form, as reflected in the three-year-old Miranda. On the *other* side of this 'death'—when Prospero reaches the island—lies *the freeing of Ariel*, in which these now newly activated powers find their first expression. The 'island' is, of course, a literal feature of Prospero's story but is itself allegorically significant, standing as it were for some final 'resting-place' of power in the Ego to which Prospero has come along with Miranda, the only two who can *properly* inhabit this ultimate 'region'.[27] One must not overlook in this allegorical context, as well, the use that is made of the 'boat' to get to the 'island', or, indeed, the 'books' with which, we are told, Prospero was at this time supplied, though it would be naïve of us to suppose (along with Caliban) that Prospero's powers continue to depend directly on his books, for they are powers that derive by this point from within his very Ego (symbolically reflected to us in the 'staff' that he later bears).

Ariel, we learn, was confined to a tree for over twelve years by the witch Sycorax 'in her most unmitigable rage' (I.ii.276), Sycorax being unable to undo her act. In the tremendous dramatization of this 'rage'[28] we have the *supersensible* extension of all that Shakespeare had had to contend with *from the time he started out* on his momentous progress in tragedy, going back at least as far as *Hamlet*.[29] Along this way comes *also* the more rapid *emergence* from tragedy that begins with *Pericles* and continues for another three years, to the time when Prospero is made to re-live that whole progress through tragedy, when he is violently thrown out to 'sea'. Miranda literally marks that emergence, being about three at the time.

'Crying to the sea', which sympathetically 'roars' back to him, Prospero at this point unconsciously unites *with Ariel's own 'groaning' of twelve years* while the latter is confined to the tree. Prospero and Ariel are in this way *identified* in their role as 'sacrificial' victims, and, uniting himself with Ariel's suffering, Prospero now finds the further power *to free* this great Spirit. He does so by a power of 'compassion' that he has learned from his own comparable suffering—at the other extreme from the 'rage' that has caused it. What Prospero then frees, with the compassionate freeing of Ariel, *is his own power of supersensible vision*. Ranging suddenly through powers of Imagination, Inspiration, and Intuition, he comes into a power of magical action that derives *from* his progression through supersensible worlds. Presumably, then, such power of action (simultaneously a power of compassion) becomes available in what one might call an *early* Intuitive phase, when the secrets of the fixed stars—the secrets of the I—are first plumbed. This condition is symbolically reflected to us in the three year old Miranda. From here Prospero will develop his capacity for Intuition still further, to the point that characterizes his powers when we first encounter him in the play, by which time Miranda, now fifteen, has 'come of age'.[30]

4
'Rapt in Secret Studies'

In Rudolf Steiner's account, the momentous change that takes place in the Renaissance is from an experience in the 'Intellectual or Mind Soul' *as well as* remnants of the 'Sentient-Soul' experience ('spiritual instinctive understanding' formerly rooted in the senses)—respectively, an older 'faith', and 'love in sensual terms', as described above (see p.126)—to experience in the 'Consciousness Soul'. This great change, reflected in Shakespeare himself over the course of his tragic progress, would be the occasion for a new experience of an old wisdom, which has since become a possible experience for us. Steiner elsewhere gives a further account of what Christian Rosenkreutz was the first to achieve fully:

> *Man has learnt to relate to the Sophia through his consciousness soul, to associate her directly with human beings. This happened during the consciousness soul age. The Sophia has therefore become the Being that elucidates man. Once having entered into humanity, she has to take up this human nature and set it objectively before mankind. She detaches herself again but takes with her what man is and places herself outside him, no longer merely as Sophia but as Anthroposophia as that Sophia who has passed through the soul of man, through man's being, and henceforth bears this being of man within herself.*[31]

Steiner also speaks of a *counter*-tendency at that time, massive evidence of which we find, as we have seen, in Shakespeare's own tragic heroes (see above pp.126-127 and 145-146). Steiner cites a 'power' at that time that

> *wants to keep [man], with his consciousness, in spiritual realms that were adapted for him in ancient times. It wants to prevent pure thinking, directed towards the understanding of physical existence, from flowing into his dream-like, imaginative conception of the world. It is able to hold back, in the wrong way, man's power of perception from the physical world. It is not, however, able to maintain in the right way the experience of the old Imaginations. And so it makes man reflect imaginatively, and yet, at the same time he is not able to transplant his soul completely into the world in which the Imaginations have their true value.*

This transition from one epoch of knowledge to the other is directly reflected in the new effort of will that Christian Rosenkreutz accomplishes, as portrayed in *The Chymical Wedding*, setting him apart from the other rival aspirants to higher knowledge. When, on the second day, those who are given to the older form of seeking enter the Castle, *he* remains behind in the hall, subsequently allowing himself to be fettered. There follows, on the third day, the 'weighing of the souls', as Steiner describes it, 'to ascertain whether to their own weight *as man* [purified, that is, of their old sensual tendencies] they [the aspirants] have added what corresponds to the seven other weights.'[32] The 'weight of the (seven liberal) arts' has had to become [in this sense] 'weight of soul' in accordance with the 'true world content' of the new age[33], and on this basis, the illegitimate intruders are now expelled, while Rosenkreutz himself is allowed to proceed. This momentous development from the *Wedding* corresponds in Shakespeare's presentation to that fateful moment when Prospero evolves from his position in the liberal arts 'without a parallel' (I.ii.74) to that further climactic point where he becomes finally '*transported* / And *rapt* in secret studies' (76-77). From here he is given up more fully to *the great epochal 'death' of that time* and the expansion that follows from this into a fresh experience of the old powers. The process of expansion is clinched for Prospero when he is finally cast out to 'sea': '*transported*… in secret studies' already *implies* this further development. There, as we have seen, Prospero experiences those successive transformations of his consciousness, for which he has prepared.[34]

It is at this very point that the candidate for higher knowledge stands poised for that *further* progress in the faculties of Imagination, Inspiration, and Intuition that Steiner's own productive life fully illustrates in *our* time. Steiner would himself be able to speak from direct experience not only of the further faculties of Imagination, Inspiration, and Intuition, but also of more far-reaching experiences still—the whole proceeding from a *first* stage of 'study' corresponding to a full grasp and exercise of what it is now in our power to do as inheritors of these new developments. Such 'study' would involve *for us*, initially, a consideration of Steiner's extensive 'science of the spirit', and so the seven steps of *modern* Rosicrucian spiritual initiation, as Steiner elaborated on these[35]:

1. Studium—the study of the science of spirit

2. Imagination

3. Inspiration

4. Intuition

5. Correspondence between Microcosm and Macrocosm

6. Living into the Macrocosm

7. Divine Bliss

Shakespeare's Prospero, as we shall see, goes a similar route, from his own starting-point in a study of the liberal arts, which he then takes further. His participation in the more far-reaching stages beyond Intuition we glean by reflection, in his further 'initiation' of Ferdinand culminating in his 'marriage' to Miranda. Shakespeare, writing out of his own time, was, however, building on the course of *alchemical* initiation as re-established by Christian Rosenkreutz through his Chemical Wedding. The further progression of events, from the time *The Tempest* opens, repeats the structure of that *earlier* form of initiation quite literally (I follow the account of that initiation as given by Paul Allen Marshall whose further elucidations I quote below[36]; the applications to *The Tempest* are my own).

1. The prima materia massa confusa

This characterizes the state of things at the beginning of the process of Transmutation.

... Prospero's subjection to tragedy and to treachery up to the tempest he raises (the death of his wife, his abduction and further exiling, his dispossession from state) ...

2. The sevaratio, divisio

This separation or clarification of the Elements concerns the factors at work in the process.

... Initially, Miranda's 'saving' action at sea: Prospero's story (of initiation) as narrated by him: his 'studies' and successive transformations of consciousness through Imagination, Inspiration and Intuition: the separate presentation of Ariel, Caliban, Ferdinand ...

3. The conjunctio

A uniting of 'male and female', that is, the active and passive natures of the Elements involved.

... Ariel's music: Ferdinand's first sight of Miranda (Imagination) and his inspired words about her (Inspiration), including his effusions about her in III.i ...

4. The mortificatio calcinatio

This is the 'mystical death' of the substance, the central point in the series.

... Ferdinand's 'trial': his separation from Miranda; the parallel judgment of Prospero's enemies; Ferdinand's purifying 'death' (Intuition), corresponding to Prospero's own development (in Imagination, Inspiration and Intuition) up to that point ...[37]

5. The ablutio, baptisma

This 'washing' or 'whitening' leads to the re-uniting of the soul of the element to its dead body.

... Ferdinand's release: Miranda *given* to Ferdinand by Prospero, *reflecting Prospero's further progression in initiation* beyond Intuition ...

6. The albedo, tinctura alba, resurrectum

This bursting out of the 'reborn' or 'purified' element into many colors is imaged in the peacock's tail.

... The masque played out before Ferdinand and Miranda, cosmically blessing their marriage to come ...

7. The rubedo

This denotes the appearance of the King (Red) and the Queen (White), who celebrate their 'Chemical Wedding', thus completing the process.

... The projected wedding of Ferdinand and Miranda (as purified Ego and Higher Ego, respectively) ...

In the end, Andreae's *Chymical Wedding* is more obviously devoted to the inner processes of initiation than is *The Tempest* which from its opening assumes these processes as a given and builds on them in covert structural form (only those who have kept their eye on the inner development (across several plays) will be able to follow Shakespeare up to this point). Perhaps Shakespeare did not feel he could say how these processes operated exactly; perhaps he did but assumed that a more open account of them to a dramatic audience would fail to go over as intended. Whatever the case, a significant link can be traced between the two works that establishes *The Tempest* as profoundly rooted in the same tradition of inner progress through spiritual worlds.

Thus in Andreae's *Wedding* we find the same link-up to the sphere of the 'Great Ocean' of which Steiner speaks in connection with the vision of the Masters of Chartres and their heirs. (It seems one can assume from Andreae's work a continuous tradition dating back to the time of that earlier cultural era.) Thus on the fifth day of Rosenkreutz' initiation, we hear of a journey that he takes by ship (along with the few other aspirants who are successful) across a 'Sea' to an 'Island' on which the seven-tiered 'Tower of Olympus' is erected[38] where the great 'chymical' process is to be accomplished. This point in the structure of the action of *The Chymical Wedding*—as in *The Tempest*—corresponds to progress into the sphere of Intuition. It is part of a whole *sequence* of successive transformations that begins in the *Wedding* when the seven 'weights', which stand for the seven liberal arts, are borne on the third day by the seven virgins who appear in the Wedding's opening ceremony led by the Queen Virgin who stands for Theology; her own 'greatest' weight is borne symbolically by the Virgin Alchemy with whom she seems to be united and who has accompanied the candidates for initiation from the outset.[39]

This *first* great transformational stage has its direct counterpart in the structure of the progress among the Masters and their heirs where, building on the study of the liberal arts, one brought one's soul into the right relationship with the planetary system, passing on into the sphere of Inspiration. In the *Wedding*, this stage in the progress is transcended through a further 'hanging up', or sacrifice, of the weights to the 'Honour of God'. Beyond this action comes the further procession to the 'House of the Sun' whence the journey proceeds across the 'Sea' to the 'Tower' on the 'Island'—into the sphere of Intuition. At this point Christian Rosenkreutz, along with the others, attends, through an intensive process of concentrated alchemy, on the re-birth of young King and young Queen.

The alchemical basis of Rosenkreutz' initiation, by which it is distinguished from the progress, into spiritual worlds, of the Chartres Masters, is especially pronounced in this section. The different basis is finally expressive of the possibility of a new concentrated self-consciousness in the midst of the vast expansion in vision and in power to be found in both cases.[40] Surrounding the amazing re-birth of young King and Queen in the *Wedding* is the dramatic resurrection of a 'Bird' from the 'dissolved' substance of the dead bodies of the 'Kings' whose solemn 'be-heading' initially launches the new process. The correspondence in this case is with the series that extends from the 'mortificatio calcinatio' through to the 'resurrectum'. (In the *Wedding*, the Bird is itself be-headed and its blood used to feed the 'Images' that are created out of the Bird's ashes and that are finally given life as the re-born young King and Queen.) Among other congruent points of structure, one should note also the appearance, towards the end of the *Wedding*, of the young King and Queen at a game of Chess (*vide* Ferdinand and Miranda), 'only it had other laws; for it was the Vertues and Vices one against another, where it might be ingeniously observed with what Plots the Vices lay in wait for the Virtues, and how to re-encounter them again.'

There seems no doubt that with *The Tempest* Shakespeare was referring his own tremendous progress in spiritual vision, which he had conducted over the course of many years, to a long tradition of progress through spiritual worlds running from the medieval Masters of Chartres (in the twelfth century) right through to Andreae's *Chymical Wedding* (in the early seventeenth). We note, what's more, the uncanny structural congruencies in Shakespeare's later work with what Frances Yates has called the 'Rosicrucian Enlightenment' covering those extraordinary European developments, beginning in Shakespeare's own time, that seemed to offer hope in a new social order *based on* Rosicrucian principles of spirit-knowledge.[41] Shakespeare's primary focus on Ferdinand and Miranda in *The Tempest* could certainly be, and was, made to serve the hopes that were being placed in contemporary terms in the new order promised specifically around the projected Wedding of Princess Elizabeth to the Elector Palatine. Those great social hopes came to nought, were violently squelched, but Rudolf Steiner draws the following moral from the eventual outcome:

> But progress in human evolution is possible only when personalities of an attitude similar to that of Johann Valentin Andreae oppose the retarding forces of certain world-currents by others of a truly constructive nature.[42]

It is, of course, easy in hindsight to second-guess the outcome of history, and any superiority about this, in any sense, would be contemptible, but it may be that we should indeed be searching out some other, long-term moral to Shakespeare's association with the Rosicrucian incision into history at this time (as in Steiner's focus on a greater 'progress in human evolution' extending beyond the particulars of that time). Shakespeare's relation to the Rosicrucian Enlightenment, as we understand this in strict historical terms, I take to be peripheral. His very long course of development, running through his extended series of many tragedies into the later romances, was, I believe, in the end his own; it testifies *independently* to the new possibility that Rosenkreutz' initiation brings in, with the passage from the older Intellectual-Soul age, in which Shakespeare begins (there are strong remnants in his time also from the Sentient-Soul age) into the new, modern Consciousness-Soul age into which we ourselves are born.[43] Behind this greater historical development, as I have indicated, lies the transmutation (taking the form of a sacrificial death *into* human consciousness) of the traditional Sophia into the Anthropos-Sophia of our time. The moral to be drawn from Shakespeare's production finally is this: he was among the first to break into supersensible realms on the basis of a new development of self-conscious knowledge of the kind that belongs to our own epoch to this day.

5
The Alchemical Extension and the New Life

Also in the *alchemical* experience we detect that same background of expansive progression into spiritual worlds that I have emphasized is the one that principally concerns us in understanding Shakespeare's evolution through his last plays. For the alchemist, concentration on the material transformations that were brought about before his eyes was an occasion for the far more significant, corresponding transformations that were taking place in his soul, and it is in this context that we recognize that same progression into the sphere of the Great Ocean, associated with an extraordinary development of the faculty of Intuition, *behind* the stage of the process that has been described as the *mortificatio calcinatio*:

> All is changed by a total destruction of life which will yet flower again ... The glowing ash is ... **placed on a ship to sail the dark seas** to an unknown destination ... **In this long voyage in the vessel over the dark waters** (the purified 'materia prima' is passing through sessions of slow heating in a vessel ...), the planets surround the sufferer, and each one, being also a metal, beams influences which balance up to a new life, compounded of all life ...[44]

Shakespeare would have recognized in the alchemical progress not only another confirmation of the extraordinary experience through which he had ranged, but also a model as to where that experience might take one *further*. He could look back upon his immersion in tragedy as another form of engagement with the *prima materia massa confusa* taken right up, through the many extraordinary transformations that follow, into the *sevaratio* of Miranda's astounding emergence from that process. Ferdinand's appearance onto the scene is itself part of a series—Miranda, Ariel, Caliban, Ferdinand—representing a continuation of the *sevaratio*. In this *sevaratio* 'the elements that had separated were also opposites'[45], and so alongside Prospero and Miranda on the one hand, we find Sycorax and Caliban on the other. Ted Hughes has described the significance of Caliban well where he speaks of a residual deposit of the whole tragic process, now separated out from the higher development on the other side: 'in stunned, half-animal form ... [and, for the first time, as tragic evil] baffled ...'[46] For his part, Ferdinand has already been through a process of higher development, evolving from the anterior figures of Lysimachus and Florizel in whom he originates, having in some sense then already attended on the previous events of purification and redemption of the Ego in *Pericles* and *The Winter's Tale*. The further inter-association among Miranda, Caliban and Ferdinand at this point reflects a stage of the alchemical experience in which all the substances are still combining, even as they are in the process of separating out through the additional influence of the *conjunctio* that now firmly binds Ferdinand to Miranda.

In the alchemical development the transformation among the substances is a graphically pictorial one, involving red and white as well as pigments of green-blue and brown descending into black. They stand respectively for the individual Ego (red) about to be reformed in the Higher Ego (white) on emerging from the tragic process (black). Miranda as Higher Ego might be imagined in white. Ferdinand, as the individual Ego about to be reformed, from his first appearance would be in red. Caliban and the company he attracts—Stephano, Trinculo—embody on the other side the baser residuum of the tragic process, and so might appear in any number of combinations of dark-green/brown, or black. The whole of *The Tempest* might be seen as a drama involving these pictorial forces, beginning with the opening scene during which all the characters might be imagined in black or in associated colours of dark brown and green. The court party emerges on shore later, however, conceivably in various forms of a new combination of black, white, and red, open as they are by then to the influences of reforming action on the island. There is also a general darkening at a certain point, as all the substances and forces at work seem to vanish into a concentration of black mass, the process of the *nigredo*, or blackening[47], leading to the central point of the *mortificatio calcinatio*. The corresponding moment in Shakespeare's play coincides with the deepest point of Ferdinand's trial, which interestingly is not directly represented in the play. Combining the play's contrasting, developing scenes into one continuous experience, we thus arrive at a full picture of the alchemical processing of substances as the adept might be imagined working on them as part of the long process of his own development in spiritual powers.

When Ferdinand appears in IV.i, *re*-emerging from the process of his *mortificatio*, one imagines him suddenly in a more sensationally luminous red, reflecting the great 'washing' or 'whitening' through which he has passed and is still passing (Miranda herself one imagines in a more sensationally luminous white). This is the fifth stage of *the ablutio* or 'new life', associated expressly in the alchemical development with the image of the re-birth of the Phoenix from its ashes (the emergent 'Bird' of Andreae's *Chymical Wedding*).[48] Prospero's evolution now takes him *beyond* the Intuition in which he has worked right through the *mortificatio*, into the next stage described, in modern Rosicrucianism, as the Correspondence between Microcosm and Macrocosm. We are given an intimation of what this involves when Prospero 'gives' Miranda away. His voice is for the first time in the play altered, suddenly more open and confiding of his extraordinary strengths and purposes; he has found in Ferdinand another in whom some understanding of the reaches of human evolution can now be assumed:

> *If I have too austerely punished you,*
> *Your compensation makes amends; for I*
> *Have given you here a third[49] of mine own life,*
> *Or that for which I live ...*
> > *... O Ferdinand*
> *Do not smile at me that I do boast her off,*
> *For thou shalt find she will outstrip all praise*
> *And make it halt behind her.*
> FERD.   *I do believe it,*
> *Against an oracle.*
> (IV.i.1-12)

Accompanying this first eruption of 'the new life' is a sequel involving the joy and celebration of the masque, which highlights, among other things, Iris' rainbow presence and the colorful peacocks that draw Juno's chariot. As we have it in the alchemical development, at this point:

> *The white became red, then golden, then it burst into a coruscation of colour, the Peacock's Tail ...*[50]

Corresponding to this account is the bursting out of highly colouristic speech and song in this section of Shakespeare's play, bringing together and harmonizing, through the figures of Ceres and Juno, Earth and Heaven. But the evolution cannot stop here: there must be a further impulse to extend the fruits of this accomplishment beyond the limits of the present, and so we reach the *resurrectum*. We pass on from the 'Paradise'[51] that Ferdinand recognizes of his perfected state of being with Miranda (being the 'heaven' and 'earth' of his previous solemn vow of allegiance to her) to the further 'passion' that now drives Prospero to break up the masque, looking ahead towards a still greater goal. In the alchemical development,

> *This is the end of the Paradise Garden ... [and] [i]t is a problem to move into another state, for this beautiful dreamland is not the answer to the mysteries, it is simply the beauty of the universe in its ineffable orderliness. So mankind has to go on the journey into timelessness ... and it is then that the soul who truly understands that the* **materia prima**, *the matter of the universe, is somehow within him is faced by illumination.*[52]

This supreme moment would seem to coincide with the moment of Prospero's disturbed 'passion', as a further quote suggests:

> *The expected light was something utterly beyond the imagination. It was something in which the adept was engulfed and altered. The experience was not to be described in terms which we can fully understand. We hear of the terror as well as the beauty, and note that the adept was often a changed personality after the experience. The ecstatic experience was the crown of the alchemist's life, but it was not always comforting. We have two Christian parallels, in St. Paul who was waylaid and shattered with the Light on the Damascus road, and ever afterwards went on his way towards martyrdom; and in St. Francis of Assisi who suffered the vision which implanted most painful stigmata to add to his virtues and complete absorption as well as his physical breakdown ...*[53]

Lecturing long before the account of latter-day historians of alchemy, Rudolf Steiner explicitly identified true alchemy as an early form of Rosicrucian practice. Ultimately, it was designed to bring the practitioner-devotee into a climactic condition in which he could share in Rosenkreutz' fundamental experience, which Steiner tells us *was* an experience 'of the event of Damascus', 'a repetition of the vision of Paul on the road to Damascus.'[54] The Higher Ego, which has been in process of developing in Imagination, Inspiration, and Intuition, is at this point taken over by what modern Rosicrucian Anthroposophy has described as the True Ego in which alone the resurrected Christ Himself is revealed, through the mediation of His greatest servant on earth, who, since the thirteenth century, has been Christian Rosenkreutz.[55] In Prospero's case the moment of transfiguration shows all the marks of a disturbance that comes from bearing the intensity of a progressive expansion that seems to know no bounds, which seems to anticipate prophetically the dissolution of the world (there would seem to be a further structural link with the process of Christ's Ascension):

> And—like the baseless fabric of this vision—
> The cloud-capped towers, the gorgeous palaces,
> The solemn temples, the great globe itself,
> Yea, all which it inherit, shall dissolve,
> And like this insubstantial pageant faded,
> Leave not a rack behind.
> (IV.i.151-156)

In Prospero's fulfilled relationship to Ferdinand, there has been a turning back, as it were, *into* the creation out of the sphere of Intuition, thus effecting the Correspondence between Microcosm and Macrocosm, and this sublime accomplishment crystallizes now in the idea of bringing that creation forward, a bringing forward that is clearly a matter of Living *back* into the Macrocosm. Profoundly upsetting, in this context of progressive creation, must seem the intractable perversity of a Caliban or for that matter the whole group of those who have conspired against Prospero, to whom his attention must now turn. No doubt another part of the disturbance that characterizes Prospero's ecstatic breakthrough comes from this necessary further diversion of consciousness away from creative expansion back to the grating perversity that continues to try him immediately.

An infinite loneliness comes upon Prospero from his consciousness of the vast disparity between the powers he now wields and the grotesque offensiveness of a human nature that continues to insist on its own perversity. The loneliness is intensified the more by the temptation Prospero has sensed to meet such perversity with severest judgment. It seems, consequently, inevitable that Prospero should feel the paradoxical compulsion in such circumstances to 'give up' his powers, as if he understood that, from this 'deed' of renunciation, these powers would have to return (at a later date) with still greater force, if there is to be a chance of dealing with the powers of resistance that remain, which he also sees at work in himself.[56] Be that as it may, there follows a choice of virtue *over* vengeance, as all are presently accommodated and everything moves on towards the moment at which Prospero will draw back the curtain to reveal Ferdinand and Miranda to the chastised Alonzo and court party. It is the moment that anticipates the final stage of the *rubedo* or the Wedding proper, projected for the return to Naples.

Already one is given in the present scene an intense intimation of what this Wedding will be like, which modern Rosicrucianism has characterised in relation to the prospect of Divine Bliss. All is in the mode of intensest religious awe, and for a moment one has some understanding of what world dissolution would feel like, as even Antonio—who will finally balk at enlightenment—is irresistibly drawn into an infinite wonder. All is centred in Miranda's miraculous Higher influence and the tremendous effect her introduction now has on the whole of the real world. At this moment we have reached the point of the greatest possible enlightenment *for* the world, given its present circumstances, and we must wonder at the great sacrifice Prospero's act of bestowal entails, though it is the point to which Shakespeare *had to* come to test the value of all that he had gained from his experience.

Elsewhere (see Part Two, pp.141-142) I have described the profound extension of terms implied in the transition from *Pericles* to *The Winter's Tale*. This transition corresponds to a progress in the power of Higher Ego out of the more limited sphere of influence in the Mind, in which it originates, into the still greater sphere that unites the Mind with Nature and the further world of the 'wandering stars': the greater world of Inspiration, as I describe this here (in Part Three). Beyond *The Winter's Tale* lies the further embodiment of the Higher Ego in the power of Intuition, as we have seen. Shakespeare has worked his way *forward* to this point by first working his way *through* the new Age of the Consciousness Soul. Unconsciously, Shakespeare was following the lead of Christian Rosenkreutz. That Shakespeare should then revert in *The Tempest* to what had become outmoded forms of alchemical-Rosicrucian expression, which his own evolution transcends, is merely an indication that no new language or appropriate ideas for that evolution had yet been supplied. That evolution for Shakespeare, as for Rosenkreutz, extends *beyond* the older terms and rather underlies them in a form that only *later* modern Rosicrucian Anthroposophy accounts for. Hence the necessity at a certain point of throwing ourselves beyond the immediate terms of Shakespeare's presentation onto the further elucidations Anthroposophy provides. The coming of those elucidations in our time would have to wait on the necessary *further* development, over the course of those centuries, of the Anthroposophia Being through which the new age is brought in at the time of the Renaissance.[57]

Modern Rosicrucian Anthroposophy informs us that the Higher Ego or Spirit Self will come *fully* into its own only centuries from now, when the Age of the Consciousness Soul has run its course. There will then be a further Age of Imagination equal in length to the Age of the Consciousness Soul, and another Age of Inspiration after that, until we reach the boundaries of Intuition etc.[58] Still more lies beyond that, as we have seen, corresponding to a still further time in which the True Ego will manifest further, from which spring in turn the still greater (almost unimaginable) faculties that evolve from Intuition. Of *these* sublime faculties we only have a concrete idea today in relation to the Life of Christ out of which they spring, and here, only an Anthroposophical Christology can begin to shed light on that relation. Suffice it to say that the fifth stage of the Rosicrucian initiation (the Correspondence between Microcosm and Macrocosm) mediates the influence of the Life of Christ Jesus before His Passion, from the time of His first miracle to His last. At one end of this Life is the miracle at Cana, when Christ Jesus learns to find a relation with His mother as 'the woman who had become virgin again'[59]. This condition is progressively added to right through to His last miracle, when Christ initiates Lazarus, raising him back to life from death. From here He is then ready to pass on, through His Passion and Death, to the Resurrection. The analogy at this point is with Prospero passing on from his initiation of Ferdinand who has himself claimed a relation to the virgin force expressed through Miranda (the mediated force of the mother herself). In the sixth stage (the Living into the Macrocosm), there is the further reflection in Prospero of Christ's influence in the Resurrection, which has continued since the Event at Palestine and is later channeled by Christian Rosenkreutz. It was in Christian Rosenkreutz' power to mediate that influence up to a certain point and in one way in an earlier age, and to another point and in another way, as we have seen, from the time of the Wedding to this very day. For it is a matter of a continuous development over time, a progressively greater and greater prophetic intimation of the evolving powers as we proceed from age to age.

A Further Note on
the Higher Ego in Shakespeare

As we have seen (in Part Two, p.138), re-emerging from the vortex of tragic time is for Shakespeare (along with Prospero, who inherits this whole process in the end) a matter *first* of coming through into the Imaginative Soul-world apart, a result of the extraordinary birth of a Higher Ego out of the tragic existence in which Shakespeare's mind is at one point seemingly irreversibly submerged. This is the extraordinary, unanticipated moment of Marina's birth and further life, from which we gather those sublime qualities in which the Higher Ego first manifests itself. Marina is, as Lysimachus notes, 'a [master-] piece of virtue' (IV. vi.109)[60], a phrase that Prospero will echo later in speaking of Miranda's mother, and Marina is indeed born of the self-sacrificing action of this very same mother, who bears the whole burden of tragedy, at this earliest stage of her intercession as Thaisa.

This Higher Ego comes forth as the inviolable counter-force to tragedy, at once connected to it and yet beyond its reach. There can be consequently no possibility of degrading or desecrating this Ego's existence, as Marina so simply insists to the Bawd:

> BAWD.   *... and you shall live in pleasure.*
> MARINA. *No.*
> (IV.ii.72-73)

Also, having a transcendent existence, this Ego can bear no relation to the import of depraved suggestion:

> *I understand you not.*
> (120)

The Higher Ego is, however, no less connected to the whole burden of tragedy than is the tragic Ego, as Marina's words to Pericles imply:

> *... she speaks,*
> *My lord, that, may be, hath endur'd a grief*
> *Might equal yours, if both were justly weigh'd.*
> (V.i.187-189)

The Higher Ego has, in fact, separated out as an entity beyond tragedy's downward pull, and it is just the strength of this Higher Ego that it does float about inviolable in its own Imaginative Soul-world apart, from which heights it lifts up the other side of itself, the Ego in its tragic, downtrodden state. One need not labour the relation that these terms have to the later Romantic Imagination. Indeed one has here nothing less than a short view of how and in what form the world of the Imagination comes forth—namely as part and parcel of a Higher Ego that manifests itself in it. Penetrating that world in the case of Shakespeare's experience is to encounter also the presence of many other powers that crystallize around the Higher Ego, notably Cerimon, e.g., who stands in a tremendous relation to the mother, on whose 'revival' he attends. And what are we to make of the mysterious 'maid' who is Marina's constant companion and must appear alongside her in the recovery of Pericles? Or Helicanus who faithfully attends on the overridden Pericles? Or Lysimachus, a further power who comes to 'court' Marina and will eventually 'marry' her? These same figures appear again in the representation of *The Winter's Tale*, respectively as Paulina (Cerimon), Camillo (Helicanus) and Florizel (Lysimachus). We notice also the greater and greater prominence given to the suitor-figure, as we go along: Lysimachus, Florizel and, finally, Ferdinand. An Imaginative allegory on an altogether grand scale is thus contained in the progressive representation of this expanding world across Shakespeare's last plays.

There is in Shakespeare's case, in fact, a continual outgrowth as we have seen, taking us ultimately far beyond the terms of the Romantic Imagination. For, although there is something of the Higher Ego among the Romantics and something of its further union with Nature—something of Imagination and something of Inspiration—the Higher Ego is not yet fully channeled, is not yet directly perceived, and so as yet is only partially if magnificently productive. And it is in this respect that Shakespeare's account of the Higher Ego in his last plays, as illuminated by Steiner's science of the spirit, takes the further lead into a future inheritance of which we have had but the first intimations thus far.

Endnotes

Introductory Overview:
On Shakespeare's Muse

1. As Sonnet 86 bears out: 'I was not sick of any fear from thence.'

2. This statement is technically accurate. However, the notion of comedies has been stretched to include the so-called 'problem comedies,' which I see rather as serious problem plays with comedy also problematically thrown in, much as in the case of Shakespeare's late 'tragicomedies' or 'romances', although these plays are obviously conceived as contending with tragic problems in a final spirit of triumph. The controversies will continue. For my own position, see my further comments on these matters on pp.97-98 of my book, *Shakespeare, the Goddess, and Modernity* (Bloomington, IN: iUniverse Inc., 2012).

3. All references in this 'Introductory Overview' to *The Complete Works. The Arden Shakespeare*, ed., Richard Proudfoot, Ann Thompson, and David Scott Kastan (London: Thomson Learning, 2006).

4. See Raymond Waddington, *English Language Notes*, vol. XXVII, no. 2, 1989, pp. 27-42.

5. For a detailed account of the historical situation, see my essay 'Outbraving Luther' in *Shakespeare the Man*, ed., R. W. Desai (Baltimore, ML: Fairleigh Dickinson University Press, 2014), p. 160 bottom, including the endnotes.

6. This is Hiram Haydn's eloquent translation in *The Counter-Renaissance* (New York: Harcourt, Brace and World Inc., 1950), p. 417. See, further, n. 20 to 'Otherworldly Hamlet' below.

7. An interesting comparison suggests itself with Jacques Maritain's appalled *rejection* of Luther's thought in *Three Reformers* (London: Sheed and Ward, 1932). I say 'comparison' rather than 'contrast' because Shakespeare was no less appalled by Luther's thought, even if *he* acts on the assumption that what Luther was saying was true.

8. A creative examination that extends over eight years or so. After *Othello* and *King Lear*, in which the obsession with libido especially intensifies, Shakespeare's examination deepens further with *Macbeth* and then broadens out with *Antony and Cleopatra, Coriolanus,* and *Timon of Athens.*

9. 'Esto peccator': be a sinner; 'pecca fortiter': sin boldly. Haydn in *The Counter-Renaissance,* p.418 was literally quoting, from a translation from the French, Lucien Febvre's free re-rendering of Luther's actual text from the letter of 1 August to Philip Melancthon, where we read: 'you must bear a true and not a fictitious sin ... Be a sinner and sin boldly', *Luther's Works,* ed., Jaroslav Pelikan and Helmut Lehmann (St. Louis and Philadelphia: Concordia Publishing and Fortress Press, 1958-1986), vol. 48, pp.281-282.

See, further, my essay 'Outbraving Luther', cited above, p.178n.17 for more on Febvre's text: there I state my case for supposing that Febvre's type of hyped-up Catholic work-over of Luther was how the matter would have come across to Shakespeare in his day.

10. References to *The Complete Plays,* ed., J.B. Steane (London: Penguin, 1986).

11. In bringing this remarkable vision forward Marlowe was building on a bridge that links *Dr. Faustus* directly back to *Tamburlaine.* Faustus' quest, like Tamburlaine's emergence, is associated with a *general* emancipation of forces: political-historical forces in the case of Tamburlaine, the profoundest metaphysical forces in the case of Faustus. Marlowe's context generally is the very great one of the Counter-Renaissance in which man appears in 'the infinite capacity' of his universal faith. See Hiram Haydn, the chapter 'Elizabethan Romanticism and the Metaphysical Ache' in *The Counter-Renaissance,* p.358ff.

12. Editorially it is far from clear that the first two lines I quote take question marks, as in the extent texts.

13. See his *Marriage of Heaven and Hell.*

14. The extent of their power over Faustus is finally measured with reference to his exaggerated expression of despair at the end of the play where he says:

> *The serpent that tempted Eve may be saved,*
> *But not Faustus.*
> (V.ii.44-45)

When, early on, Faustus speaks of offering 'lukewarm blood of new-born babes' to Belzebub (I.v.14), he is already possessed by the dark forces with whom he has made contact. His talk of serving his own 'appetite' (11) is also given to us in the context of his possession, having in fact no relation to the noble ends he serves in his own person. The later forms of escapist sensuality that Faustus chooses are likewise the expression of his subjected state, attractively individualistic though these may appear to us to be especially in the case of the invocation of Helen. Even Faustus knows that his involvement with Helen signifies (on the analogy of the collapse of Troy) the tragic collapse of that romantic Wittenberg he had projected as the symbol of a redeemed Europe when he first set out on his quest.

One might also mention here, to complete the account, that where Faustus appears to be willing evil upon the Old Man at the end, his words are intended as rhetorical bravado, to deflect the punishments threatened to him by Lucifer. Careful attention to the tone of these words will reveal that Faustus is not actually willing this action; the words are brought to bear upon the Old Man only because the forces that Lucifer represents choose to translate these words into deeds, as one expression of the phantasmagoria of despair Lucifer and company impose upon Faustus.

Close reading of Marlowe's text will indeed confirm the fundamental nobleness of his hero as this contrasts with the depravity that is wilfully thrust upon him, without his free choice, by the play's dark forces. On the other hand, Marlowe was not in the least minimizing the tragic awfulness of a humankind that thinks itself ready to deal with these forces.

15. See V.i.35-V.ii.94. It follows from what I have already argued about the Old Man that his destruction at the hands of Lucifer constitutes a highly subtle and complex action if, as I am claiming, the Old Man is himself a phantasmagoric creation of this Lucifer and his devils. He is like the Angels to whom Faustus never directly reaches out: a voice in Faustus' subconscious mind whose destruction spells the point at which Faustus passes beyond the possibility of hope. I.e., in the destruction of the Old Man we are confronted with the point at which Faustus is led to *believe* or *think* the destruction of his hope final.

16. I offer a full, detailed reading of the play in these terms in Part One of this book, in the section on 'Sexuality': see below, pp.53-57.

17. Matters that I deal with at length throughout Part One of this book. Bound up with this effort of 'justification', in spite of Hamlet's new knowledge, is the faith he continues to reserve in the moral probity of human nature, which he seeks to vindicate especially in his confrontation with his mother, where he seems to offer a definite plan of recovery. See especially the section from Part One: 'On Revenge'.

18. See my detailed account of this situation in the section 'On *Othello*' in my book, *Shakespeare, the Goddess, and Modernity* (Bloomington, IN: iUniverse Inc.), pp. 103-113. See, also, below pp. 25-26, including n.21.

19. Cf. Luther: 'it [sin] was born in me; as soon as I was formed in the womb, I was a sinner. For the flesh and blood of which I was made were sin ... That which father and mother contribute is itself already sin'. *Luther's Works*, vol. 36, pp. 354-355.

20. Compare *Hamlet*:

> HAMLET. *Ha, ha! Are you honest?*
> OPHELIA. *My lord?*
> HAMLET. *Are you fair?*
> OPHELIA. *What means your lordship?*
> HAMLET. *That if you be honest and fair, your honesty should admit no discourse to your beauty.*
> OPHELIA. *Could beauty, my lord, have better commerce than with honesty?*
> HAMLET. *Ay, truly, for the power of beauty will sooner transform honesty from what it is to a bawd than the force of honesty can translate beauty into his likeness. This was sometime a paradox, but now the time gives it proof.*
> (III.i.103-115)

*****

> GERTRUDE. *What have I done, that thou dar'st wag thy tongue*
> *In noise so rude against me?*
> HAMLET.   *... Such an act*
> *That blurs the grace and blush of modesty,*
> *Calls virtue hypocrite, takes off the rose*
> *From the fair forehead of an innocent love*
> *And sets a blister there, makes marriage vows*
> *As false as dicers' oaths—O, such a deed*
> *As from the body of contraction plucks*
> *The very soul, and sweet religion makes*
> *A rhapsody of words. Heaven's face does glow,*
> *O'er this solidity and compound mass*
> *With heated visage, as against the doom,*
> *Is thought-sick at the act.*
> ....
> GERTRUDE.   *... Ay me, what act*

That roars so loud and thunders in the index?
(III.iv.39-52)

21. Cf. Iago:

Not to affect many proposed matches
Of her own clime, complexion and degree,

....

Foh! One may smell in such a will most rank,
Foul disproportion, thoughts unnatural ...
(III.iii.233-237)

See on this score my essay 'Outbraving Luther' in *Shakespeare the Man*, p.180: 'what takes Othello over and clinches Iago's effect on him (all this in III.iii) is not, in fact, the thought that Cassio and Desdemona are engaged with each other so much as that Desdemona's sexual will *has* that overwhelming character that Iago ascribes to her. If not 'the maiden never bold', then, in fact, one who already had her 'will', which she would surely have needed to satisfy and did with Othello, at the time denying her many other, more passionless suitors, though now (Iago pretends) the need for 'satisfaction' has driven her elsewhere.'

22. See also Chapter 3 of *Shakespeare, the Goddess, and Modernity*, p.93: 'As for Desdemona's love or kindness, what value can *it* still have *through all the horror of her death*? The appalling horror of that death overwhelms the scene: I speak here also of the way we are drawn into the excruciating physical horror of that death. What possible meaning can Desdemona's love for Othello have in the midst of that action, and once he has become her murderer? We live at the end with the finality of that situation, and any further expression of his love for her, which returns to him afterwards, only appears to us the more horrible as it is now rendered null. We feel the same about her commendations to him when she dies. They have been rendered null, can no longer have any application to him, no matter how hard we want to believe it.'

23. See my discussion of this violence in *Shakespeare, the Goddess, and Modernity*, the section on 'The Worst of Depravity', p.31 *passim*.

24. See Nicholas Brooke, 'The Ending of *King Lear*', from *Shakespeare: 1564-1964*, ed., Edward A. Bloom (Providence, RI: Brown University Press, 1964), pp.86,84.

25. The following passage, from *Shakespeare, the Goddess, and Modernity* p.94, will throw further light on my view of the relative devastation in the comparison of *King Lear* with *Macbeth*: 'If I speak of this scene [the ending of *King Lear*] as 'the point of greatest devastation' in Shakespeare, 'the farthest extremity of a stifled humanity', this is because here love is involved to the very utmost and it is crushed, pulverized, negated. In *Macbeth* love is not there; there isn't even a possibility of love in the *Macbeth*-world, which is what makes that world already a far less human world. If still great devastation, there is less devastation here in human terms, because love has quite disappeared from the scene. There is certainly "greatness of soul" in Macbeth, on a scale that is unsurpassable in its own way, but this greatness has been radically divorced from love from the start. That is a deeper tragedy perhaps, but beyond where we could wish ourselves to be, and certainly beyond any power of recourse. Hence my relative account of *King Lear* and *Macbeth*.

26. '[T]he most withering indictment' because evil could no longer be thought to come simply from those of evil race.

Otherworldly Hamlet, and The New Tragedy

1. John Dillenberger, ed., *Martin Luther: Selections from His Writings* (New York: Doubleday, 1961), p.xxviii.

2. For a close account of the many parallels between the action in *Hamlet* and Luther's life and thought, see the article by Raymond Waddington in *English Language Notes*, vol. XXVII, no. 2, 1989, pp.27-42. I discuss this article further in my contribution to *Shakespeare the Man*, ed., R. W. Desai (Baltimore, ML: Fairleigh Dickinson University Press, 2014): see 'Outbraving Luther', p.177n.6. See also n.5 to the 'Introductory Overview'.

3. Martin Luther, 'Preface to the Complete Edition of Luther's Latin Writings', from *Martin Luther*, ed., Dillenberger, p.11.

4. *Ibid.*, p.11.

5. Dillenberger, *Martin Luther*, p.xxix.

6. *Ibid.*, p.xxix.

7. All quotations are taken from the edition by Lily B. Campbell, ed., *The Mirror for Magistrates* (Cambridge: Cambridge University Press, 1938).

8. See Alwin Thaler, 'Literary Criticism in *A Mirror for Magistrates*', *JEGP* 49, 1950, no. 1.

9. See John Lydgate, *The Fall of Princes*, ed., Henry Bergen (London:

Oxford University Press, 1967), Book I, l.477, p.14.

10. Howard Baker, *Induction to Tragedy* (Louisiana: Louisiana State University Press, 1939), p.111.

11. Thomas Kyd, *The Spanish Tragedy*, ed., Philip Edwards (London: Methuen, 1959; rpt., 1973).

12. From 'The Theme of Damnation in *Dr. Faustus*', *Marlowe: 'Doctor Faustus': A Casebook*, ed., John Jump (London: Macmillan, 1969), p.95.

13. See 'Appendix I', scene xii, from the Revels edition, ed. John Jump (London: Methuen, 1962), pp.115-116. The fact that the Emperor's speech belongs to the 1604 A-text of Marlowe's play, which is no longer regarded, and has not been for some time, as the authoritative text— the A-text having been judged by Greg (originally) to be a memorial reconstruction by actors of the original prompt-book for provincial performance—this, it would seem, decisive fact does not at all detract from my argument here insofar as the very supposition of a speech in these terms, as such evidence suggests, by someone *not* Marlowe, merely lends support to my claim about a *general* Renaissance concern.

14. All references in Part One are to the Peter Alexander Text (London: Collins, 1951).

15. For more on Richard II's comparable predicament, the reader may wish to consult Chapters 7 and 8 of my book, *Shakespeare, the Goddess, and Modernity* (Bloomington, IN: iUniverse Inc., 2012).

16. See *The Time Is Out of Joint* (London: Andrew Dakers, 1948), p.28.

17. See G.K. Hunter, *Dramatic Identities and Cultural Tradition* (Liverpool: Liverpool University Press, 1978).

18. Classical mythology only gives evidence of an uninterrupted egress through the gates, and from this point of view, Kyd's action represents a dramatic break with tradition. Kyd's innovation, however, corresponds to his ultimate theme which, as I show below, has to do with man's tragic separation from an otherworldly experience. Kyd frankly assumes the existence of the otherworld, but what he wishes to dramatize is the tragic realization that man no longer has available to him *full* consciousness of an otherworldly experience. Hence, the disruption in Andrea's visionary journey, which is a matter of *aborted* egress or the sudden deflation of vision. The otherworld had always been, traditionally, the locus of the dream-vision.

19. For an extensive consideration of dream-vision literature up to the reign of Henry VIII, see A.C. Spearing, *Medieval Dream Poetry*

(Cambridge: Cambridge University Press, 1976). As for the Elizabethans, it would take Shakespeare, with his acute sense of its dramatic possibilities, to revitalize this material to greatest effect—as in Clarence's dream from *Richard III*, where the dream-vision structure merges with the material of the marvellous journey into hell (with its echo of Kyd) to serve the projection of a powerful representation of the self-revolt that attends on moral guilt:

> *No, no, my dream was lengthen'd after life.*
> *O, then began the tempest to my soul!*
> *I pass'd, methought, the melancholy flood*
> *With that sour ferryman which poets write of,*
> *Unto the kingdom of perpetual night.*
> *The first that there did greet my stranger soul*
> *Was my great father-in-law, renowned Warwick,*
> *Who spoke aloud 'What scourge for perjury*
> *Can this dark monarchy afford false Clarence?'*
> *And so he vanish'd. Then came wand'ring by*
> *A shadow like an angel, with bright hair*
> *Dabbled in blood, and he shriek'd out aloud*
> *'Clarence is come—false, fleeting, perjur'd Clarence,*
> *That stabb'd me in the field by Tewksbury.*
> *Seize on him, Furies, take him unto torment!'*
> *With that, methoughts, a legion of foul fiends*
> *Environ'd me, and howled in mine ears.*
> *Such hideous cries that, with that very noise,*
> *I trembling wak'd, and for a season after*
> *Could not believe but that I was in hell,*
> *Such terrible impression made my dream.*
> (I.iv.43-63)

20. This is Haydn's eloquent translation in *The Counter-Renaissance* (New York: Harcourt, Brace and World Inc., 1950), p.417. In Pelikan, *Luther's Works*, ed., Jaroslav Pelikan and Helmut Lehmann (St. Louis and Philadelphia: Concordia Publishing and Fortress Press, 1958-1986), vol. 1, p.168, we read: 'lust alone can be cured by no remedy'.

21. See Nicholas Brooke, *Shakespeare's Early Tragedies* (London: Methuen, 1968), p.186.

22. For more on the details of this situation, see my essay 'Outbraving Luther' in *Shakespeare the Man*, p.162 bottom, including endnote 20: 'What otherwise seemed like a legitimate love or 'blossoming' between himself and his wife had its basis in fact in an 'appetite' for which the

father has been judged [re: 'Why, she would hang on him / As if increase of appetite had grown / By what it fed on'] ... [We are]drawn here into the disturbing view that nature itself, even in its seemingly most positive aspect, constitutes *sub specie aeternitatis* a condition of sin. 'As long as we are here [in this world],' Luther says, 'we have to sin', *Luther's Works*, vol. 48, p. 282.

23. See E. M. W. Tillyard, *Shakespeare's Problem Plays* (Toronto: Toronto University Press, 1950), p. 24.

24. See D. G. James, *The Dream of Learning* (London: Oxford at the Clarendon Press, 1951), particularly pp. 38-43; Arthur Sewell, *Character and Society in Shakespeare* (Oxford: Clarendon Press, 1951), p. 77; Douglas Bush, *Shakespeare and the Natural Condition* (Cambridge, MA: Harvard University Press, 1956), particularly pp. 83-84.

25. See Arthur Sewell, *Character and Society*, p. 77.

26. See A. W. Von Schlegel, from *Dramatic Art and Literature*, 1809-1811, as quoted by A. C. Bradley, *Shakespearean Tragedy* (London: Macmillan, 1974; orig. pub., 1904), p. 83; S. T. Coleridge, *Coleridge on Shakespeare*, ed., Terence Hawkes (Harmondsworth: Penguin Books, 1969), p. 174; Edward Dowden, *Shakspere: His Mind and Art* (London: Kegan Paul, Trench, Trubner, 1892), p. 133. For a modern re-statement of this position, see H. B. Charlton, *Shakespearian Tragedy* (Cambridge: Cambridge University Press, 1948), p. 93. For an eloquent *attack* freeing Hamlet from the charge of irresolution, see A. C. Swinburne, *A Study of Shakespeare* (London: William Heinemann, 1920; first pub., Chatto and Windus, 1879), pp. 168-169.

27. See Patrick Cruttwell, 'The Morality of *Hamlet*: 'Sweet Prince' or 'Arrant Knave'?' from *Hamlet*, ed., J. R. Brown and Bernard Harris, *Stratford-Upon-Avon Studies* 5 (London: Edward Arnold, 1963), p. 111.

28. See A. C. Bradley, *Shakespearean Tragedy*, p. 79; J. D. Wilson, *What Happens in 'Hamlet'* (London: University Press, 1935, rpt., 1962) pp. 72,84; H. D. F. Kitto, *Form and Meaning in Drama* (London: Methuen, 1956; rpt., 1964) pp. 286-287; H. B. Charlton, *Shakespearian Tragedy* (Cambridge: Cambridge University Press, 1948), pp. 86-87; and Kenneth Muir, *Shakespeare: 'Hamlet'* (London: Edward Arnold, 1963; rpt., 1969), p. 56.

29. For emphasis on the Ghost as a symbol of fate, see I.iv.81; for manifestations of an overwhelming desire to get the Ghost to speak, see I.i.49-51; I.i.127-139; and particularly, I.iv.40-44, where the desire to get the Ghost to speak overrides the consideration of whether it is good or evil.

30. See J. M. Robertson, *The Problems of 'Hamlet'* (London: George Allen Unwin Ltd., 1919), p.74; A. J. A. Waldock, *'Hamlet': A Study in Critical Method* (London: Cambridge University Press, 1931), p.66; Helen Gardner, *The Business of Criticism* (London: Oxford at the Clarendon Press, 1959), p.46; and Harry Levin, *The Question of* Hamlet (New York: Oxford University Press, 1959), pp.56-57. Harold Jenkins has, in his Arden edition of the play (London: Methuen, 1982), himself brought up this major stumbling block in the appraisal of Hamlet's predicament, with prominent allusion to L. C. Knights, *An Approach to 'Hamlet'*, and Eleanor Prosser, *Hamlet and Revenge*.

31. See A. C. Bradley, *Shakespearean Tragedy*, p.96: 'the demand on him, in the name of everything dearest and most sacred, to arise and act'; and G. Wilson Knight, *The Wheel of Fire* (London: Methuen, 1961; first pub., 1930), p.20: 'to cleanse, to create harmony'.

32. See particularly A. C. Bradley, p.141; and J. D. Wilson, p.72.

33. See Levin, p.56.

34. See Muir: *Shakespeare: 'Hamlet'*, p.67.

35. Levin, pp.83-85.

36. Levin, p.34.

37. See Gardner, p.46; Wilson Knight, p.36.

38. See Peter Alexander, *Hamlet, Father and Son* (London: Oxford at the Clarendon Press, 1955), pp.144-145; A. C. Bradley, p.80.

39. See D. G. James, *The Dream of Learning*, pp.45-46.

40. See Waldock, p.43.

41. See Kitto, p.315.

42. See Maynard Mack, 'The World of *Hamlet*', *The Yale Review*, xli, 1951-1952, p.508.

43. Mack, p.522.

44. Kitto, p.315.

45. Mack, p.522.

46. Levin, pp.34-35. Emphasis mine.

47. In *Shakespeare's Life and Art* (New York: New York University Press, 1967; orig. pub., 1961), cited by Jenkins, p.140.

48. See II.ii.547-549: 'all his visage wann'd / Tears in his eyes, distraction in's aspect, / A broken voice' etc.

49. See Roy Walker, *The Time is Out of Joint* (London: Andrew Dakers, 1948), p.152.

50. See E. E. Stoll, *Art and Artifice in Shakespeare* (London: Methuen, 1963; orig. pub. Barnes and Noble, 1933), pp.127-128.

51. See El Greco's painting, *Burial of the Count Orgaz.*

Othello's Sacrifice, and Romantic Tradition

1. Except for the first of the four quotes, for which I have favoured the Lowrie translation (Princeton: Princeton University Press, 1941, rpt.1970), p.33, see Soren Kierkegaard, *Fear and Trembling*, tr., Alastair Hannay (Harmondsworth: Penguin, 1985), pp.81,58,75.

2. Ivor Morris, *Shakespeare's God: The Role of Religion in the Tragedies* (London: Allen and Unwin, 1972), p.339.

3. All references in Part Two are to *The Riverside Shakespeare*, ed., G. Blakemore Evans (Boston: Houghton Mifflin Co., 1974).

4. Helen Gardner, 'The Noble Moor' from *Shakespeare's 'Othello': A Casebook*, ed., John Wain (London: Macmillan, 1971), p.161.

5. Gardner, p.161.

6. *Fear and Trembling*, pp.60,65,66.

7. *Fear and Trembling*, p.90.

8. *Fear and Trembling*, pp.75-76.

9. See Hiram Haydn, *The Counter-Renaissance* (New York: Harcourt, Brace and World, 1950), especially the section 'The Denial of Limit: The Romanticists'. See also n.11 to the 'Introductory Overview'.

10. David Bevington, ed., *Medieval Drama* (Boston: Houghton Mifflin Co., 1975), pp.308-321.

11. Samuel Johnson, *Johnson on Shakespeare*, ed., Walter Raleigh (London: Oxford University Press 1908), p.200.

12. Sidney Lanier, *Shakespeare and His Forerunners*, vol.I, pp.300-301; cited by Alwin Thaler, *Shakespeare's Silences* (Cambridge, MA: Harvard University Press, 1929), p.3.

13. A. C. Bradley, *Shakespearean Tragedy* (London: Macmillan Press, 1904), pp.13-14. See also pp.19ff.

14. Graham Hough, *A Preface to 'The Faerie Queene'* (London: Gerald Duckworth and Co. Ltd., 1962), p. 107.

15. *A Preface to 'The Faerie Queene',* p. 105.

16. F. R. Leavis, 'Tragedy and the Medium', from *The Common Pursuit* (London: Chatto and Windus, 1952), p. 130.

17. L. C. Knights, *Some Shakespearean Themes* (London: Chatto and Windus, 1959), p. 23.

18. G. Wilson Knight, *The Wheel of Fire* (London: Methuen and Co. Ltd., 1961; rpt., 1972; orig. pub. Oxford University Press, 1930), p. 11.

19. The general approach and viewpoint outlined here have been thoroughly researched by S. Viswanathan in the context of 'The Rise of the Poetic Interpretation of Shakespeare' in his book *The Shakespeare Play As Poem* (Cambridge: Cambridge University Press, 1980). My own aim in this book is to set this tradition in criticism back farther than Viswanathan does, though he himself acknowledges at one point that 'The term 'incarnation' was originally employed by Wordsworth with reference to poetic language' (p. 46 n. 11).

20. Alwin Thaler, *Shakespeare's Silences,* p. 12.

21. Blackwood's *1849,* cited by Kenneth Muir in the Arden *Macbeth* (London: Methuen, 1951), p. 139n.

22. W. H. Clemen, *The Development of Shakespeare's Imagery* (London: Methuen, 1961; first pub., 1951), p. 151.

23. Frank Kermode in his Introduction to the Arden edition of *The Tempest* (London: Methuen, 1954), p. lxxviii.

24. It is revealing of the representational significance of this action of touching or pointing to the breast to compare what John Bulwer has to say about it in his *Chironomia,* London, 1644: 'The touch doth most availe in a sharpe and inflamed stile, when the motions of the minde are by Action unfolded: As when an Oratour would expresse an incredible ardour of love lodged in his bosome, and cleaving to his very marrow; or grief deeply settled in his yearning bowells...' (pp. 39-40; the symbol 'ſ' for 's' modernized.)

25. For the last line of this speech, I have adopted M. R. Ridley's rendering from the Arden edition of the play (London: Methuen, 1958).

26. '... the very noblest man whom even omnipotence or Shakespeare could ever call to life': Algernon Swinburne, *A Study of Shakespeare* (New York: AMS Press, 1965), pp. 176-177.

27. James Bulman, *The Heroic Idiom in Shakespearean Tragedy* (Newark: University of Delaware Press, 1985).

28. A tradition that, interestingly, Viswanathan omits to identify and acknowledge in his otherwise thorough survey and review of modern Shakespeare criticism in *The Shakespeare play as poem*. What makes this omission interesting is the indication it offers of Viswanathan's own biased absorption in the form of criticism that opposes itself to this tradition later, as if this tradition, or the opposition to it, had never been. Glossing the situation in this way, Viswanathan misses the occasion to observe the immense significance of this opposition/impasse for the future course of Shakespeare criticism. As I argue below, we were left with a situation that remained unresolved, the whole situation of modern Shakespeare criticism up to that time falling from that point into disarray, and this from the insufficiency of the general method that had motivated it up till then, that method being, implicitly, the method of Romantic Imagination, as argued below. See:

Farnham, Willard, *The Medieval Heritage of Elizabethan Tragedy* (Oxford: Basil Blackwell, 1963; orig. pub., 1936).

Baker, Howard, *Induction to Tragedy* (Louisiana: Louisiana State University Press, 1939).

Prior, Moody, *The Language of Tragedy* (Bloomington: Indiana University Press, 1947).

Leech, Clifford, *Shakespeare's Tragedies* (London: Chatto and Windus, 1950).

James, D. G., *The Dream of Learning* (London: Oxford at the Clarendon Press, 1951).

Alexander, Peter, *Hamlet: Father and Son* (London: Oxford at the Clarendon Press, 1955).

Bush, Douglas, *Shakespeare and the Natural Condition* (Cambridge, MA.: Harvard University Press, 1960).

Watson, Curtis, *Shakespeare and the Renaissance Concept of Honor* (Princeton: Princeton University Press, 1960).

Rosen, William, *Shakespeare and the Craft of Tragedy* (Cambridge, MA: Harvard University Press, 1960).

Waith, Eugene, *The Herculean Hero* (New York: Columbia University Press, 1962).

Brower, Ruben, *Hero and Saint* (Oxford: Oxford at the Clarendon Press, 1971).

29. *Shakespearean Tragedy*, p.165.

30. *Shakespearean Tragedy*, pp.234-235.

31. *The Wheel of Fire*, pp.221,236.

32. Barbara Everett, 'The New King Lear', in *Shakespeare's 'King Lear': A Casebook*, ed., Frank Kermode (London: Macmillan, 1969), pp.187-188.

33. 'On the Tragedies of Shakespeare', from *Lamb's Criticism*, ed., E. M. W. Tillyard (Cambridge: Cambridge University Press, 1923), pp.45-46.

34. 'The New King Lear', pp.199-200.

35. Helen Gardner, '*Othello*: A Retrospect, 1900-1967', in *Shakespeare Survey 21*, ed., Kenneth Muir (Cambridge: Cambridge University Press, 1968).

36. At a certain level, of course, both *King Lear* and *Macbeth* are themselves grounded in such qualities of individuality and concentration. In spite of their obviously 'giant' nature, both display and emerge themselves from some 'correspondence with the forms and events of human affairs' (to quote Wilson Knight). Indeed, without that correspondence, these plays could hardly reflect the way they do upon a vision of human destiny. What is more, the negative comparison of *Othello* with the later achievements (in point of fact, only two or three years 'later') in respect of power of passion, strikes one as obviously misplaced. It has never been doubted that Othello himself is anything less than gigantic. Swinburne, for instance, spoke of the titanic quality of the later Shakespearean tragic heroes and included, of course, his Othello, prized so immemorially, among the list he gives. Bradley himself called attention to something 'colossal' about these same heroes— 'huge men', adding, in his introduction to the subject of the great tragedies, that 'Othello is the first of these men ...' Indeed, a breakthrough had first to be made. That breakthrough once made, we might naturally expect to find progression and evolution, explaining the relatively greater, expanded power of *Lear* and *Macbeth* as creations following immediately on *Othello*.

37. John Bayley, *Shakespeare and Tragedy* (London: Routledge and Kegan Paul, 1981), pp.8-15 *passim*.

38. T.B. Tomlinson, *A Study of Elizabethan and Jacobean Drama* (Cambridge: Cambridge University Press, 1964).

39. F.R. Leavis, *Education and the University* (London: Chatto and Windus, 1948). L.C. Knights, *Some Shakespearean Themes* (London:

Chatto and Windus, 1959).

40. *A Study of Elizabethan and Jacobean Drama*, p.36.

41. *A Study of Elizabethan and Jacobean Drama*, p.27. Tomlinson's passage ends with a quotation from L. C. Knights.

42. Owen Barfield, *Romanticism Comes of Age* (Middletown, CT: Wesleyan University Press, 1966), p.20.

43. *Romanticism*, p.15.

44. From the thirteenth chapter of the *Biographia Literaria*, ed., James Engell and W. Jackson Bate (Princeton: Princeton University Press, 1983), vol. I, p.299. The value of Coleridge's terms can only be grasped, of course, in the context of his entire discussion which begins, and is substantially presented, in the twelfth chapter of the *Biographia*.

45. *Romanticism*, p.100.

46. *Romanticism*, pp.129-130.

47. Terry Eagleton, *Literary Theory* (Minnesota: University of Minnesota Press, 1983), p.42. Eagleton's account proceeds in (seemingly deliberate) ignorance of the whole Romantic philosophical tradition and what *it* is making of the 'intuitive'. Coleridge is himself building on that tradition in the definition he offers of the Imagination.

48. F. R. Leavis, *The Living Principle* (London: Chatto and Windus, 1975).

49. From this view, the reader will gather my proposal of a Romantic provenance for the method also of the later 'meta-heroic' critics (rallied here under Leavis' banner), most of whom, among those I cite, Viswanathan (in *The Shakespeare play as poem*) sees as working within a view of the 'poetic interpretation' of Shakespeare that he thinks distinctively modern. With its 'insistence on 'intimations' and indirect suggestions in poetry, and the appeal to faculties other than the conscious' (p.44) and its 'basic presupposition that poetry is a unique mode of discourse, unparaphraseable, especially in rational prose and direct statement' (p.43), Viswanathan acknowledges the possibility of seeing this movement as 'a continuation of the Romantic movement' (p.45). He himself cites the opinion of Frank Kermode (*Romantic Image*) and Graham Hough (*Image and Experience*) to that effect. But he resists this view, claiming that 'as a matter of fact, the ideal hankered after, however difficult in practice, was the co-extensive development, fusion or function in unison of the emotional and the imaginative sensibilities, and of the faculty of reason and judgment' (p.45). But it is wrong to assume a desired separation of these functions in the Romantic approach to the Imagination. We are, in any case, on firm ground for dealing with the tragic fortunes of modern post-Romantic Shakespeare criticism (fortunes that Mr. Viswanathan, publishing in 1980, could not really foresee) only by returning to the provenance of its major modes in the Romantic method of Imagination. Without that strategy, we have no other way of grasping or approaching the tragedy with any hope of pursuing a solution.

50. 'Austrian-born Rudolf Steiner (1861-1925) became a respected and well-published scholar, particularly known for his work on Goethe's scientific writings. After the turn of the 19th century, he began to develop his earlier philosophical principles into an approach to methodical research of psychological and spiritual phenomena. His multi-faceted genius has led to innovative and holistic approaches in medicine, science, education (Waldorf schools), special education, philosophy, religion, economics, agriculture (the Bio-dynamic method), drama, the new art of eurhythmy, and other fields. In 1924, he founded the General Anthroposophical Society, which today has branches throughout the world' [from the jacket cover of *Christianity as Mystical Fact* (New York: Anthroposophic Press, 1972)].

51. *Romanticism Comes of Age*, p.130.

52. *Romanticism*, p.30.

53. *Romanticism*, p.15.

54. *Romanticism*, p.16.

55. *Romanticism*, p.16.

56. *Romanticism*, p.37.

57. *Romanticism*, pp.15-16.

58. Sergei O. Prokofieff, *Rudolf Steiner and the Founding of the New Mysteries* (London: Rudolf Steiner Press, 1986), p.72.

59. Part One of this book reprints, with revisions, *Otherworldly Hamlet* (Montreal: Guernica Editions, 1991). All of the material of *Otherworldly Hamlet* was written by 1981. I became a member of the Anthroposophical Society in 1989.

60. *Romanticism*, p.142.

61. See the account by Hiram Haydn in 'Elizabethan Romanticism and the Metaphysical Ache', from *The Counter-Renaissance* (cited above—see n.9—and in the 'Introductory Overview', n.11), pp.358-373: 'On the one hand, an assertive ideal of unlimited freedom, on the other the sense of transiency. And since most of these thinkers and writers among the Elizabethans applied the ideal of unlimited freedom to the limited goods of mortal life— especially the goods of sensuous love and beauty—they were really treating a naturalistic position with a romanticist attitude. The resultant conflict is everywhere apparent in Elizabethan literature' (p. 361).

62. *Romanticism*, p. 110.

63. *The Wheel of Fire*, p. 140.

64. *The Wheel of Fire*, p. 42.

65. *The Wheel of Fire*, p. 34.

66. *The Wheel of Fire*, p. 28.

67. *The Wheel of Fire*, p. 34.

68. See Peter Manns, *Martin Luther: An Illustrated Biography* (New York: Crossroad Publishing Co., 1982), p. 180, where Manns speaks of 'The patience and indulgence [Luther] showed his numerous friends, colleagues and brothers who, like Karlstadt, Johann Bugenhagen, Justus Jonas, or Wenzeslaus Link, were suddenly in very much of a rush to extinguish the 'burning fire' …' Manns adds that 'it was not Luther who abandoned the monastery, as the mass of his fellow friars did before him and an entire army of monks and nuns did in the sixteenth century … Of course, Luther bears a share of responsibility for this development, but … it is not his fault that monks, nuns, and priests misused the call to 'freedom' nor is he the actual cause of this regrettable turn of events.' Manns' conclusion is that 'it was rather that the monastery collapsed around [Luther], as it were. Monasticism was losing its bloom and leaves, like trees in autumn.'

69. See endnote n. 9 to the 'Introductory Overview'.

70. Here I would include Lear along with Hamlet and Othello. The exception to this pattern, of course, is Macbeth in whom an utmost violence is *directly* at work. Its effect in the world of *Macbeth*, nevertheless, is in keeping with the overall pattern. The violence drives one character to acknowledge that 'all is the fear, and nothing is the love' (IV.ii.12). This is not to be seen simply as a failure of moral nature in the characters of the *Macbeth*-world. What *Macbeth* asks us to contemplate is a species of violence, and a degree of such violence, in the development of which all manner of love has vanished. With *Macbeth* we have moved beyond that point where faith in love is still being tragically affirmed.

71. For Johnson on *Othello*, see above p.94. For Johnson's comment on the ending of *King Lear*, see *Johnson on Shakespeare*, cited above in n.11, pp.162-163.

72. Nicholas Brooke, 'The Ending of *King Lear*' from *Shakespeare: 1564-1964*, ed., Edward A. Bloom (Providence, RI: Brown University Press, 1964), pp.86;84.

73. See Bulman, *Heroic Idiom*.

74. Rudolf Steiner, *Christianity as Mystical Fact* (New York: Anthroposophic Press, 1972), pp.16-18.

75. The four quotations are from separate sections of Barfield's work: respectively pp.79-80; p.98; pp.101-102; pp.127-128. I have adjusted Barfield's second diagram to bring this into line with my own diagrams in the rest.

76. There is more, of course, to the foregrounding of these characters. They seem to step out of their, dramatically, literal situation directly into our presence in the theater, in keeping with the additional masque-like qualities of this play.

77. Rudolf Steiner, *The Gospel of St. Luke* (London: Rudolf Steiner Press, 3rd edn., 1975), p.23.

78. Combining both Marina and Perdita, Miranda, in this picture, *is* the full 'wonder' of the higher world itself, now fully perceived in the Ego. In another sense of her name, Miranda also 'mirrors' this higher world to us: in herself, as literal personage. (The name 'Miranda' contains both senses, of 'wonder' and of 'mirroring'.) At the same time, the world (as we know it) is, in her, 'mirrored' back to us, as it were through the 'eyes' of the higher world. Hence, Miranda's view of the Milan-party: 'O brave new world / That hath such people in it' (V.i.184-185).

79. John Middleton Murry, 'Romanticism and the Tradition', from *Defending Romanticism*, ed., Malcolm Woodfield (Bristol: Bristol Classical Press, 1989), p.142.

80. 'Romanticism and the Tradition', p.142.

81. 'Romanticism and the Tradition', p.143: 'In the greater spirits the wheel turns full circle; in the lesser, it turns half or quarter of the way.'

82. In this way, Steiner fulfills the quest for that 'future synthesis' for which Murry, in the essay 'Towards a Synthesis', was looking, back in 1927: 'Objective synthesis is nugatory unless it rests upon a subjective synthesis of which it is the harmonious and orderly projection ... Shakespeare's solution, or his system, was simple—it was the re-assertion of tragedy ... Not that I suggest that a new synthesis could unfold itself simply through a complete exploration of the implications of Shakespeare's tragedy, considered as experience ... my intention is merely to indicate the significance of Shakespeare, and the tragedy which he created, as a symbol and touchstone of a future synthesis. I believe that there will be no essential element in that synthesis that is not implied in Shakespeare; and that, whereas the poetic synthesis of medievalism in Dante was subsequent to the philosophic and religious synthesis in St. Thomas, it stands in the very nature of the present epoch that the poetic synthesis should come first and the philosophical synthesis long afterwards' (from *Defending Romanticism*, pp.196-198).

It is ironic that at the time he was writing these words, Murry should have been ignorant of Steiner, making so much of Shakespeare only because he had not traced out what comes to fulfilment in Steiner. In Theosophy circles in the London of Murry's day, Steiner's name would have been circulating for years if only because he had challenged its structures so radically, and Steiner himself came to London, as the representative of the Anthroposophy he had founded, to lecture just before he died, in 1924. Barfield, I know from first-hand knowledge in an interview I had with him, was among those who had the chance to see Steiner lecture at that time, though there never was a personal meeting between them. It is interesting to note, too, that Yeats was familiar with Theosophy through his wife, and that both may also have known and heard of, and even read, Steiner. Murry's fate is certainly amongst the most dramatic testimony in our critical history (judging from his words in the passage I cite) of the consequences of limiting our focus strictly to the immediate terms of our activity, whether this be literature, sociology, psychology, or history. The need is for a reference point to that further *outside* element that we had failed, or refused, to look into that finally synthesizes all.

83. Rudolf Steiner, *Anthroposophical Leading Thoughts* (London: Rudolf Steiner Press, 1973), p.108.

84. 'The Ending of *King Lear*', p.87.

85. See *Knowledge of the Higher Worlds* (London: Rudolf Steiner Press, l969), pp.191-192.

86. *Knowledge of the Higher Worlds*, pp.194-195.

Prospero's Powers:
Shakespeare's Last Phase

1. References in Part Three are to the Arden edition of *The Tempest*, ed. Virginia Mason Vaughan and Alden T. Vaughan (London: Thomas Learning, 2006).

2. An end-point equivalent with the ending of *King Lear*, as we have seen above, on p.131.

3. Nor is Prospero the Presenter of these plays alone but of a great many that precede them, of *Hamlet* and *Macbeth* certainly, but also *Othello* and, most notably, *King Lear*. Certainly we need to entertain a new and more ambitious idea of Shakespearean dramatic production, one that would make any presentation of *The Tempest* contingent on a prior viewing at least of the two main plays that precede it as its informants as well as on some form of major rehearsal of Shakespeare's momentous progress through the tragedies.

4 Stephen Orgel, ed., *The Tempest* (Oxford: Oxford University Press, 1987), p.106n.

5. In *The Golden Age of Chartres* (Edinburgh: Floris Books, 1987).

6. *The Golden Age*, p.81.

7. Querido provides us with a detailed chart. See *The Golden Age*, p.75:

Liberal Arts	leading to the sphere of	foremost representative
Astronomica (embodies the ritual of the stars)	Saturn	Ptolemy
Geometrica (measures)	Jupiter	Euclid
Arithmetica (counts)	Mars	Pythagoras
Musica (sings)	Sun	Pythagoras
Rhetorica (paints the words)	Venus	Cicero
Dialectica (teaches the true)	Mercury	Aristotle
Grammatica (speaks)	Moon	Donatus

8. *The Golden Age*, pp.74,93.

9. Lecture of 13 July, 1924, given in Dornach. Reprinted in *Karmic Relationships* (London: Rudolf Steiner Press, 1977), pp.87-89.

10. Lecture of 13 July, 1924. For a remarkable account of the difference between the 'planetary' and the 'starry' worlds as these latter bear further on the structure of the zodiac, see the anthroposophist, Sergei O. Prokofieff, 'The Starry Script as a Key' from *The Twelve Holy Nights and the Spiritual Hierarchies* (London: Temple Lodge Press, 1993).

11. Lecture of 13 July, 1924, p.92.

12. In the case of Perdita, as described above p.142; in the case of Miranda, see pp.143-144. See also, as for Marina, p.138.

13. In his *Theosophy* (Hudson, NY: Anthroposophic Press, 1988), p.122.

14. 'Upper Devachan' in Steiner's account from *Theosophy*, and the 'World of Reason' in his account from *Theosophy of the Rosicrucian* (London: Rudolf Steiner Press, 1981).

15. *Rosicrucianism and Modern Initiation* (London: Rudolf Steiner Press, 1982), p.45.

16. *Rosicrucianism*, p.44.

17. *Rosicrucianism*, p.50.

18. *Rosicrucianism*, pp.51,53.

19. Lecture of 24 December, 1920. Reprinted in *The Search for the New Isis, the Divine Sophia* (Spring Valley, NY: Mercury Press, 1983).

20. Lecture of 24 December, 1920. Italics mine.

21. See n.34.

22. Andreae's *Chymical Wedding* was published in 1616—roughly four years after *The Tempest*, and on a textual basis, the historical influence would *seem* to run through John Dee, via the English dramatists including Shakespeare, *thence* to Andreae. However, in his record of the Chemical Wedding, Andreae was building on a visionary experience he had had in his youth at the age of 18, and a manuscript of Andreae's *Chymical Wedding* it would seem was being 'read' as early as 1604, according to Carlo Pietzner, the translator of Rudolf Steiner's essay on the *Wedding*, as published in *A Christian Rosenkreutz Anthology*, ed., Paul Marshall Allen (Blauvelt, NY: Rudolf Steiner Publications, 1968). In any case, Andreae's *Wedding* purports to record an experience that takes place *over 150 years earlier*, and presumably there would also have been an *esoteric* development long before Dee, with its own influences, from the time of the actual Wedding of 1459. This is the situation I assume in my chapter, deferring to Rudolf Steiner's acute testimonial indications about the historical significance of the *Wedding* when one refers this work back to such an esoteric development. There had already been a long (Rosicrucian) alchemical tradition, before Christian Rosenkreutz undergoes the Wedding that was to re-establish alchemical practice on a different basis.

23. See 'The Chymical Wedding of Christian Rosenkreutz' from *A Christian Rosenkreutz Anthology* (cited in the previous note) p.41. Steiner's essay was published in 1917.

24. 'The Chymical Wedding of Christian Rosenkreutz', p.40.

25. Lecture of 3 February, 1913. Cited by Sergei O. Prokofieff, *The Twelve Holy Nights*, p.88. See also below, p.164.

26. Shakespeare's depiction of this 'death' should not be confused with the still greater and more complex death of the Sophia over a much longer period of time as this is given to us in Gnostic literature (see Hughes, *Shakespeare and the Goddess of Complete Being*, London: Faber, 1992, p.351ff.) and in Anthroposophical literature (see Sergei O. Prokofieff, *The Heavenly Sophia and the Being Anthroposophia*, London: Temple Lodge Press, 1996, pp.182-183). The 'death' of the mother in Shakespeare reflects the *other* great, *topical* event of this time—'the passage of the Sophia through man'. *This* latter 'passage' is a purely supersensible event—experienced by Christian Rosenkreutz (from what we know) more or less without upheaval. However, as an event undergone by Shakespeare through his tragic heroes—with all the attachments to the world at that time that these heroes reflect to us—this 'passage' takes the form *in the plays* of a very great upheaval. In *Shakespeare the tragic visionary*, the passage is experienced as a great 'death', although, as we discover in the later romances, this 'death' turns out to be sacrificially 'borne' *by* the mother.

27. Until Prospero's experience 'at sea', there is no indication of his having as yet acquired *magical* power from his 'studies', but he has certainly done so by the time he safely reaches the island he is to inhabit (as he says himself, with the help of 'providence divine'—I.ii.159). There, his first achievement is to free Ariel from the pine tree to which the sorceress, Sycorax, has horribly confined this 'spirit' for 'a dozen years'— (I.ii.279). Clearly Prospero has come into his power of magic *as a direct result* of what he has, in the meantime, experienced 'at sea'.

28. Powerfully rendered in Peter Greenaway's film, entitled *Prospero's Books*.

29. Ted Hughes (in *The Goddess of Complete Being*) traces the 'tragic quest' back literally twelve years, to Jacques in *As You Like It*. It is in the figure of Jacques, Hughes argues, that Shakespeare first makes the conscious decision to undertake the quest. My own reading (as given in the next sentence of my text) differs from Hughes's reading where he associates this beginning with Prospero's exile at sea.

30. We must consequently assume that the twelve years that intervene—from the time of the sea-adventure to the tempest that is raised—represent a further *narrative* time additional to the autobiographical sequence, as if the action were being projected into the future, which is where we take up when the action begins. All this, though strange and unusual, would seem to be in keeping with the frankly utopian nature of this play.

31. Lecture of 3 February, 1913, cited by Sergei O. Prokofieff in 'The Cosmic Aspect of the Sophia' from *The Twelve Holy Nights*, pp. 87-88.

32. 'The Chymical Wedding of Christian Rosenkreutz', pp. 37-38.

33. 'The Chymical Wedding', p. 37.

34. The *basis* of this 'progress' or 'expansion' in spiritual vision, paradoxically, is a series of continuous acts of 'dissolution'—*extensive* acts of 'will' in the precise sense S. T. Coleridge himself expounds in the *Biographia* (cited in Part Two n. 44), p. 250:

> *Again, the spirit (originally the identity of object and subject) must in some sense **dissolve** this identity, in order to be conscious of it ... But this implies an act, and it follows therefore that intelligence or self-consciousness is impossible, except by and in a will. **The self-conscious spirit therefore is a will**; and freedom must be assumed as a ground of philosophy, and can never be deduced from it.*

Some years later (in the *Philosophy of Freedom*, London: Rudolf Steiner Press, 1964, p. 173), Steiner would clarify the same understanding:

> *the free act of will consists in the fact that, firstly, through the intuitive element, the activity that is necessary for the human organism is checked and repressed, and **then** replaced by the spiritual activity of the idea-filled will ... man is unfree insofar as he cannot complete the process of suppressing the organic activity.*

(See my edited collection, *The Thinking Spirit: Rudolf Steiner and Romantic Theory* (Lincoln, NE: iUniverse Inc., 2007), p.65ff, for a full contextualization of this matter.)

It is also in this same sense that Mary Anne Atwood, a profound student of alchemical writing and philosophy, observed:

> *Alchemy is the art of fermenting the human vital spirit in order to purify it and finally to 'dissolve it', so that the essence can be reconstructed through a regeneration or transmutation.*

(Cited by Paul Marshall Allen in *The Time Is At Hand! The Rosicrucian Nature of Goethe's 'Fairy Tale of the Green Snake and the Beautiful Lily' and the Mystery Dramas of Rudolf Steiner* (Hudson, NY: Anthroposophical Press, 1995), p.89.)

35. See the account as given by Paul Marshall Allen in *The Time Is At Hand!* p.91.

36. From *The Time Is At Hand!* p.91.

37. Ferdinand's situation at this point might be referred to *Prospero's Books*, specifically to the scene where Ferdinand is lying halfway up the stairs as if crucified (cf. Ferdinand's 'wooden slavery'—III.i.62). In the film presentation, Prospero is at the top of the stairs, Miranda at Ferdinand's side.

38. One can only speculate on the symbolism of the Tower, but I would propose that, in its seven-tiered form, it is a recapitulatory emblem of the seven-part process of the Rosicrucian initiation, as outlined above.

39. Rudolf Steiner identifies these Virgins as Theology and Alchemy in his essay 'The Chymical Wedding' cited above, pp.43-44.

40. This difference emerges immediately from a comparison of *The Wedding* with, for example, the *Anti-Claudianus* of Alain de Lille who was one of those Masters. The latter work will be familiar to English readers from C. S. Lewis' treatment of it in his *Allegory of Love.*

41. See Frances Yates, *The Rosicrucian Enlightenment and Shakespeare's Last Plays.* I say 'uncanny' because Shakespeare's main focus on a daughter and her lover in his last plays anticipates by a few years the later situation of James's daughter, Elizabeth, and the Count Palatine. James himself does not appear to have had anything to do with the Rosicrucian scheme of that time and only wished to distance himself from it, for political reasons.

42. In his essay, 'The Chymical Wedding', p.45.

43. Steiner's dates for these respective ages: The Sentient-Soul Age, to the time of the birth of the ancient Greek civilization (from 2800–700 B.C.); the Intellectual-Soul Age, which includes the Middle Ages (from 700 B.C.–1400 A.D.), the Consciousness-Soul Age, beginning at the time of the Renaissance (from 1400 A.D.–3500 A.D.). All approximative dates.

44. C. A. Burland, *The Arts of the Alchemists* (New York: Macmillan, 1962), p.141.

45. Burland, p.71.

46. In *The Goddess of Complete Being*, cited above, p.462.

47. Burland, p.71.

48. Cf. Burland, p.72: 'The dews distilled and the flames reflected fell on the black mass, which reddened and glowed, and then whitened ... Then came the Phoenix, the strange flashing white jewel, the flower, the expanding feathers of white fire.'

49. Miranda, the mother, and Prospero constitute the three.

50. Burland, p.72.

51. IV.i.124.

52. Burland, p.142.

53. Burland, p.144.

54. See *Esoteric Christianity and the Mission of Christian Rosenkreutz* (London: Rudolf Steiner Press, 1984), pp.39-45 *passim*.

55. See Sergei O. Prokofieff, *The Twelve Holy Nights*, pp.90-91, and also the chapter, 'The Great Servants of the Sophia: Rudolf Steiner and Christian Rosenkreutz', from *The Heavenly Sophia and the Being Anthroposophia*, pp.125-128.

56. This is Richard Ramsbotham's idea, shared privately. Cf. Prospero, with reference to Caliban: 'This thing of darkness I / Acknowledge mine'.

57. For a detailed account of this further development, see Sergei O. Prokofieff, *The Heavenly Sophia and the Being Anthroposophia*, p.68ff.

58. See endnote 43 for the dating of these epochs.

59. See Rudolf Steiner, *The Gospel of St. John and Its Relation to the Other Gospels* (Spring Valley, NY: The Anthroposophic Press, 1982), pp.190-192; also p.158 and p.167. See also Sergei O. Prokofieff, *The Heavenly Sophia and the Being Anthroposophia*, pp.123-124.

60. References to the Arden edition of *Pericles*, ed., F. D. Hoeniger (London: Thomas Learning, 2006).

117

Accuse me thus: that I have scanted all
Wherein I should your great deserts repay,
Forgot upon your dearest love to call,
Whereto all bonds do tie me day by day;
That I have frequent been with unknown minds,
And given to time your own dear-purchased right;
That I have hoisted sail to all the winds
Which should transport me farthest from your sight.
Book both my wilfulness and errors down,
And on just proof surmise accumulate;
Bring me within the level of your frown,
But shoot not at me in your wakened hate;
Since my appeal says I did strive to prove
The constancy and virtue of your love.